DOMESDAY BOOK

Nottinghamshire

History from the Sources

DOMESDAY BOOK

A Survey of the Counties of England

LIBER DE WINTONIA

Compiled by direction of

KING WILLIAM I

Winchester
1086

DOMESDAY BOOK

text and translation edited by

JOHN MORRIS

28

Nottinghamshire

edited from a draft translation prepared by

Celia Parker and Sara Wood

PHILLIMORE
Chichester
1977

1977

Published by

PHILLIMORE & CO. LTD.,

London and Chichester

Head Office: Shopwyke Hall,
Chichester, Sussex, England

© John Morris, 1977

ISBN 0 85033 147 1 (case)
ISBN 0 85033 148 X (limp)

*Printed in Great Britain by
Titus Wilson & Son Ltd.,
Kendal*

NOTTINGHAMSHIRE

Introduction

The Domesday Survey of Nottinghamshire

Notes
Index of Persons
Index of Places
Systems of Reference
Maps
Technical Terms

History from the Sources
General Editor: John Morris

The series aims to publish history
written directly from the sources
for all interested readers, both
specialists and others. The first
priority is to publish important
texts which should be widely
available, but are not.

DOMESDAY BOOK

The contents, with the folio on which each county begins, are:

Domesday Book is termed *Liber de Wintonia* (The Book of Winchester) in column 332c

INTRODUCTION

The Domesday Survey

In 1066 Duke William of Normandy conquered England. He was crowned King, and most of the lands of the English nobility were soon granted to his followers. Domesday Book was compiled 20 years later. The Saxon Chronicle records that in 1085

> at Gloucester at midwinter ... the King had deep speech with his counsellors ... and sent men all over England to each shire ... to find out ... what or how much each landholder held ... in land and livestock, and what it was worth ... The returns were brought to him.[1]

William was thorough. One of his Counsellors reports that he also sent a second set of Commissioners 'to shires they did not know, where they were themselves unknown, to check their predecessors' survey, and report culprits to the King.'[2]

The information was collected at Winchester, corrected, abridged, chiefly by omission of livestock and the 1066 population, and fair-copied by one writer into a single volume. Norfolk, Suffolk and Essex were copied, by several writers, into a second volume, unabridged, which states that 'the Survey was made in 1086'. The surveys of Durham and Northumberland, and of several towns, including London, were not transcribed, and most of Cumberland and Westmorland, not yet in England, was not surveyed. The whole undertaking was completed at speed, in less than 12 months, though the fair-copying of the main volume may have taken a little longer. Both volumes are now preserved at the Public Record Office. Some versions of regional returns also survive. One of them, from Ely Abbey,[3] copies out the Commissioners' brief. They were to ask

> The name of the place. Who held it, before 1066, and now?
> How many *hides*?[4] How many ploughs, both those in lordship and the men's?
> How many villagers, cottagers and slaves, how many free men and Freemen?[5]
> How much woodland, meadow and pasture? How many mills and fishponds?
> How much has been added or taken away? What the total value was and is?
> How much each free man or Freeman had or has? All threefold, before 1066,
> when King William gave it, and now; and if more can be had than at present?

The Ely volume also describes the procedure. The Commissioners took evidence on oath 'from the Sheriff; from all the barons and their Frenchmen; and from the whole Hundred, the priests, the reeves and six villagers from each village'. It also names four Frenchmen and four Englishmen from each Hundred, who were sworn to verify the detail.

The King wanted to know what he had, and who held it. The Commissioners therefore listed lands in dispute, for Domesday Book was not only a tax-assessment. To the King's grandson, Bishop Henry of Winchester, its purpose was that every 'man should know his right and not usurp another's'; and because it was the final authoritative register of rightful possession 'the natives called it Domesday Book, by analogy

---

[1] Before he left England for the last time, late in 1086.   [2] Robert Losinga, Bishop of Hereford 1079-1095 (see *E.H.R.* 22, 1907, 74).   [3] *Inquisitio Eliensis,* first paragraph.   [4] A land unit, reckoned as 120 acres.   [5] *Quot Sochemani.*

from the Day of Judgement'; that was why it was carefully arranged by Counties, and by landholders within Counties, 'numbered consecutively ... for easy reference'.[6]

Domesday Book describes Old English society under new management, in minute statistical detail. Foreign lords had taken over, but little else had yet changed. The chief landholders and those who held from them are named, and the rest of the population was counted. Most of them lived in villages, whose houses might be clustered together, or dispersed among their fields. Villages were grouped in administrative districts called Hundreds, which formed regions within Shires, or Counties, which survive today with minor boundary changes; the recent deformation of some ancient county identities is here disregarded, as are various short-lived modern changes. The local assemblies, though overshadowed by lords great and small, gave men a voice, which the Commissioners heeded. Very many holdings were described by the Norman term *manerium* (manor), greatly varied in size and structure, from tiny farmsteads to vast holdings; and many lords exercised their own jurisdiction and other rights, termed *soca*, whose meaning still eludes exact definition.

The Survey was unmatched in Europe for many centuries, the product of a sophisticated and experienced English administration, fully exploited by the Conqueror's commanding energy. But its unique assemblage of facts and figures has been hard to study, because the text has not been easily available, and abounds in technicalities. Investigation has therefore been chiefly confined to specialists; many questions cannot be tackled adequately without a cheap text and uniform translation available to a wider range of students, including local historians.

Previous Editions

The text has been printed once, in 1783, in an edition by Abraham Farley, probably of 1250 copies, at Government expense, said to have been £38,000; its preparation took 16 years. It was set in a specially designed type, here reproduced photographically, which was destroyed by fire in 1808. In 1811 and 1816 the Records Commissioners added an introduction, indices, and associated texts, edited by Sir Henry Ellis; and in 1861-1863 the Ordnance Survey issued zincograph facsimiles of the whole. Texts of individual counties have appeared since 1673, separate translations in the Victoria County Histories and elsewhere.

This Edition

Farley's text is used, because of its excellence, and because any worthy alternative would prove astronomically expensive. His text has been checked against the facsimile, and discrepancies observed have been verified against the manuscript, by the kindness of Miss Daphne Gifford of the Public Record Office. Farley's few errors are indicated in the notes.

[6] *Dialogus de Scaccario* 1,16.

The editor is responsible for the translation and lay-out. It aims at what the compiler would have written if his language had been modern English; though no translation can be exact, for even a simple word like 'free' nowadays means freedom from different restrictions. Bishop Henry emphasized that his grandfather preferred 'ordinary words'; the nearest ordinary modern English is therefore chosen whenever possible. Words that are now obsolete, or have changed their meaning, are avoided, but measurements have to be transliterated, since their extent is often unknown or arguable, and varied regionally. The terse inventory form of the original has been retained, as have the ambiguities of the Latin.

Modern English commands two main devices unknown to 11th century Latin, standardised punctuation and paragraphs; in the Latin, *ibi* ('there are') often does duty for a modern full stop, *et* ('and') for a comma or semi-colon. The entries normally answer the Commissioners' questions, arranged in five main groups, (i) the place and its holder, its hides, ploughs and lordship; (ii) people; (iii) resources; (iv) value; and (v) additional notes. The groups are usually given as separate paragraphs.

King William numbered chapters 'for easy reference', and sections within chapters are commonly marked, usually by initial capitals, often edged in red. They are here numbered. Maps, indices and an explanation of technical terms are also given. Later, it is hoped to publish analytical and explanatory volumes, and associated texts.

The editor is deeply indebted to the advice of many scholars, too numerous to name, and especially to the Public Record Office, and to the publisher's patience. The draft translations are the work of a team; they have been co-ordinated and corrected by the editor, and each has been checked by several people. It is therefore hoped that mistakes may be fewer than in versions published by single fallible individuals. But it would be Utopian to hope that the translation is altogether free from error; the editor would like to be informed of mistakes observed.

The preparation of this volume has been greatly assisted by a generous grant from the Leverhulme Trust Fund.

Conventions

*	refers to a note to the Latin text.
[ ]	enclose words omitted in the MS.

b. = bovate; c. = carucate.
( ) enclose editorial explanations.

*I*N BVRGO SNOTINGEHAM FVER .CLXXIII.

burgenſes.7 xix . uiłłi . Ad hc̄ Burgū adiacent . vi.

car̃ tre ad głđ regis.7 unū p̃tū.7 ſiluæ minutæ . vi.

q̃ʒ łḡ.7 v . laſ̃.H̄ terra partita fuit inſ̃ xxxviii.

burgenſes.7 de cenſu tre 7 opib burgenſiū redđ

lxxv . ſoł 7 vii . den.7 de duobʒ monetarijs . xl . ſolid.

Inibi habuit cōm Toſti . i . car̃ træ . de cuj træ

ſoca habeƀ rex . ii . denar̃.7 ipſe comes tciū.

Hugo.f.Baldrici inuenit . cxxxvi . hōēs man̄.

modo ſuꝫ . xvi . min̄ . Ipſe tam̃ hugo in terra

comitis|ſtatuit . xiii . dom quæ antea n̄ fuerant.

apponens eas in cenſu ueteris burgi.

In Snotingehā . ē una æccła in dn̄io regis . in qua ia

cent . iii . manſiones burgi,7 v . bouatæ træ de ſup̃

dictis|carucatis cū ſaca 7 ſoca.7 ad eand æcclam

p̃tiñ . v . acræ træ 7 dimidia . de qua rex hſ̃ ſacā 7

ſocā . Burgenſes hn̄t . vi . caruc|ad aranđ.7 xx.

borđ.7.xiiii . çarucas . In aqua Trente ſoliti eraꝫ

piſcari.7 m̊ querelā faciuꝫ q̃đ piſcari ꝓhibent̃.

T.R.E. redđ Snotinghā . xviii . liƀ . m̊ redđ . xxx.

7 x . liƀ de moneta.

NOTTINGHAMSHIRE

B In the Borough of NOTTINGHAM

1 Before 1066 there were 173 burgesses and 19 villagers.
To this Borough are attached 6 carucates of land, liable to
the King's tax; one meadow; underwood 6 furlongs long
and 5 wide. This land was divided between 38 burgesses;
from the dues of the land and the work of the burgesses it
pays 75s 7d; from two moneyers 40s.

2 Therein Earl Tosti had 1 carucate of land; from the
jurisdiction of this land the King had two pennies; the
Earl had the third himself.

3 Hugh son of Baldric, the Sheriff, found 136 men living there;
now there are 16 less. However, Hugh erected 13 houses himself,
which were not there before, on the Earl's land, in the new
Borough, and placed them among the dues of the old Borough.

4 In Nottingham is a church, in the King's lordship, in whose
(land) lie 3 residences of the Borough and 5 bovates of
land, of the said 6 carucates, with full jurisdiction; to this
church belong 5½ acres of land, of which the King has
full jurisdiction.

5 The burgesses have 6 carucates of land for ploughing, and 20
smallholders and 14 ploughs.

6 They were accustomed to fish in the river Trent, and now they
make a complaint because they are forbidden to fish.

7 Before 1066 Nottingham paid £18; now it pays £30, and £10
from the mint.

ꝼRoger de buſli hͭ in Snotinghā. III. manſioñ.
in quibʒ ſedent. XI. dom reddentes. IIII. ſoł 7 VII.
ꝼWiłłs peurel hͭ. XLVIII. dom mercatoʒ   ꝼdeñ.
reddentes. XXXVI. ſoł. 7 XII. dom eꝗtū. 7 VIII. bord.
ꝼRadulf de burun hͭ. XIII. dom eꝗtū. in una
harū manet unus mercator. ꝼGulbtus. ꝼmercatores.
                                .IIII.domʾ.
ꝼRadulf fili Hubti hͭ. XI. dom. in his maneɴ. III.
ꝼGoisfrid Alſelin hͭ. XXI. domū. 7 Aitard II. dom.
                              pbr   as
ꝼIn Crofta pbri ſunt. LXV. dom. 7 in his hͭ rex
ſacā 7 ſocā. Æcclͣa cū omibʒ ꝗ ad eā ptineɴ. ualet
p annū centū ſolidos. ꝼRicard freſle hͭ. IIII. dom.
ꝼIn foſſato burgi. ſunt. XVII. dom. 7 aliæ. VI. dom.
ꝼWiłło peurel cceſſit rex. X. acras terræ. ad
faciendū pomeriū.
ꝼIn Snotingehā hͭb rex Edw. I. caͬ træ cū głͩ.
Tͬra. II. caͬ. Ibi hͭ m rex. XI. uiłł hñtes. IIII. caͬ.
7 XII. aͨs pͭti. In dñio nichil. T.R.E. uał. III. lib. m ſim.
ꝼIn Snotingehā. Aqua Trentæ 7 foſſa. 7 uia uerſus
eboracū cuſtodiunt. ita ut ſiquis impedierit
tranſitū nauiū. 7 ſiꝗs arauerit uel foſsā fecerit
in uia regis infra duas pticas. emendare hͭ
p. VIII. libras.

8 Roger of Bully has 3 residences in Nottingham, in which 11
   houses are sited, which pay 4s 7d.

9 William Peverel has 48 merchants' houses which pay 36s,
   and 12 horsemen's houses and 8 smallholders.

10 Ralph of Buron has 13 horsemen's houses; a merchant lives
    in one of them.

11 Wulfbert, 4 houses.

12 Ralph son of Hubert has 11 houses; 3 merchants live in them.

13 Geoffrey Alselin has 21 houses, and Aitard the priest 2 houses.

14 In the priests' croft there are 65 houses; the King has full
    jurisdiction in them.

15 Annual value of the church, with all that belongs to it, 100s.

16 Richard Frail has 4 houses.

17 In the Borough ditch are 17 houses, and 6 other houses.

18 To William Peverel the King assigned 10 acres of land, to
    make an orchard.

19 In Nottingham King Edward had 1 carucate of land with the tax.
    Land for 2 ploughs. Now the King has 11 villagers, who have 4
    ploughs and 12 acres of meadow. Nothing in lordship.
    Value before 1066 £3; now the same.

20 In Nottingham the river Trent and the dyke and the road
    to York are so protected that if anyone hinders the passage of
    ships, or if anyone ploughs or makes a dyke within 2 perches
    of the King's road, he has to pay a fine of £8.

IN BVRGO DERBY.T.R.E.erant.ccxl.iii.

burgenſes manentes.7 ad ipſu burgu adiacent

xii.car tre ad gld.quas.viii.car poſs arare.

H terra partita erat int.xl.i.qui 7 xii.car

habebant.Duæ partes regis.7 tcia comitis.de

cenſu 7 theloneo 7 forisfactura 7 de omi cſuetu

dine.In eod burgo erat in dnio regis.i.æccla.

cu.vii.clericis q̇ teneb.ii.car træ libere   in

ceſtre.Erat 7 altera æccla regis ſimilit.in qua

vi.clerici teneb.ix.bou træ in Cornun 7 Detton

ſimilit libera.In ipſa uilla erą́.xiiii.molend.

Modo ſuą́ jbi.c.burgenſes.7 alii.xl.minores.

Centu 7 iii.maňs ſunt waſtæ.quæ censu reddeb.

Ibi ſunt m̂ x.molend.7 xvi.ac p̊ti.

Silua minuta.iii.q̇ż lg.7 ii.lat.

T.R.E.reddeb int tot xxiiii.lib.m̂ cu molend

7 uilla Ludecerce reddit.xxx.lib./7 ix.uilł hnt.ii.car.7 xii.ac p̊ti.

Co In Ludecerce ht rex.ii.car træ ad gld.Tra.iii.car.Ibi.i.ſoch.

The translation of this column is given in the Derbyshire volume.

In Derbẏ h̄ abb̄ de Bertone . 1 . moliñ . 7 1 . maſ trᵃ̄ᵉ

cū ſaca 7 ſoca . 7 11 . maſ de q̇bƷ h̄ rex ſocā . 7 xiii . ac̋s

⌐Goiſfrid alſelin h̄ . 1 . ᵃ̄ᵉcclam . q̇ fuit Tochi.   ⌐ṗti.

⌐Radulf . f . Hubti . 1 . ᵃ̄ᵉcclam . q̇ fuit Leuric . cū . 1 . car̄ trᵃᵉ,

⌐Norman de Lincolia . 1 . ᵃ̄ᵉcclam q̇ fuit . Brun

⌐Edric h̄ ibi . 1 . ᵃ̄ᵉcclam . q̇ fuit Coln patris ej

⌐Hugo h̄ . 11 . maſuras 7 1 . piſcar̄ cū ſaca 7 ſoca.

⌐Henric de ferrarijs . iii . maſur̄ cū ſaca 7 ſoca ſimil.

⌐Oſmer p̄br h̄ . 1 . bou trᵃᵉ cū ſaca 7 ſoca.

⌐Goduin p̄br . 1 . bou trᵃᵉ ſimilit̄

⌐Ad feſtū S̄ Martini redduɲ̄ burgenſes regi

xii . trabes annonᵃᵉ . de q̇ h̄ abb̄ de bertone . xl .

⌐Adhuc in eod̄ burgo ſunt . viii . maſurᵃᵉ ⌐garbas.

cū ſaca 7 ſoca . Hᵃᵉ fuer̄ Ælgar . m̊ ſunt regis.

⌐Duo nūmi regis 7 tcius comitis qui exeuɲ̄ de
In Derberie   t cenſu
apletreu Wapent̄ . ſunt in manu uicecomitis.

teſtim̄ duarū ſcirarū .

⌐De Stori Anteceſſore Walterij de Aincurt dn̄t

qd̄ ſine alicuj licentia potuit facere| ᵃᵉcclam in

ſua tra 7 in ſua ſoca , 7 ſuā decimā mittere q̇ uellet.

The translation of this column is given in the Derbyshire volume.

In Snotingehā scȳre & in Derbiſcȳre. pax regis
manu uel ſigillo data. ſi fuerit infraɔ̃ta.
emdat p. xviii. hundrez. Vnūqdꝗ hund.
viii. lib. Huj emdationis lr̃ rex. ii. partes.
comes tciā. Ideſt xii. hd emdant regi. 7 vi. coin.

Siꝗs ſcđm legē exulat fuerit pro aliꝗ reatu.
nullus pter regē pacē reddere poteſt ei.
Tain hn̄s pluſquā. vi. maneria. non dat træ
releuationē niſi regi tantū. viii. lib.
Si hr̃. vi. tantū uel min. uicecomiti dat re
leuationē. iii. Markas argenti. ubicunꝗ ma
neat in Burgo uel extra.
Si tain hn̄s ſacā 7 ſocā forisfecerit trā ſuā.
int regē & comite hn̄t medietatē træ ej atꝗ
pecúniæ. 7 legalis uxor cū legitimis hæredibꝛ
ſi fuerint hn̄t aliā medietatē.

Hic notant qui habuer ſocā 7 ſacā 7 Thol 7 Thaim
7 c̄ſuetudinē regis. ii. denarioꝛ.
Archieps eborac ſup maneria ſua. 7 Godeua
comitiſſa ſup Neuuercā Wapent. 7 Vlf feniſc
ſup trā ſuā. Abb de Burg ſup Colingeham.
Abb de Bertune. Hugo con ſup marcheton.
Eps de Ceſtre. Tochi. Suen. f. Suaue. Siuuard barn
Azor f. Saleuæ. Vlfric cilt. Elſi jllinge. Leuuin. f Aluuin.
Ælueua comitiſſa. Goda comitiſſa. Elſi. f. Caſchin.
ſup Wercheſſope. Henric de ferrar ſup Ednodes
tune 7 Dubrige 7 Breilesfordham. Walter de
Aincurt ſup Granebi 7 Mortune 7 Pinneſleig.

[SHIRE CUSTOMS]

1   In Nottinghamshire and in Derbyshire, if the King's peace,   280 c
given by his hand or seal, be broken, a fine is paid through
the 18 Hundreds; each Hundred, £8. The King has two
parts of this fine, the Earl the third; i.e., 12 Hundreds pay
the fine to the King, 6 to the Earl.

2   If anyone be exiled according to the law for any crime, no one
but the King can restore peace to him.

3   A thane who has more than 6 manors does not pay death-duty on
his land, save only to the King, £8. If he has only 6 or
less, he pays death-duty to the Sheriff, 3 silver marks,
wherever he may live, within the Borough or outside.

4   If a thane who has full jurisdiction should forfeit his land,
the King and the Earl between them have the half of his land
and of his money; his lawful wife, with his lawful heirs, if any,
have the other half.

5   List of those who had full jurisdiction and market rights
and the King's customary dues of two pence

The Archbishop of York
over his manors

Countess Godiva
over Newark Wapentake

Ulf Fenman
over his land

The Abbot of Peterborough
over Collingham

The Abbot of Burton

Earl Hugh
over Markeaton

The Bishop of Chester

Toki

Swein son of Swafi

Siward Bairn

Azor son of Saleva

Young Wulfric

Alfsi Illing

Leofwin son of Alwin

Countess Aelfeva

Countess Gytha

Alfsi son of Kaskin
over Worksop

Henry of Ferrers
over Ednaston
and Doveridge
and Brailsford

Walter of Aincourt
over Granby
and Morton
and Pilsley

Ho₹ omĩum nemo haƀe potuit ͧtciũ denaͬ
comitis nifi ei ͨcceſſu.7 Hoc ꝙdiu uiueret.
p̄ter Archiep̄m 7 Vlf fenifc 7 Godeue comitiſsā.

⌐Sup foca ꝙ jacet ad Cliftune. debet habere
comes ͧtciā parte omĩum c͠fuetudinũ 7 opum.

Of all these, none could have the Earl's third penny, unless with his assent, and that for as long as he lived, except for the Archbishop and Ulf Fenman and the Countess Godiva.

6 Over the jurisdiction which lies in Clifton the Earl ought to have the third part of all customary dues and works.

LIST OF LANDHOLDERS IN NOTTINGHAMSHIRE   280 d

1	King William	20	Ilbert of Lacy
2	Count Alan	21	Berengar of Tosny
3	Earl Hugh	22	Hugh son of Baldric
4	The Count of Mortain	23	Hugh of Grandmesnil
5	The Archbishop of York	24	Henry of Ferrers
6	The Bishop of Lincoln	25	Robert Malet
7	The Bishop of Bayeux	26	Durand Malet
8	The Abbey of Peterborough	27	Osbern son of Richard
9	Roger of Bully	28	Robert son of William
10	William Peverel	29	William the Usher
11	Walter of Aincourt	30	The King's Thanes
12	Geoffrey Alselin	IN RUTLAND	
13	Ralph son of Hubert	1	The King
14	Ralph of Limesy	2	Countess Judith
15	Ralph of Buron	3	Robert Malet
16	Roger of Poitou	4	Oger
17	Gilbert of Ghent	5	Gilbert of Ghent
18	Gilbert of Tison	6	Earl Hugh
19	Geoffrey of La Guerche	7	Albert Clerk

TERRA REGIS.

B RNEDESELAWE WAPENTAC.

In *DVNEHAM* cū . IIII . Bereuuitis . Pagenehil
Wimentun Derluuetun Suanesterne . habuit
rex Edvv . v . car tre 7 dim ad gld . Tra . XII . car.
jbi hr m rex . II . car in dnio.7 L uitt 7 III . bord
hntes . x . car.7 I molin . III . folidoƷ .7 I . pifcaria
x . folid 7 VIII . den.7 cxx . acs pti . Silua paftit
VI . q̊Ʒ lḡ .7 IIII . lat . T.R.E . reddeb . xxx . lib 7 VI.
fextar mett . m . xx . lib cū oib q ibi ptineſ.

§ **I**n Draitone . II . car 7 III . bou / Soca hvi maner.
7 v . pars uni bou ad gld . Tra . v . car . Ibi . xvi.
foch 7 xvII . uitt hnt . xIII . car.7 xx . acs pti.
Silua paftit . I . q̊Ʒ lḡ .7 dimid lat.

§ **I**n Marcha . III . car træ 7 dim ad gld . Tra . x . car.
Ibi xxv . fochi.7 xv . uitt hnt . x . car . Ibi æccta
7 pbr.7 xL . ac pti.7 filuæ min aliqtulum.

§ **I**n Grenleige . II . bou 7 vI . pars uni bouatæ ad gld.
Tra . II . car . Ibi . v . foch 7 I . bord hnt . II . car . Silua
past . IIII . q̊Ʒ lḡ .7 IIII . lat.

§ **I**n Ordefhale . I . bou tre ad gld . Tra . I . car . Ibi . II . foch
hnt . I . car.7 III . acs pti.7 III . acs filuæ.

§ **I**n Graue dim bou træ ad gld . Tra . I . bou.7 II . ac pti . Wasta . ē.

§ **I**n Vpetone . I . bou træ ad gld . Tra . I . car . Ibi . IIII . fochi
7 II . bord hnt . I . car 7 dim.7 III . acs pti . Silua past . II.
q̊Ʒ lḡ .7 I . lat.

§ **I**n Normentone . I . bou træ 7 dim ad gld . Huj tre medietas
ptin ad dune   altera ad bodmefceld . Wasta . ē . Silua
past . III . q̊Ʒ lḡ .7 II . lat.

BASSETLAW Wapentake

1 M. In DUNHAM, with the four outliers, RAGNALL, WIMPTON,
DARLTON and ' SWANSTON ' King Edward had 5½ c.
of land taxable. Land for 12 ploughs.
The King now has 2 ploughs in lordship and
   50 villagers and 3 smallholders who have 10 ploughs.
   1 mill, 3s; 1 fishery, 10s 8d; meadow, 120 acres;
   woodland pasture 6 furlongs long and 4 wide.
Before 1066 it paid £30 and 6 sesters of honey; now £20
with everything that belongs there.

Jurisdiction of this manor.
2 S. In (East) DRAYTON 2 c., 3 b. and the fifth part of 1 b. of
land taxable. Land for 5 ploughs.
   16 Freemen and 17 villagers have 13 ploughs.
   Meadow, 20 acres; woodland pasture 1 furlong long and ½ wide.

3 S. In (East) MARKHAM 3½ c. of land taxable. Land for 10 ploughs.
   25 Freemen and 15 villagers have 10 ploughs.
   A church and a priest; meadow, 40 acres; some underwood.

4 S. In (Little) GRINGLEY 2 b. of land the sixth part of 1 b. of
land taxable. Land for 2 ploughs.
   5 Freemen and 1 smallholder have 2 ploughs.
   Woodland pasture 4 furlongs long and 4 wide.

5 S. In ORDSALL 1 b. of land taxable. Land for 1 plough.
   2 Freemen have 1 plough.
   Meadow, 3 acres; woodland, 3 acres.

6 S. In HEADON ½ b. of land taxable. Land for 1 ox.
   Meadow, 2 acres. Waste.

7 S. In UPTON 1 b. of land taxable. Land for 1 plough.
   4 Freemen and 2 smallholders have 1½ ploughs.
   Meadow, 3 acres; woodland pasture, 2 furlongs long and 1 wide.

8 S. In NORMANTON (-by-Clumber) 1½ b. of land taxable.
   One half of this land belongs to Dunham, the other to Bothamsall.
   Waste.
   Woodland pasture 3 furlongs long and 2 wide.

ⓂIn *BODMESCEL*. ħƀ Tosti. xii . bou tre ad gld . Tra

viii . car̄ . Ibi nc̄ hr̄ rex . v . uilt . 7 i . borđ cū . ii . car̄.

7 i . moliñ . viii . foliđ . 7 xl . ac̄s p̄ti . Silua paſt dim

lev lḡ . 7 iiii . q̇ꝫ lḡ . T.R.E . ualt . viii . liƀ . m̊ . lx . foliđ.

§ In Elchefleig . iiii . bou træ ad glđ . Soca hvi man.

Tra . ii . car̄ . Ibi æccta 7 pƀr . 7 vi . focħ cū . i . car̄ 7 dim.

7 i . moliñ . iiii . foliđ . 7 filuæ minutæ modicū.

§ In Mortune 7 altera Mortune x . bou tre ad glđ . Tra . iiii.

car̄ . Ibi . vii . focħ 7 i . borđ hn̄t . iiii . car̄ . Silua paſtit

ii . q̇ꝫ lḡ . 7 i . lat̄.

§ In Baburde 7 Odestorp 7 Ordeshale | vi . bou træ 7 dim

ad glđ . Tra . iii . car̄ . Waſt e . p̄ter . i . uilt 7 ii . borđ . cū

dimiđ car̄ . Ibi . x . ac̄ p̄ti.

§ In Ranesbi . 7 Suderdefhale . v . bou træ ad glđ . Tra . i . car̄

7 dim . Waſta . e.

281 b

§ In Ranebi . ii . car̄ træ ad gld . Tra . iiii . car̄ . Waſta . e.

§ In Madreffeig . xi . bou træ ad gld . Tra . iii . car̄ . Ibi . xii.

focħi 7 ii . uilti 7 iii . borđ hn̄t . vi . car̄ 7 dimiđ . p̄ti . iii . q̇ꝫ

lḡ . 7 i . lat̄ . Silua paſt . i . lev lḡ . 7 i . q̇ꝫ 7 dim lat̄.

§ In Lund 7 Barnebi . vi . bou tre 7 dim . 7 iii . pars uni bou

ad glđ . Ibi . iii . focħ hn̄t . i . car̄ . 7 iii . ac̄s p̄ti 7 dim . Silua paſt

ii . q̇ꝫ lḡ . 7 dim lat̄.

ⓂIn *GRIMESTVNE* . iiii . bou tre   ad gld . Tra . ii . car̄.

Ber In Mamesfed . Ibi . iii . focħ 7 iii . borđ hn̄t . ii . car̄.

7 ii . ac̄s p̄ti . Silua paſt dimid lev lḡ . 7 iiii . q̇ꝫ lat̄.

§ Ibide . i . bou tre 7 dim ad gld . Tra . ii . boū . Soca hvi man.

Ibi . ii . focħ hn̄t dim car̄ . In Schidrintune dim bou ad gt̄.

9   M. In BOTHAMSALL Earl Tosti had 12 b. of land taxable.
Land for 8 ploughs. The King now has
5 villagers and 1 smallholder with 2 ploughs.
1 mill, 8s; meadow, 40 acres; woodland pasture ½ league
long and 4 furlongs [wide].
Value before 1066 £8; now 60s.

Jurisdiction of this manor.
10   S. In ELKESLEY 4 b. of land taxable. Land for 2 ploughs.
A church and a priest; 6 Freemen with 1½ ploughs.
1 mill, 4s; a little underwood.

11   S. In MORTON and the other MORTON 10 b. of land taxable.
Land for 4 ploughs.
7 Freemen and 1 smallholder have 4 ploughs.
Woodland pasture 2 furlongs long and 1 wide.

12   S. In BABWORTH 2½ b , in 'ODSTHORPE' 4½ b. and in ORDSALL 1 b ;
in all 7½ b. of land taxable. Land for 3 ploughs. Waste except for
1 villager and 2 smallholders with ½ plough.
Meadow, 10 acres.

13   S. In RANBY 3 b. and in SOUTH ORDSALL 2 b; 5 b. of land taxable.
Land for 1½ ploughs. Waste.

14   S. In RANBY 2 c. of land taxable. Land for 4 ploughs. Waste.   281 b

15   S. In MATTERSEY 11 b. of land taxable. Land for 3 ploughs.
12 Freemen, 2 villagers and 3 smallholders have 6½ ploughs.
Meadow 3 furlongs long and 1 wide; woodland pasture 1
league long and 1½ furlongs wide.

16   S. In LOUND and BARNBY (Moor) 6 b. of land, *and ½ and the third part
of 1 b.* taxable.
3 Freemen have 1 plough.
Meadow, 3½ acres; woodland pasture 2 furlongs long and ½ wide.

17   M. In GRIMSTON 4 b. of land ... taxable. Land for 2 ploughs.
Outlier in Mansfield.
3 Freemen and 3 smallholders have 2 ploughs.
Meadow, 2 acres; woodland pasture ½ league long
and 4 furlongs wide.

Jurisdiction of this manor.
18   S. There also 1½ b. of land taxable. Land for 2 oxen.
2 Freemen have ½ plough.

19   In KIRTON ½ b. taxable.

§ In Wilgebi 7 Waleſbi . ii . boú tre ad gld . Tra . i . cař . Ibi

iiii . ſocħi hñt . i . car . Silua paſt . iiii . ptic l̄g . 7 iiii . lat̄.

§ In Beſtorp 7 Carletone . iiii . boú træ ad gld . Tra . i . car.

Ibi . iiii . ſocħ 7 iii . borđ hñt . ii . cař . 7 xxx . ačs ſiluæ paſtil.

In Franesfeld ħt rex . i . boú træ ad gld . ppe Snotingeħa.

BROCOLVESTOV WAPENTAC

ꝏ In MAMESFELDE 7 Scħegebi 7 Sutone habuit rex

Edw . iii . car tre 7 vi . boú ad gld . Tra . ix . cař.

Ibi ħt rex . ii . cař in dñio . 7 v . ſocħ de . iii . bouat huj træ.

7 xxxv . uilt 7 xx . borđ cū . xix . car 7 dim . 7 i . molin

7 unā piſcariā . xxi . ſolid . 7 xx . iiii . ač p̄ti . Silua paſtil

ii . lev l̄g . 7 ii . lat̄ . Ibi . ii . æcclæ 7 ii . p̄ri.

In Warſope . i . boú . In Clune . iiii . boú . In Carbtone . ii . cař.

In Clunbre . iii . boú . In Butebi . ii . cař . In Tureſbi . vi . boú.

In Scotebi 7 Torp 7 Rouuetone . ii . cař . In Edeneſtou . i . cař.

In Grimeſtone . dim car . In Ecringhe . iii . boú . In Mapelbec . ii . bō.

In Beſtorp . ii . boú . In Carentune . ii . boú . In Schitrintone . i . boú 7 đ.

In Wilgebi . i . boú 7 dim . In Almuntone dim bō . In Caretone . iiii . cař

Int totū . xiii . car træ 7 vi . boú 7 dim ad gld.

In Wareſope . i . boú træ . q tenet q̄dā cæc in elemoſina de rege.

ubi ħt . i . borđ cū . vi . bob in car.

In Torp . iiii . pars uni boú træ Waſta . ē . q jacet in Mamesfeld.

B In Grimeſtone . iiii . boú træ ad gld . Tra . ii . cař . BEREW

Ibi ħt rex . i . cař . 7 viii . uilt 7 i . borđ . hñtes . ii . cař.

Silua paſt . vi . q̄⁊ l̄g . 7 iiii . lat̄   BEREW

B In Edeneſtou . i . cař tre ad gld . Tra . ii . cař . Ibi æccla

7 p̄br 7 iiii . borđ hñt . i . cař . Silua paſt dim lev l̄g . 7 dim lat̄.

20 S. In WILLOUGHBY and WALESBY 2 b. of land taxable. Land for 1 plough.
4 Freemen have 1 plough.
Woodland pasture 4 perches long and 4 wide.

21 S. In BESTHORPE 2, and CARLTON (-on-Trent) 2, 4 b. of land taxable.
Land for 1 plough.
4 Freemen and 3 smallholders have 2 ploughs.
Woodland pasture, 30. acres.

22 In FARNSFIELD the King has 1 b. of land taxable near Nottingham.

In BROXTOW Wapentake

23 M. In MANSFIELD and the outliers SKEGBY and SUTTON (-in-Ashfield)
King Edward had 3 c. and 6 b. of land taxable. Land for 9
ploughs. The King has 2 ploughs in lordship.
5 Freemen with 3 b. of this land; 35 villagers
and 20 smallholders with 19½ ploughs.
1 mill and 1 fishery, 21s; meadow, 24 acres; woodland
pasture 2 leagues long and 2 wide ; 2 churches and 2 priests.

24 In WARSOP 1 b.; CLOWN 4 b.; CARBURTON 2 c.; CLUMBER 3 b.;
BUDBY 2 c.; THORESBY 6 b.; SCOFTON, PERLETHORPE and RAYTON 2 c.;
EDWINSTOWE 1 c.; GRIMSTON ½ c.; EAKRING 3½ b.; MAPLEBECK 2 b.;
BESTHORPE 2 b.; CARLTON (-on-Trent) 2 b.; KIRTON 1½ b.;
WILLOUGHBY 1½ b.; OMPTON 1½ b.; CARLTON (-in-Lindrick) 4 c.
In total 13 c. and 6½ b. of land taxable.

25 In WARSOP 1 b. of land, which a blind man holds in alms from
the King, where he has
1 smallholder, with 6 oxen in a plough.

26 In PERLETHORPE the fourth part of 1 b. of land. Waste;
it lies in Mansfield (lands).

27 B. In GRIMSTON 4 b. of land taxable. Land for 2 ploughs. Outlier.
The King has 1 plough and
8 villagers and 1 smallholder who have 2 ploughs.
Woodland pasture 6 furlongs long and 4 wide.
Outlier.

28 B. In EDWINSTOWE 1 c. of land taxable. Land for 2 ploughs.
A church and a priest and 4 smallholders have 1 plough.
Woodland pasture ½ league long and ½ wide.

§ In Mapelberg . II . boū ⁊ træ ad gld . Tra . IIII . boū . Ibi . III .

ſocħ hñt . I . caɍ

§ In Carletone . II . caɍ . In Scotebi ⁊ Reneton . ⁊ Torp . II . caɍ

~~In Ronebi . II . car træ~~ . H . ē . ᵛ̶ɪ̶ . ad gld . Soca de Mamesfeld

Waſtæ ſunt.   Iᴛ Soca in Wardebec Wapentac.

§ In Tilne . II . boū ⁊ træ . ⁊ IIII . pars . I . boū ad gld . Tra . I . caɍ . Ibi . II . ſocħ

⁊ I . uilt ⁊ I . borđ hñt . VI . boū in caɍ . Ibi . II . molini . XXXII . ſolịđ .

⁊ VI . ac̈ p̈tı . Valet . XL . ſol.

281 c

§ In Cledretone . XII . bɔū tıæ ad glđ . Tra . IIII . caɍ .

Ibi . XXII . ſocħi ⁊ XI . uilt hñt . IX . caɍ . Hi ſocħiⱿ ad glđ .

reddeƀ . XX . ſol de c̃ſuetudine . T.R.E . |Fentune dım car.

§ In Litelburg . IIII . boū træ ad gld . Tra . I . caɍ . Ibi

XIIII . ſocħ ⁊ II . uilt ⁊ IIII . borđ . hñt . V . caɍ . P̈tū

III . q̂⁊ ⁊ X . uirg lḡ . ⁊ II . q̂⁊ laɍ . Ħ ſoca ualeᴛ . x.

§ In Eſtretone . II . caɍ træ ad gld . Tra . VI . caɍ . Ibi

XX . IIII . ſocħ ⁊ XI . uilt ⁊ VII . borđ hñt . VIII . caɍ .

P̈tū . I . lev lḡ . ⁊ I . q̂⁊ laɍ . Silua paſt . I . lev lḡ . ⁊ v .

q̂⁊ laɍ . Ħ ſoca ualeᴛ . XL . ſol.

§ In Wateleie . II . boū træ ad gld . Tra . II . caɍ . Ibi . VI .

ſocħ ⁊ I . uilt hñt . II . caɍ . Silua paſt . I . lev ⁊ I . q̂⁊

lḡ . ⁊ ⁊ I . q̂⁊ ⁊ dım laɍ . T.R.E . uaᴛ . III . ſol . m̊ . VII . s .

§ In Wacheringħā . XII . boū træ ⁊ dım ad gld . Tra

IIII . caɍ . Ibi . XIII . ſocħ ⁊ II . uilt ⁊ III . borđ hñt

IIII . caɍ . P̈tū . VI . q̂⁊ lḡ . ⁊ IIII . laɍ . Silua . VIII . q̂⁊

lḡ . ⁊ IIII . laɍ . Vaᴛ . XX . ſol.

§ In Miniſtretone . V . boū træ ⁊ . IIII . pars uni boū

ad gld . Tra . I . caɍ . Ibi . V . ſocħ ⁊ VI . uilt ⁊ I . borđ

hñt . I . caɍ . P̈tū . I . q̂⁊ lḡ . ⁊ dım q̂⁊ laɍ . Vaᴛ . VII . ſol.

29 S. In MAPLEBECK 2 b. of land taxable. Land for 4 oxen.
3 Freemen have 1 plough.

30 S. In CARLTON (-in-Lindrick) 2 c.; in SCOFTON, RAYTON and
PERLETHORPE 2 c. *In RANBY,* from Bothamsall, *2 c. of land*;
that is, 4 taxable. Jurisdiction of Mansfield, Waste.

Also Jurisdiction in OSWALDBECK Wapentake.

31 S. In TILN 2 b. and the fourth part of 1 b. of land taxable.
Land for 1 plough.
2 Freemen, 1 villager and 1 smallholder have 6 oxen
in a plough.
2 mills, 32s; meadow, 6 acres.
Value 40s.

32 S. In LEVERTON 12 b. of land taxable. Land for 4 ploughs.   281 c
22 Freemen and 11 villagers have 9 ploughs.
These Freemen paid 20s in customary dues before 1066.

33   In FENTON ½ c. taxable.

34 S. In LITTLEBOROUGH 4 b. of land taxable. Land for 1 plough.
14 Freemen, 2 villagers and 4 smallholders have 5 ploughs.
Meadow 3 furlongs and 10 virgates long and 2 furlongs wide.
Value of this jurisdiction 10s.

35 S. In STURTON (-le-Steeple) 2 c. of land taxable. Land for 6 ploughs.
24 Freemen, 11 villagers and 7 smallholders have 8 ploughs.
Meadow 1 league long and 1 furlong wide; woodland
pasture 1 league long and 5 furlongs wide.
Value of this jurisdiction 40s.

36 S. In WHEATLEY 2 b. of land taxable. Land for 2 ploughs.
6 Freemen and 1 villager have 2 ploughs.
Woodland pasture 1 league and 1 furlong long and 1½
furlongs wide.
Value before 1066, 3s; now 7s.

37 S. In WALKERINGHAM 12½ b. of land taxable. Land for 4 ploughs.
13 Freemen, 2 villagers and 3 smallholders have 4 ploughs.
Meadow 6 furlongs long and 4 wide; woodland 8 furlongs
long and 4 wide.
Value 20s.

38 S. In MISTERTON 5 b. and the fourth part of 1 b. of land taxable.
Land for 1 plough.
5 Freemen, 6 villagers and 1 smallholder have 1 plough.
Meadow 1 furlong long and ½ wide.
Value 7s.

§ In Wifetone . 1 . car̄ tre ad glđ . Ṫra . 11 . car̄ . Ibi . vii .

foch 7 vii . uiłł . 7 1111 . borđ . hūt vi . car̄ . P̈tū . 11 . q̂ƶ

lḡ . 7 11 . lat̄ . Silua past̄ x1111 . q̂ƶ lḡ . 7 i1ii . lat̄ . Valet

§ In Clauorde . 1 . car̄ træ 7 vi . boū ad glđ.   ⌠x . fot̄ .

Ṫra . 111 . car̄ . Ibi . x11 . foch 7 1 . uiłł 7 xv111 . borđ hūt

. x . car̄ . p̈tū . 11 . q̂ƶ lḡ . 7 1 . q̂ƶ 7 dim lat̄ . Silua past̄

x . q̂ƶ lḡ . 7 vi . q̂ƶ lat̄ . Valet xxvi . fot̄ . 7 i1ii . den̄ .

§ In Claureburg . 11 . boū træ 7 1111 . pars uni boū ad gld .

Ṫra . 1 . car̄ . Ibi . 11 . foch 7 1 . uiłł 7 1 . borđ hn̄tes . vi . boū

in car̄ . 7 11 . molin̄ . xxx . 11 . fot̄ . 7 vi . acs p̈ti . Val̄ . xl . fot̄ .

§ In Wellun 7 Simentone . v . boū træ 7 i11 . pars uni boū

ad gld . Ṫra . 11 . car̄ . Ibi . v . foch 7 1 . uiłł 7 1 . borđ . hūt

11 . car̄ . P̈tū . 1 . q̂ƶ 7 dim lḡ . 7 1 . q̂ƶ 7 x . pticas lat̄ . Silua

past̄ . 1x . q̂ƶ lḡ . 7 11 . q̂ƶ 7 dim lat̄ . Val̄ . x . fot̄ 7 v111 . den̄ .

§ In Greneleig . 11 . boū træ 7 dim ad gld . Ṫra . 1 . car̄ . Ibi

vi . foch 7 1 . uiłł 7 1 . borđ . hūt . 11 . car̄ . Silua past̄ . vi . q̂ƶ

lḡ . 7 1111 . lat̄ . Val̄ . x . fot̄ .   ⌠ad pifcē regis .

In Sandebi ten un̄ uiłł . 1 . ortū . redđ fat̄ in bigredic

ꝋ In ERNEHALE . ħƀ Rex Edw . 111 . car̄ træ ad glđ . Ṫra

111 . car̄ . Ibi ħ rex . 1 . car̄ . 7 xx . uiłł 7 1111 . borđ . hn̄tes

v11 . car̄ . Silua past̄ p loca . 111 . lev lḡ . 7 111 . lat̄ . T.R.E.

uat̄ . 1111 . liƀ . 7 11 . fextar̄ mełł . m̊ . v111 . liƀ . 7 vi . fext̄ mełł .

In Broncote . vi . bō fre ad gld . Ṫra . vi . bo̅ .   ꝫ SOCA huj' Manerii . ꝫ

ꞂB In Waletone . 1 . car̄ træ ad gld . Ṫra . 1 . car̄ . BER Waſta . ē

39 S. In WISETON 1 c. of land taxable. Land for 2 ploughs.
7 Freemen, 7 villagers and 4 smallholders have 6 ploughs.
Meadow 2 furlongs long and 2 wide; woodland pasture
14 furlongs long and 4 wide.
Value 10s.

40 S. In CLAYWORTH 1 c. and 6 b. of land taxable. Land for 3 ploughs.
12 Freemen, 1 villager and 18 smallholders have 10 ploughs.
Meadow 2 furlongs long and 1½ furlongs wide; woodland
pasture 10 furlongs long and 6 furlongs wide.
Value 26s 4d.

41 S. In CLARBOROUGH and TILN 2 b. and the fourth part of 1 b. of
land taxable. Land for 1 plough.
2 Freemen, 1 villager and 1 smallholder who have 6 oxen
in a plough.
2 mills, 32s; meadow, 6 acres.
Value 40s.

42 S. In WELHAM and *SIMENTONE* 5 b. and the third part of 1 b. of land
taxable. Land for 2 ploughs.
5 Freemen, 1 villager and 1 smallholder have 2 ploughs.
Meadow 1½ furlongs long and 1 furlong 10 perches wide;
woodland pasture 9 furlongs long and 2½ furlongs wide.
Value 10s 8d.

43 S. In (Little) GRINGLEY 2½ b. of land taxable. Land for 1 plough.
6 Freemen, 1 villager and 1 smallholder have 2 ploughs.
Woodland pasture 6 furlongs long and 4 wide.
Value 10s.

44 In SAUNDBY a villager holds 1 garden; he pays salt, in Bycarr's
Dike, for the King's fish.

45 M. In ARNOLD King Edward had 3 c. of land taxable.
Land for 3 ploughs. The King has 1 plough and
20 villagers and 4 smallholders who have 7 ploughs.
Woodland pasture, in various places, 3 leagues long and 3 wide.
Value before 1066 £4 and 2 sesters of honey; now £8 and 6
sesters of honey.

Jurisdiction of this manor.

46 In BRAMCOTE 6 b. of land taxable. Land for 6 oxen.

47 B. In WOLLATON 1 c. of land taxable. Land for 1 plough.
Outlier. Waste.

§ In Lentone. IIII. boũ træ ad gld. Soca in Ernehale. Wasta. e̅.

§ In Brocheleſtou. I. boũ tre ad gld̄. Waſta. e̅. Soca in Ernehale.

In Bileburch. I. boũ tre. ad gld̄.

281 d

BINGAMESHOV WAPENT.

ⓂⒾn OSCHINTONE. h̅b̅ rex Edw. III. car̅ træ ad gld.

Tra. x. car̅. Ibi h̅r̅ rex. III. car̅. 7 III. ſoch de. I. car̅

hui træ. 7 xix. uill 7 xi. bord. h̅ntes. xiiii. car̅.

Ibi æccla 7 II. p̅bri h̅ntes. I. car̅. 7 I. boue̅. 7 nouies. xx.

ac̅s p̅ti. T.R.E. ual̅. xxx. lib̅ ad numer̅. m̅ xx. lib̅.

B̅ In Scarintone. II. car̅ tre ad gld. BEREW HVI MAN̅.

Tra. III. car̅. Ibi h̅r̅ rex. II. car̅. 7 xxiii. uill 7 iiii. bord

◉ Tra. III. car̅. h̅ntes. v. car̅ 7 dim. In STANTVN. vii. boũ 7 iii ac̅ træ ad gld̄. ◉

Ibi. x. ſochi
7 III. bord. S̅In Toruertune. xii. boũ tre ad gld. Tra. iiii. car̅.

cũ. III. car̅
7 lx. ac p̅ti. Ibi. I. ſochs 7 xvi. uill. h̅ntes. vii. car̅. Ibi p̅br

S̅In Screuintone. I. car̅ tre ad gld. Tra. III. car̅. Ibi. III.

ſoch 7 II. uill 7 I. bord. h̅nt. I. car̅ 7 dim. 7 viii. ac̅s p̅ti.

S̅ In Coleſtone. IIII. boũ 7 IIII. ac̅ tre ad gld. Tra. I. car̅,

Ibi. v. ſoch h̅nt. I. car̅ 7 dim.

S̅ In Aſlachetone. I. boũ træ ad gld̄. Ibi arat. I. uills.

ⓂIn NEVBOLD. h̅b̅ Morcar. III. car̅ tre ad gld̄. Tra

viii. car̅. Ibi h̅r̅ rex. III. car̅. 7 xiii. ſoch 7 xiii. uill

7 III. bord h̅ntes. vii. car̅. 7 II. ac̅s ſilue min̅. Ibi p̅br

7 æccla. T.R.E. ual̅. iiii. lib̅. m̅. x. lib̅.

ⓂIn BROTONE, h̅b̅ Algar. II. car̅ tre ad gld̄. Tra. vii. car̅.

Ibi h̅r̅ rex. II. car̅. 7 xxiii. uill. 7 iiii. bord. h̅ntes vii. car̅

7 I. molin̅. v. ſolid. 7 c. ac̅s p̅ti. T.R.E. ual̅. III. lib̅. m̅. IIII.

48 S. In LENTON 4 b. of land taxable. Jurisdiction in Arnold. Waste.

49 S. In BROXTOW 1 b. of land taxable. Waste. Jurisdiction in Arnold.

50 S. In BILBOROUGH 1 b. of land taxable.

BINGHAM Wapentake   281 d
51 M. In ORSTON King Edward had 3 c. of land taxable.
   Land for 10 ploughs. The King has 3 ploughs and
      3 Freemen with 1 c. of this land and 19 villagers
      and 11 smallholders who have 14 ploughs.
   A church and 2 priests who have 1 plough and 1 ox;
      meadow, 180 acres.
   Value before 1066 £30 at face value; now £20.
   Outlier of this Manor.

52 B. In SCARRINGTON 2 c. of land taxable. Land for 3 ploughs.
   The King has 2 ploughs and
      23 villagers and 4 smallholders who have 5½ ploughs.

53   In STAUNTON 7 b. and 3 acres of land taxable. Land for 3 ploughs.
   10 Freemen and 3 smallholders with 3 ploughs.
   Meadow, 60 acres.

54 S. In THOROTON 12 b. of land taxable. Land for 4 ploughs.
   1 Freeman, 18 villagers and 1 smallholder who have 7 ploughs.
   A priest.

55 S. In SCREVETON 1 c. of land taxable. Land for 3 ploughs.
   3 Freemen, 2 villagers and 1 smallholder have 1½ ploughs.
   Meadow, 8 acres.

56 S. In (Car) COLSTON 4 b. and 4 acres of land taxable.
   Land for 1 plough.
      5 Freemen have 1½ ploughs.

57 S. In ASLOCKTON 1 b. of land taxable. 1 villager ploughs there.

58 M. In 'NEWBOLD' Earl Morcar had 3 c. of land taxable.
   Land for 8 ploughs. The King has 3 ploughs and
      13 Freemen, 13 villagers and 3 smallholders who have
         7 ploughs.
   Underwood, 2 acres. A priest and a church.
   Value before 1066 £4; now £10.

59 M. In (Upper) BROUGHTON Earl Algar had 2 c. of land taxable.
   Land for 7 ploughs. The King has 2 ploughs and
      23 villagers and 4 smallholders who have 7 ploughs.
   1 mill, 5s; meadow, 100 acres.
   Value before 1066 £3; now £4.

Ƀ In Torp.x.boū t̄ræ ad gld.T̄ra.x.boƀ.BEREW.

Wafta.ē.Ibi.xii.āc p̄ti.Val.ii.ſot.T.R.E.xl.ſot.

� In *FLINTHA* ħƀ Eluuin.xiiii.bou t̄ræ 7 iii partes

uni bou ad gld̄.T̄ra.v.car̄.Ibi hℲ rex.ii.car̄ in dn̄io.

7 v.ſoch 7 iiii.uilt 7 v.bord̄ hn̄tes.iii.car̄.Ibi æccła

7 pƀr hn̄s dim car̄.7 lx.āc p̄ti.Silua min̄.iii.q̄ꝗ

7 dim lḡ.7 i.q̄ꝗ lat̄.T.R.E.ual.lx.ſot.m̄ xl.

In Cheniueton.iii.bou t̄ræ ad gld.T̄ra.iiii.boū.Ibi.i.

ſoch hℲ dim car̄.7 i.āc p̄ti.

In Notintone hℲ rex.i.car t̄ræ ad gld.T̄ra.ii.car̄.

Ibi.xi.uilt hn̄t.iiii.car̄.7 xii.aĉs p̄ti.Valet.iii.liƀ

★ In *MERINGE* Witts ħƀ.vi.bō 7 dim ad gld̄.

In *MISNE* hℲ rex.iii.boū ad gld̄.Tofti habuit.Ibi sℲ.vi.

uilti cū.iii.car̄.Soca in *CIRCETON*.

Ibid̄ dim bou ad gld̄.Ad Lefton jacet.Ibi.i.uilts.

Wido teñ 7 Alured̄ de eo.

282 c

TERRA ALANI COMITIS.

Ꝉn *SIBETORP*.ħƀ Vnſpac.ii bou t̄ræ 7 dim ad

gld̄.T̄ra.i.car̄.Alan comes hℲ Fredgis de eo tenet.

7 ibi hℲ.i.car̄.7 iiii.ſoch de una bou tre.7 ii.bord̄

hn̄tes.i.car̄.Ibi pƀr 7 æccła.ad quā ptiñ.iiii.pars tre.

Ibi.x.āc p̄ti.T.R.E.xx.ſot.m̄.xii.ſot.

Ꝉbidē hℲ Osƀn.i.bou t̄ræ 7 iii.aĉs ad gld̄.T̄ra dim

car̄.Ibi pƀr.7 ii.bord̄.7 iiii.āc p̄ti.T.R.E.ual.x.ſot.

╭ m̄.iiii.ſot.

60 B. In THORPE (in-the-Glebe) 10 b. of land taxable.
  Land for 10 oxen. Outlier. Waste.
    Meadow, 12 acres.
  Value 2s; before 1066, 40s.

61 M. In FLINTHAM Alwin had 14 b. and 3 parts of 1 b. of land taxable.
  Land for 5 ploughs. The King has 2 ploughs in lordship and
    5 Freemen, 4 villagers and 5 smallholders who have 3 ploughs.
    A church and a priest who has ½ plough; meadow, 60 acres;
      underwood 3½ furlongs long and 1 furlong wide.
  Value before 1066, 60s; now 40 [s].

62 In KNEETON 3 b. of land taxable. Land for 4 oxen.
  1 Freeman has ½ plough.
  Meadow, 1 acre.

63 In SNEINTON the King has 1 c. of land taxable. Land for 2 ploughs.
  11 villagers have 4 ploughs.
  Meadow, 12 acres.
  Value £3.

[NEWARK Wapentake]
64 In MEERING William had 6½ b. taxable.

[BASSETLAW Wapentake]
65 In MISSON the King has 3 b. taxable. Tosti had it.
  6 villagers with 3 ploughs.
  Jurisdiction in Kirton (-in-Lindsey).
66 There also ½ b. taxable. It lies in Laughton (lands).
  1 villager.
  Guy holds it and Alfred from him.

Page 282 a,b is blank

2   **LAND OF COUNT ALAN**   282 c

[NEWARK Wapentake]
1 M. In SIBTHORPE Ospak had 2½ b. of land taxable. Land for 1 plough.
  Count Alan has it. Fredegis holds from him. He has 1 plough and
    4 Freemen with 1 b. of land; 2 smallholders who
      have 1 plough.
    A priest and a church, to which a fourth part of the land belongs;
      meadow, 10 acres.
  [Value] before 1066, 20s; now 12s.

2 M. There also Osbern has 1 b. and 3 acres of land taxable.
  Land for ½ plough.
    A priest; 2 smallholders.
    Meadow, 4 acres.
  Value before 1066, 10s; now 4s.

ᛒ In SIRESTVNE. ha
buit Ailric. III. bou
ad gld. Tra. I. car 7 dim.
Ibi. III. fochi hnt eas.
Ibi. XII. ac pti. Robt ten
de comite Alano.
Olī. XL. fot. m̄. XX. folid.

In CARLETVNE
.x. bou ad gld.
Ibi sf . III. uilli
cū. I. car. Witts ten.

In CLEDRETONE
habuer Godric
7 Vlmar. VII. bŏ træ
7 qntã parte uni bou
ad gld. Hanc trã
tenuer Alan com̄
7 Rog de busli
ufq; nē. Tra. II.
car. Val. XX. fot.

In SVDTONE. hb Witts fili Sceluuard. II. car træ
7 VI. bou ad gld. Tra. V. car. Ibi Herueus hŏ comitis. A.
ht. II. car. 7 XIII. foch de medietate træ huj. 7 XVII. uitt.
7 III. bord. hntes. VIII. car. Ibi pbr 7 æccla. 7 III. pifcariæ.
7 c. ac pti. Silua past. I. lev lg. 7 dim lev lat. T.R.E. 7 m̄

ᛗ In RODINTVN. hb Leuiet. XII. bou træ ad gld ᚠuat. II. lib.
Tra. IIII. car. Ibi comes in dnio. ht. I. car. 7 VI. foch. 7 VII. uitt
hntes. III. car. Ibi. LV. ac pti. T.R.E. uat. LX. fot. m̄ XXX. fot.

ᛗ In CHENIVETONE. hb Elfi. I. car tre ad gld. Tra XII. bou.
Ibi comes ht. I. car. 7 III. foch 7 V. uitt. hntes. II. car.
Ibi pbr 7 dim æccla. 7 I. molin. X. fot. 7 V. ac pti. T.R.E. uat
XX. fot. m̄ XL.

ᛗ IBIDE. hb Vluric. I. car træ ad gld. Tra XII. bou. Ibi
un uitts. ē 7 I. bord.

ᛗ In TIRESWELLE. hb Vlmar. VI. bou tre. 7 III. parte
uni bou ad gld. Tra. IIII. car. Robt de mofters hŏ com̄
ht. I. car. 7 VIII. uitt 7 V. bord. hntes. IIII. car. 7 XL. acs pti.
Silua past. IIII. q̃ɋ lg. 7 I. q̃ɋ 7 dim lat. T.R.E 7 m̄ uat XL. fot.

M . In SYERSTON Alric had 3 b. taxable. Land for 1½ ploughs.
3 Freemen have them.
Meadow, 12 acres.
Robert holds from Count Alan.
[Value] formerly 40s; now 20s.

[LYTHE Wapentake]
M. In SUTTON (-on-Trent) William son of Scaldward had 2 c.
and 6 b. of land taxable. Land for 5 ploughs.
Hervey, Count Alan's man, has 2 ploughs and
13 Freemen, with half of this land and 17 villagers and
3 smallholders who have 8 ploughs.
A priest and a church; 3 fisheries; meadow, 100 acres;
woodland pasture 1 league long and ½ league wide.
[Value] before 1066 and now £4.

In CARLTON (-on-Trent) 1 b. taxable.
3 villagers with 1 plough. William holds it.

[RUSHCLIFFE Wapentake]
M. In RUDDINGTON Leofgeat had 12 b. of land taxable.
Land for 4 ploughs. Count Alan has 1 plough in lordship and
6 Freemen and 7 villagers who have 3 ploughs.
Meadow, 55 acres.
Value before 1066, 60s; now 30s.

[BINGHAM Wapentake]
M. In KNEETON Alfsi had 1 c. of land taxable. Land for 12 oxen.
Count Alan has 1 plough and
3 Freemen and 5 villagers who have 2 ploughs.
A priest and ½ church; 1 mill, 10s; meadow, 5 acres.
Value before 1066, 20s; now 40[s].

M . There also Wulfric had 1 c. of land taxable. Land for 12 oxen.
1 villager and 1 smallholder.

[OSWALDBECK Wapentake]
M. In TRESWELL Wulfmer had 6 b. and the third part of 1 b. of
land taxable. Land for 4 ploughs. Robert of Moutiers, Count
Alan's man, has 1 plough and
8 villagers and 5 smallholders who have 4 ploughs.
Meadow, 40 acres; woodland pasture 4 furlongs long
and 1½ furlongs wide.
Value before 1066 and now 40s.

In LEVERTON Godric and Wulfmer had 7 b. and the fifth part
of 1 b. of land taxable. Count Alan and Roger of Bully held
this land until now. Land for 2 ploughs.
Value 20s.

.III. TERRA HVGONIS COMITIS.

Ⓜ In SVDTONE. hb Harold. I . car tre 7 dim ad glđ.

Tra . I . car . Hugo com m hr . Robt ~~fili Willi~~ de eo ten.

7 ibi hr . I . car 7 dim .7 III . foch 7 VI . uilt . hntes . III . car

7 dim .7 I . molin XX . folid .7 XV . acs pti . T.R.E .7 m ual

S In Normanton . II . bou træ 7 II . part . I . bou ⌐XL . fol.

ad glđ . Tra . I . car . Wafta . ē . Ibi . III . ac pti . T.R.E . ual

Ⓜ In BONITONE . hb Harold . VI . bou tre ⌐V . fol . m . III . fol.

ađ glđ . Tra . II . car . Ibi Robt ho comitis hr . III . foch.

.II. 7 V . uilt hntes . II . car 7 dim . Ibi . X . ac pti . T.R.E .7 m ual

Ⓜ In CHINESTAN . hbr Leuuin 7 Ricard . III . bou ⌐XX . fol.

træ 7 dim ad glđ . Tra . X . bou . Ibi m un⁹ fochs hr dim

car .7 IX . acs pti . T.R.E . ual . XXX . fol . m . X . fol.

.IIII. TERRA COMITIS MORITON.

282 d

Ⓜ In NORMANTVNE hb Stori X . bou tre ad glđ.

Tra . II . car . Nc comes de morit hr . Alden de eo tenet.

7 Ibi hr . I . car .7 II . foch .7 II . uilt .7 III . borđ . hntes . II . car.

Ibi . XV . ac pti . T.R.E . ual . XL . fol . m . XXX.

Ⓜ In SVDTONE . hb Stori dim car træ ad glđ . Tra XII . bou.

Ibi nc . I . car in dnio .7 V . ac pti . T.R.E . ual XXX . fol . m . XX.

Ⓜ In GATHA . hb Stori . II . car træ 7 III . bou 7 dim ad glđ .7 . V . acs.

Tra . VI . car . Ibi comes . R . in dnio hr . III . car .7 III . foch.

7 XX . uilt 7 II . borđ . hntes . IX . car .7 qt XX . acs pti . T.R.E.

ual . LX . fol . m XL . fol. ⌐ In Leche . II . bou træ ad glđ . SocA huj Ⓜ.

3   LAND OF EARL HUGH

[RUSHCLIFFE Wapentake]

1 M. In SUTTON (Bonington) Harold had 1½ c. of land taxable.
Land for 1 plough. Earl Hugh now has it. Robert *son of William* holds from him. He has 1½ ploughs.
   3 Freemen and 6 villagers who have 3½ ploughs.
   1 mill, 20s; meadow, 15 acres.
Value before 1066 and now 40s.

Jurisdiction.

2 S. In NORMANTON (-on-Soar) 2 b. and 2 parts of 1 b. of land taxable. Land for 1 plough. Waste.
   Meadow, 3 acres.
Value before 1066, 5s; now 3s.

3 M. In (Sutton) BONINGTON Harold had 6 b. of land taxable.
Land for 2 ploughs. Robert, the Earl's man, has
   3 Freemen and 5 villagers who have 2½ ploughs.
   Meadow, 10 acres.
Value before 1066 and now 20s.

4 M. 2 In KINGSTON (-on-Soar) Leofwin and Richard had 3½ b. of land taxable. Land for 10 oxen.
   1 Freeman now has ½ plough under Earl Hugh.
   Meadow, 9 acres.
Value before 1066, 30s; now 10s.

4   LAND OF THE COUNT OF MORTAIN   282 d

[RUSHCLIFFE Wapentake]

1 M. In NORMANTON (-on-Soar) Stori had 10 b. of land taxable.
Land for 2 ploughs. Now the Count of Mortain has it.
Haldane holds from him. He has 1 plough and
   2 Freemen, 2 villagers and 3 smallholders who have 2 ploughs.
   Meadow, 15 acres.
Value before 1066, 40s; now 30[s].

2 M. In SUTTON (Bonington) Stori had ½ c. of land taxable.
Land for 12 oxen. 1 plough now in lordship.
   Meadow, 5 acres.
Value before 1066, 30s; now 20[s].

3 M. In GOTHAM Stori had 2 c, 3½ b. of land taxable, and 5 acres.
Land for 6 ploughs. Count Robert has 3 ploughs in lordship and
   3 Freemen, 20 villagers and 2 smallholders who have 9 ploughs.
   Meadow, 80 acres.
Value before 1066, 60s; now 40s.

4 In LEAKE 2 b. of land taxable. Nothing there. Jurisdiction of this manor.

ↀ In *STANTVN*.ħɓ Stori.iii.bou trǽ 7 dim ad glđ.Tra.i.car.

Ibi Alured hõ comitis hr̃.i.car.7 vi.uiłł 7 iii.borđ.

⁂cū.ii.car.Ibi xx.aᴄ̃ p̃ti.T.R.E.uał.xʟ.foł.m̃ xx.

ↀ In *CAWORDE*.ħɓ Stori.iii.bou tre.7 iii.partẽ.i.bou

ad glđ.Tra.i.car.Ibi Alured hõ com hr̃.ii.focħ.7 i.uiłł

7 i.borđ cū.i.car 7 dim.T.R.E.uał.xx.foł.m̃.x.foł.

⁂ↀ In ead Stantun.ħɓ Frane.i.bou trǽ 7 iii.part.uni bou

ad glđ.Tra dim car.Ibi.iii.uiłłi m̃ hn̄t.i.car.

In *NEVTORP*.ħɓ Æluin.i.bou trǽ ad glđ.Tra.ii.boū.

Ibi Silua past.viii.q̃ʒ lḡ.7 ii.q̃ʒ 7 dim lat.T.R.E.uał.

ii.foł.m̃ xii.den.

283 a

.V.   TERRA ARCHIEP̃I EBORAC̃SIS.

    TORGARTONE WAPENTAC.

ↀ In *SVDWELLE* cū Bereuuitis fuis.funt xxii.

    carucatæ trǽ 7 dim ad glđ.Tra.xxiiii.car.

Ibi hr̃ Archiep̃s Thomas.x.car in dñio.7 x.focħ

7 ʟxxv.uiłł.7 xxiii.borđ.hn̄tes.xxxvii.car.

Ibi.ii.molđ.xʟ.foliđ.7 pifcina 7 paffagiū.vi.foł.

De ead tra ten.vi.milites.iiii.car trǽ 7 dim.

Tres clerici.hn̄t.i.car tre 7 dim.de ea fuɴ.ii.bouatæ

in p̃benda.Duo anglici hn̄t.iii.car trǽ 7 v.bouatæ.

Ⲅ Milites hn̄t.vii.car in dñio.7 xxxv.uiłłos.7 xxviii.

borđ.hn̄tes.xxi.car.7 i.moliñ.viii.foliđ.   Ⲅiii.car.

Ⲅ Clerici hn̄t.i.car 7 dim in dñio.7 vii.uiłłos 7 v.borđ.hn̄tes

Ⲅ Anglici hn̄t.iiii.car in dñio.7 xx.uiłł 7 vʟ.borđ hn̄tes

vi.car 7 dim.

Ad Suduuelle p̃tiñ c 7 q̃t xx 7 viii.aᴄ̃ p̃ti.Silua

past.viii.lev lḡ.7 ii.q̃ʒ 7 dim lat.Terra arabił

v.lev lḡ. 7 iii.lat.

T.R.E.uał.xʟ.liɓ.m̃.xʟ.liɓ 7 xv.foliđ.

In Suduuelle numerant.xii.bereuu.

5   M. In STANTON (on-the-Wolds) Stori had 3½ b. of land taxable.
Land for 1 plough. Alfred, the Count's man, has 1 plough and
6 villagers and 3 smallholders with 2 ploughs.
Meadow, 20 acres.
Value before 1066, 40s; now 20[s].

4,6 is entered after 4,7, with transposition marks.

7   M. In KEYWORTH Stori had 3 b. and the third part of 1 b. of land
taxable. Land for 1 plough. Alfred, the Count's man, has
2 Freemen, 1 villager and 1 smallholder with 1½ ploughs.
Value before 1066, 20s; now 10s.

6   M. Also in STANTON Fran had 1 b. and 3 parts of 1 b. of land
taxable. Land for ½ plough.
3 villagers now have 1 plough.

[BROXTOW Wapentake]

8   In NEWTHORPE Alwin had 1 b. of land taxable. Land for 2 oxen.
Woodland pasture 8 furlongs long and 2½ furlongs wide.
Value before 1066, 2s; now 12d.

5   LAND OF THE ARCHBISHOP OF YORK   283 a

THURGARTON Wapentake

1   M. In SOUTHWELL with its outliers 22½ c. of land taxable.
Land for 24 ploughs. Archbishop Thomas has 10 ploughs in
lordship and
10 Freemen, 75 villagers and 23 smallholders who have 37 ploughs.
2 mills, 40s; a fishpond and a ferry 6s.
6 men-at-arms hold 4½ c. of this land. 3 clerics have 1½ c.
of land, of which 2 b. are in prebend. 2 Englishmen
have 3 c. and 5 b. of land.
The men-at-arms have 7 ploughs in lordship and
35 villagers and 28 smallholders who have 21 ploughs.
1 mill, 8s.
The clerics have 1½ ploughs in lordship and
7 villagers and 5 smallholders who have 3 ploughs.
The Englishmen have 4 ploughs in lordship and
20 villagers and 6 smallholders who have 6½ ploughs.
To Southwell belongs meadow, 188 acres; woodland pasture 8
leagues long and 2½ furlongs wide; arable land 5 leagues long
and 3 wide.
Value before 1066 £40; now £40 15s.
In Southwell 12 outliers are enumerated.

In Nordmuſchã. .I.car 7 dim̃ ad gld̃.

ꝏ In CROPHILLE.7 Hegelinge.h̃b S̃ MARIA de
7 B' Sudvvelle.II.car tre 7 dim̃ ad gld.Tra.VII.car.

Ibi h̃nt canon in dñio.II.car̃.7 v.ſoch 7 xv.uilt.

7 II.bord̃.h̃ntes vI.car̃ 7 II.boues.7 xx.aĉs p̃ti.

T.R.E.ual.Lx.ſolid̃.modo.L.

ꝏ In LANVN cũ Bereuu his.Aſcã Bechinghã.San
7 B' debi.Bolun.Burtone.Watelaie.Legretone.

VIIII.car uem træ 7 II.bou ad gld̃.Tra xxvII.car.

In dñio aulæ ſuɴ.x.bou de hac tra.Reliq̃ eſt ſoca.

Modo h̃t|Thomas ibi arch̃.IIII.car 7 dim̃.7 xxxv.uilt.

7 vI.bord̃ h̃ntes.xvI.car̃.Ibi æccła 7 p̃br.7 II.

piſcariæ.vIII to.ſolid̃.7 I.molĩn.xvI.ſolid̃.Silua

paſtil.III.lev l̃g.7 I.lev 7 dim̃ lat̃.Prati.C.

acræ.

In ſup̃dictis BER ad ipsũ ꝏ p̃tinent ſuɴ.xxxvIII.

ſoch̃i.7 xvII.uilt 7 xx.bord̃.h̃ntes.xIIII.car̃ 7 dim̃.

⌐ Suɴ 7 alii.xxxIII es.ſoch 7 vI.uilt 7 xvIII.bord̃.h̃ntes

xv.car̃.Hos cũ tra ſua ten.II.milites de archiep̃o.

★ ꝏ In Muſchã 7 Carleton.IIII.car træ 7 v.bou ad gld.

Tra.Ix.car̃ 7 dim̃. Ibi Thom arch̃ h̃t.II.car̃ in dñio.

7 xx.ſoch 7 vII.uilt 7 xvI.bord̃

h̃ntes.vI.car̃.Ibi.I.mol.II.ſolidoʒ.7 Lx vI..ac̃ p̃ti.

7 qt a7 xx ti.aĉs filuæ minutæ.T.R.E.ual.xvI.ſot.m̃.x.

★ In ROLLESTVNE Aluric habuit ꝑ ꝏ.IIII.bou 7 dim̃ ad gld̃.

283 b Tra.I.car̃.q̃ h̃nt ibi.v.uilti.Ibi.xII.ac̃ p̃ti.Olĩ.xx.ſot.M̊ ual.x.ſolid̃.

ꝏ In SVDTONE 7 Scrobi 7 Madreſſei B' Lund.I.car træ
7 B' 7 vI.bou ad gld.Tra.vI.car̃.Ibi h̃t Thom arch̃.II.

car in dñio.7 xIIII.uilt 7 vI.bord̃.h̃ntes.vI.car̃.

2   In NORTH MUSKHAM 1½ c. taxable.

BINGHAM Wapentake

3 M.
  &B. In CROPWELL (Bishop) and the outlier, HICKLING, St Mary's
of Southwell had 2½ c. of land taxable. Land for 7 ploughs.
The Canons have 2 ploughs in lordship and
    5 Freemen, 15 villagers and 4 smallholders who have 6
      ploughs and 2 oxen.
    Meadow, 20 acres.
Value before 1066, 60s; now 50 [s].

[BASSETLAW Wapentake]

4 M.
  &B. In LANEHAM, with these outliers, ASKHAM, BECKINGHAM, SAUNDBY,
BOLE, (West) BURTON, WHEATLEY and LEVERTON, 9 c. and 2 b. of land
taxable. Land for 27 ploughs. 10 b. of this land are in the
lordship of the hall; the rest is [in] the Jurisdiction. Archbishop
Thomas now has 4½ ploughs and
    35 villagers and 6 smallholders who have 16 ploughs.
    A church and a priest; 2 fisheries, 8s; 1 mill, 16s; woodland
    pasture 3 leagues long and 1½ leagues wide; meadow, 100 acres.
In the said outliers which belong to this manor are
    38 Freemen, 17 villagers and 20 smallholders who have 14½ ploughs.
    Also another 33 Freemen, 6 villagers and 18 smallholders who
      have 15 ploughs.
    Two men-at-arms hold them from the Archbishop with their land.
[Value...]

[LYTHE Wapentake]

5 M. In (South) MUSKHAM and CARLTON (-on-Trent) 4c. and 5 b. of land
taxable. Land for 9½ ploughs. Archbishop Thomas has 2 ploughs
in lordship and
    20 Freemen, 7 villagers and 16 smallholders who have 6 ploughs.
    1 mill, 2s; meadow, 66 acres; underwood, 80 acres.
Value before 1066, 16s; now 10 [s].

[THURGARTON Wapentake]

6   In ROLLESTON Aelfric had as a manor 4½ b. taxable. Land for 1 plough.
    5 villagers have it.
    Meadow, 12 acres.
Value formerly 20s; now 10s.

[BASSETLAW Wapentake]

7 M.
  &B. In SUTTON (-by-Retford) and the outliers SCROOBY and   283 b
LOUND, 1 c. and 6 b. of land taxable. Land for 6 ploughs.
Archbishop Thomas has 2 ploughs in lordship and
    14 villagers and 6 smallholders who have 6 ploughs.

Ibi vii . a̅c p̃ti . Silua past dim̄ lev 7 viii . q̃ʒ l̅g.

7 viii . q̃ʒ 7 dim̄ lat̄ . T.R.E. ual . viii . lib̄ . m̄ similit.

SOCA HVI MANER.

In Ettone . ii . car̄ . In Tilne . ii . bou̅ 7 iiii . pars . i . bou.

In Wellon 7 Simenton . v . bou̅ 7 iiii . pars . i . bou̅.

In Grenelei . i . bo̅ 7 iiii . pars . i . bou̅ . In Scafteorde . i . car̄.

In Euretone . i . car̄ 7 iii . pars . i . bou̅ . Tra h̄ est . xii . car̄.

Ibi m̄ . xxxviii . soch cu̅ xviii . uilt 7 xx bord

h̄nt . xxv . car̄ . In Tilne . i . molin̄ redd̄ . l̅xxx . solid.

In Redforde . i . mot . ptin̄ ad sudtone . In Claueburch . vi . bo̅ 7 dim̄.

P̃tu̅ iiii . q̃ʒ 7 dim̄ l̅g . 7 tantd̄ lat̄ . 7 adhuc . xlv . acs.

Silua past . ii . lev 7 dim̄ l̅g . 7 ii . lev lat̄.

In *BLIDEWORDE* h̄b̄ arch ebor . ix . bou træ ad gld̄.

Tra . iii . car̄ . Ibi h̄t Thom . v . uilt h̄ntes . ii . car̄ . 7 unu̅

molin̄ qui . e̅ in Ludeha̅ . Silua past . iii . lev l̅g . 7 i . lat̄.

In Caļuretone . vi . bou træ ad gld . Tra xii . bou . BER.

Ibi . vii . uilt 7 ii . bord h̄nt . ii . car̄ . Ibi æcc̄la 7 p̄br . 7 ii . a̅c

p̃ti . Siluæ past . viii . q̃ʒ l̅g . 7 iii . lat̄ . T.R.E. 7 m̄ ual . xl . sot.

In *OSTONE* h̄b̄ Elnod . vi . bou træ ad gld̄ . Tra . ii . car̄.

Ibi h̄t Thom . i . car̄ in d̄nio . 7 i . soch 7 i . uilt . 7 i . bord

h̄ntes . ii . car̄ . De hac tra h̄t rex . i . bou . Reliq̃ iacet

ad Blideuuorde . T.R.E. ual . xl . sot . m̄ xx.

★ In *RAVESCHEL* . iiii . bou 7 dim̄ ad gld̄ . Tra . e̅ . i car̄ . Vasta fuit 7 e̅.

Godric tenuit . Arch tenet.

In *NORTWELLE* h̄b̄ S̃ MARIA de Sudwelle xii . bou

træ ad gld . Tra . vi . car̄ . Ibi m̄ . ii . car̄ in d̄nio . 7 xxii.

uilt 7 iii . bord . h̄ntes . vii . car̄ . Ibi æcc̄la 7 p̄br . 7 i . molin̄

. xii . denar . 7 i . piscar . 7 lxx . iii . a̅c p̃ti . Silua past . ii.

lev l̅g . 7 i . lat̄ . T.R.E. ual . vi . lib̄ . m̄ . c . sot . SOCA HVI MAN.

In Osuuitorp . iiii . bou træ ad gld . Tra . ii . car̄ . Ibi . iiii . soch

Meadow, 7 acres; woodland pasture ½ league and 8 furlongs long
and 8½ furlongs wide.
Value before 1066 £8; now the same.

Jurisdiction of this manor.

8   In EATON 2 c. taxable; TILN 2 b. and the fourth part of 1 b;
WELHAM' and SIMENTON 5 b. and the fourth part of 1 b; (Little)
GRÍNGLEY 1 b. and the fourth part of 1 b; SCAFTWORTH 1 c;
EVERTON 1 c. and the third part of 1 b; Land for 12 ploughs.
     38 Freemen with 18 villagers and 20 smallholders have 25 ploughs.
In TILN 1 mill which belongs to Laneham pays 30s; in RETFORD 1 mill
belongs to Sutton; in CLARBOROUGH 6½ b.
     Meadow 4½ furlongs long and as much wide and a further
       45 acres; woodland pasture 2½ leagues long and 2 leagues wide.

[THURGARTON Wapentake]

9   M. In BLIDWORTH the Archbishop of York had 9 b. of land taxable.
Land for 3 ploughs. Archbishop Thomas has
     5 villagers who have 2 ploughs.
     A mill which is in Lowdham; woodland pasture 3 leagues
     long and 1 wide.

10   B. In CALVERTON 6 b. of land taxable. Land for 12 oxen. Outlier.
     7 villagers and 2 smallholders have 2 ploughs.
     A church and a priest; meadow, 2 acres; woodland pasture 8
     furlongs long and 3 wide.
Value before 1066 and now 40s.

11   M. In OXTON Alnoth had 6 b. of land taxable. Land for 2 ploughs.
Archbishop Thomas has 1 plough in lordship and
     1 Freeman, 1 villager and 1 smallholder who have 2 ploughs.
     The King has 1 b. of this land; the rest lies in Blidworth (lands).
Value before 1066, 40s; now 20[s.]

12   In RANSKILL 4½ b. taxable. Land for 1 plough. It was and is
waste. Godric held it; the Archbishop holds it.

[LYTHE Wapentake]

13   M. In NORWELL St. Mary's of Southwell had 12 b. of land taxable.
Land for 6 ploughs. 2 ploughs now in lordship;
     22 villagers and 3 smallholders who have 7 ploughs.
     A church and a priest; 1 mill, 12d; 1 fishery; meadow, 73 acres;
     woodland pasture 2 leagues long and 1 wide.
Value before 1066 £6; now 100s.

Jurisdiction of this manor.

14   S. In OSMANTHORPE 4 b. of land taxable. Land for 2 ploughs.

hñt.ii.car. Pti ac.viii.Silua past.iiii.q̃ᵹ lḡ.7 iii.lat.

§ In Wilgebi.iii.bou træ 7 dim ad gld.Tra.i .car.Ibi.iiii.
foch 7 iii.uilt hñt.ii.car.7 xvi.ac pti.

§ In Calneſtone.ii.bou træ ad gld.Tra.iiii.bou.Ibi.i.foch
7 v.bord hñt.i.car 7 dim.7 ii.acs pti.Silua past.iii.q̃ᵹ lḡ
In Ocretone.i.bou træ ad gld.Ibi.i.uilt 7 i.bord. ⌐7 ii.lat.
7 ii.ac pti.

In Vdeburg.vii.bou træ ad gld.Tra.ii.car.Ibi dim car
in dño.7 ii.uilt 7 i.bord hñt.i.car. Ad Suduuelle ptiñ.
Ibidē.ht.i.cleric⁹ fub arch.i.bou træ ad gld.

.VI. TERRA EPI LINCOLIENSIS.

In NEWERCHE cũ.ii.bereuuit.Baldretune

7 Farendune.habuit Godeua comitiſſa.vii.car træ
7 ii.bou ad gld.Tra.xxvi.car.Ibi eps Remig
ht.|vii.car.7 xl.ii.uilt 7 iiii.bord.hñtes.xx.car
7 dim.Ibi.x.æcclæ 7 viii.pbri hñtes.v.car.Ibi.vii.
franci hões hñt.v.car 7 dim.Ibi.i.moliñ.v.folid.
7 iiii.denar.7 i.pifcariã.Ad Neuuerche adjacen
oms ciuetudines regis 7 comitis de ipfo Wapentac.
T.R.E.reddeb.l.lib.m̃.xxxiiii.lib.Soca huj M

§ In Baldretone.vi.bou træ 7 dim ad gld.Tra.iii.car.
Ibi xxvi.foch 7 iii.bord hñt.ix.car.

★ § In Cheluintone.Sireſtune.Eluestune.Stoches.
Holtone.Cotintone.Barnebi.Wimuntorp.Simul
ad gld.iii.car 7 dim bou.Tra.x.car 7 dimid.
Ibi.lxx.vii.foch cũ.iiii.bord hñt xv.car 7 dim.
jn eis.c.lxiii.ac pti.

§ In Scornelei.Gretone.Spaldesforde.Torneſhaie.
7 Wigesleie.Herdrebi.Cotun.Simul ad gld.
vi.car 7 dim.7 dim bou.Tra xx.i.car.7 iii.bou.

4 Freemen have 2 ploughs.
Meadow, 8 acres; woodland pasture 4 furlongs long and 3 wide.

15 S. In WILLOUGHBY 3½ b. of land taxable. Land for 1 plough.
4 Freemen and 3 villagers have 2 ploughs.
Meadow, 16 acres.

16 S. In CAUNTON 2 b. of land taxable. Land for 4 oxen.
1 Freeman and 5 smallholders have 1½ ploughs.
Meadow, 2 acres; woodland pasture 3 furlongs long and 2 wide.

17 In HOCKERTON 1 b. of land taxable.
1 villager and 1 smallholder.
Meadow, 2 acres.

18 In WOODBOROUGH 7 b. of land taxable. Land for 2 ploughs. ½
plough in lordship.
2 villagers and 1 smallholder have 1 plough; it belongs to Southwell.

19 There also 1 cleric has 1 b. of land taxable under the Archbishop.

Column 283 c is blank

6   LAND OF THE BISHOP OF LINCOLN   283 d

[NEWARK Wapentake]
1 M. In NEWARK with the 2 outliers BALDERTON and FARNDON Countess
Godiva had 7 c. and 2 b. of land taxable. Land for 26 ploughs.
Bishop Remigius has 7 ploughs in lordship and
56 burgesses, 42 villagers and 4 smallholders who have 20½ ploughs.
10 churches and 8 priests who have 5 ploughs. 7 Freemen
have 5½ ploughs.
1 mill, 5s 4d; 1 fishery.
All the customary dues of the King and the Earl from this
Wapentake are attached to Newark.
Before 1066 it paid £50; now £34.
Jurisdiction of this manor.

2 S. In BALDERTON 6½ b. of land taxable. Land for 3 ploughs.
26 Freemen and 3 smallholders have 9 ploughs.

3 S. In KILVINGTON 1 b; SYERSTON 1½ b; ELSTON 1 b; (East) STOKE 1½ b;
HAWTON 2½ b; CODDINGTON 1 c; BARNBY (-in-the-Willows) 2½ b;
WINTHORPE 6½ b; altogether 3 c. and ½ b. taxable.
Land for 10½ ploughs.
77 Freemen with 4 smallholders have 15½ ploughs.
Meadow, 163 acres, in these (villages).

4 S. In (South) SCARLE 2½ c; GIRTON 1½ c; SPALFORD 3½ b; THORNEY 1 c;
WIGSLEY 7 b; HARBY 1 b; COTHAM 1 b; altogether 6½ c. and ½ b.
taxable. Land for 21 ploughs and 3 oxen.

Ibi.ᴌxxɪ.focħ 7 vɪɪ.borđ.hn̄t xxɪ.caŕ.7 dim̄.

Ibi.cc.7 q̇t xx.ac̄ p̄ti.Silua paſt.v.q̇ɻ lḡ.

ıı.7 ɪɪɪɪ.q̇ɻ lat.

ꝳ In *ELVESTVN*.ħbr Leuuin 7 Pileuuin.ɪɪ.bou̇ træ
ad għđ.Tra.ɪɪɪɪ.bou̇.Ibi.ɪ.uiħs 7 ɪɪɪ.borđ hn̄t
ɪ.caŕ.Ibi.xɪɪ.ac̄ p̄ti.T.R.E.7 m̊.uaħ.x.foliđ.
Rauenefort 7 Arnegri̇ ten̊ de epo.

ꝳ In Cotintone.ħƀ Vluric.ɪ.bou̇ træ ad għđ.Tra
ɪɪ.bou̇.Ibi ħ eꝑs dim̄ caŕ.7 ɪ.ac̄ p̄ti.T.R.E.uaħ
xᴌ.foħ.m̊.xx.

ꝳ Ibidē ħƀ Bugo.ɪ.bou̇ træ 7 dim̄ ad għđ.Tra dim̄
caŕ.Waſta.ē.Botild tenet.7 valet.ɪɪ.foħ.Ibi.ɪɪ.ac̄ p̄ti.

ꝳ In *CLITONE*.ħƀ Vluiet.vɪ.bou̇ træ|ad għđ.Tra.ɪɪɪ.
caŕ.Ibi ħ eꝑs.R.ɪɪɪ.focħ de.ɪɪɪ.bou̇ hui̇ træ.7 ɪ.borđ.
cū.ɪ.caŕ.Ibi xxx.ac̄ p̄ti.Silua paſt dim̄ lev̇ lḡ
7 ɪɪɪ.q̇ɻ lat.T.R.E.uaħ.xx.foħ.m̊.x.foħ.Radulf

ꝳ In *HERDEBI*.ħƀ Goduin.vɪ.bou̇ tre ad għđ.Tra
ɪɪ.caŕ.Ibi m̊.v.uiħi hn̄t.ɪɪ.caŕ.7 xɪɪ.ac̄s p̄ti.
Silua paſt dim̄ leu̇ lḡ.7 dim̄ lat.T.R.E.uaħ.xᴌ.foħ.

ꝳ In *CLIFTONE*.ħƀ Frane.ɪɪɪ.bou̇ træ 7 dim̄ ⌐ m̊.xx.
ad gld.Tra.xɪɪ.bou̇.Ibi eꝑs.Re.ħ.ɪ.caŕ.7 vɪ.uiħ
7 ɪɪ.borđ hn̄tes.ɪ.caŕ 7 dim̄.Ibi xɪɪɪɪ.ac̄ p̄ti.T.R.E.
uaħ xᴌ.foħ.m̊ xx.Siuuate tenet.

ꝳ Ibidē ħƀ Vluiet.ɪ.bō træ 7 dim̄ ad għđ.Tra.ɪ.caŕ.

284 a

Waſta.ē.Radulf tenet.Ibi.ē quarta pars.ɪ.æcclæ.
7 vɪɪɪ.ac̄ p̄ti.T.R.E.uaħ x.foħ.m̊.v.foliđ.

ꝳ Ibidē.ħƀ Agemund.ɪɪ.bou̇ træ 7 dim̄ ad għđ.
Tra.ɪ.caŕ.Idē Agemund ten̊ de epo.7 ħ.ɪɪ.bou̇ in
caŕ.7 ɪɪ.uiħ fimilit.ɪɪ.bou̇ in caŕ.7 vɪɪɪ.ac̄s p̄ti.
T.R.E.uaħ.x.foħ.m̊.vɪ.foħ.

71 Freemen and 7 smallholders have 21½ ploughs.
Meadow, 280 acres; woodland pasture 5 furlongs long and
    4 furlongs wide.

5 2 In ELSTON Leofwin and Pilwin had 2 b. of land taxable.
  M. Land for 4 oxen.
    1 villager and 3 smallholders have 1 plough.
    Meadow, 12 acres.
  Value before 1066 and now 10s.
      Ravensward and Arngrim hold from the Bishop.

6 M. In CODDINGTON Wulfric had 1 b. of land taxable.. Land for 2 oxen.
  The Bishop has ½ plough.
    Meadow, 1 acre.
  Value before 1066, 40s; now 20[s.]

7 M. There also Bugg had 1½ b. of land taxable. Land for ½ plough.
    Waste. Bothild holds it.
  Value 2s.
    Meadow, 2 acres.

8 M. In CLIFTON Wulfgeat had 6½ b. of land taxable. Land for 3 ploughs.
  Bishop Remigius has
    3 Freemen with 3 b. of this land and 1 smallholder with 1 plough.
    Meadow, 30 acres; woodland pasture ½ league long and 3
        furlongs wide.
  Value before 1066, 20s; now 10s.
    Ralph holds it.

9 M. In HARBY Godwin had 6 b. of land taxable. Land for 2 ploughs.
    5 villagers now have 2 ploughs.
    Meadow, 12 acres; woodland pasture ½ league long and ½ wide.
  Value before 1066, 40s; now 20[s].

10 M. In CLIFTON Fran had 3½ b. of land taxable. Land for 12 oxen.
  Bishop Remigius has 1 plough and
    6 villagers and 2 smallholders who have 1½ ploughs.
    Meadow, 14 acres.
  Value before 1066, 40s; now 20[s].
    Siwat holds it.

11 M. There also Wulfgeat had 1½ b. of land taxable. Land for 1 plough.
    Waste. Ralph holds it.   284 a
    The fourth part of 1 church; meadow, 8 acres.
  Value before 1066, 10s; now 5s.

12 M. There also Agemund had 2½ b. of land taxable. Land for 1 plough.
    Agemund still holds from the Bishop; he has 2 oxen in a plough.
    2 villagers likewise, 2 oxen in a plough.
    Meadow, 8 acres.
  Value before 1066, now 6s.

ⓂIn *Fladebvrg* h̄b Godeue .ı.car̄ 7 ııı.boū 7 dim

ad glđ.Tra.ıııı.car̄.Ibi Nigell h̄o ep̄i h̄t.ıı.car̄

7 dim.7 xvı.uill.7 v.foch de.ı.boū huj træ.h̄ntes

v.car̄.Ibi p̄br 7 æccla.7 ı.moliñ.xıı.denar̄.Silua

paſt.ı.lev l̄g.7 dim lev lat̄.T.R.E.ual.vııı.lib̄.m̊.v.

§In Normentone.vı.b̄o træ ad glđ.Tra.xıı.boū.Soca

Ibi xı.foch h̄nt.ııı.car̄.7 vı.ac̊s p̊ti.

ⓂIn *Estoches* h̄b Godeue vı.bou tre 7 ııı.parte

7 q̇ndecima.ad glđ.Tra.xıı.boū.Ibi Nigel h̄o ep̄i

h̄t v.foch 7 ıııı.borđ h̄nt.ııı.car̄.7 vı.ac̊s p̊ti.

7 Siluæ minut̄

T.R.E.   ual.xx.fol.

m̊.x.fol.

284 b

.VI. **Terra ep̄i Baiocensis.**

ⓂIn *Cotes*.h̄b Leuric.ııı.bou træ ad gld.Tra

xıı.boū.Ibi Wazeliñ h̄o ep̄i Baioc̊ h̄t.ı.car̄.

7 v.uill 7 ı.borđ h̄ntes dim car̄.7 xx.ac̃ p̊ti.

T.R.E.ual.xl.fol.m̊.xxx.

ⓂIn *Barnebi*.h̄b Vluric̊.vıı.bou træ ad glđ.

Tra.ııı.car̄.Ibi Loſuard h̄o ep̄i Baioc̊ h̄t.ı.car̄.

7 ıııı.foch de ıı.bou hui træ.7 ıx.uill 7 vı.borđ

h̄ntes.ıııı.car̄ 7 dim.Ibi p̄br 7 æccla.in q̊ jacet dim

bou de hac tra.7 ı.moliñ.v.fol.7 ıııı.den.7 xxx.ac̃

p̊ti.7 filua minuta.T.R.E.7 m̊ ual.xl.fol.

ⓂIn *Cotintvn*.h̄b Vluric.ııı.bou træ 7 dim ad gld.

Tra.xıı.boū.Ibi Loſoard h̄o ep̄i h̄t.ıı.uill 7 ıııı.

borđ cū.ı.car̄.7 ııı.ac̃ p̊ti.T.R.E.ual xx.fol.m̊.x.

In BASSETLAW Wapentake

13 M. In FLEDBOROUGH Countess Godiva had 1 c. and 3½ b. taxable.
Land for 4 ploughs. Nigel, the Bishop's man, has 2½ ploughs and
16 villagers and 5 Freemen with 1 b. of this land who have
5 ploughs.
A priest and a church; 1 mill, 12d; woodland pasture 1 league
long and ½ league wide.
Value before 1066 £8; now [£] 5.

14 S. In NORMANTON (-on-Trent) 6 b. of land taxable. Land for 12 oxen.
Jurisdiction.
11 Freemen have 3 ploughs.
Meadow, 6 acres.

15 M. In STOKEHAM Countess Godiva had 6 b. of land, and a third part and
a fifteenth taxable. Land for 12 oxen. Nigel, the Bishop's man, has
5 Freemen. 4 smallholders have 3 ploughs.
Meadow, 6 acres; underwood.
Value before 1066, 20s; now 10s.

[7]   LAND OF THE BISHOP OF BAYEUX   284 b

[In NEWARK Wapentake]
1 M. In COTHAM Leofric had 3 b. of land taxable. Land for 12 oxen.
Wazelin, the Bishop of Bayeux's man, has 1 plough and
5 villagers and 1 smallholder, who have ½ plough.
Meadow, 20 acres.
Value before 1066, 40s; now 30[s.]

2 M. In BARNBY (-in-the-Willows) Wulfric had 7 b. of land taxable.
Land for 3 ploughs. Losoard, the Bishop of Bayeux's man,
has 1 plough and
4 Freemen with 2 b. of this land and 9 villagers and
6 smallholders who have 4½ ploughs.
A priest and a church in whose (lands) lies ½ b. of this land;
1 mill, 5s 4d; meadow, 30 acres; underwood.
Value before 1066 and now 40s.

3 M. In CODDINGTON Wulfric had 3½ b. of land taxable.
Land for 12 oxen. Losoard, the Bishop's man, has
2 villagers and 4 smallholders with 1 plough.
Meadow, 3 acres.
Value before 1066, 20s; now 10[s.]

ꝳ **In** Cotintone . h̄b Leuric . v . bou tre ad gl̄d . Tra
ii . car̄ . Ibi Oudchel ſub epō h̄t dim̄ car̄ . 7 iiii . ſoch
de . iiii . bou hui træ 7 iii . bord cū dim car̄ . 7 v . ac̄ p̄ti.

ꝳ **In** Rollestone . h̄b Goduin . ii . car̄ træ 7 dim̄ ad gl̄d .
7 iiii . partē . i . bou . Tra . vi . car̄ . Ibi Loſoard hō epī
h̄t . i . car̄ . 7 xi . uill . 7 ix . bord . hn̄tes . iiii . car̄ 7 dim .
Ibi . i . molin̄ . xxvii . ſolid . 7 lxviii . ac̄ p̄ti . T.R.E. ual
viii . lib̄ . m̄ iiii . lib̄ 7 x . ſol . Ad iſt ꝳ p̄tin̄ . vii . ſoch
jᷠ Opetone 7 Colingehā.

ꝳ **In** Screvetone h̄b Toti . xii . bou træ ad gld . Tra . iii .
car̄ . Ibi Hugo nepos herb̄ti hō epī h̄t . v . ſoch 7 iiii . uill
7 i . bord hn̄tes . iii . car̄ 7 vi . boues . 7 xii . ac̄s p̄ti.
T.R.E. ual xx . ſol . m̄ . xxxii . ſol.

.VII. **Terra Sc̄i petri De Bvrg.**

ꝳ **I**n Colingehā . h̄b S̄ Petr de Burg . iiii . car̄ tre 7 dim̄ bou
ad gl̄d . Tra . xiiii . car̄ . Ibi m̄ in dn̄io ſuᷠ . ii . car̄ . 7 xxxvii .
ſoch . de ii . car̄ 7 iii . bou hui tre 7 viii . uill 7 xx . bord
hn̄tes . xiiii . car̄ . Ibi pbr 7 ii . æccl̄æ . 7 ii . mol . xx . ſolidoᷦ
7 cc . ac̄ p̄ti . Silua min . ii . q̄ᷦ l̄g . 7 i . q̄ᷦ lat . T.R.E. ual . ix . lib̄

ꝳ **I**n Nordmvschā . h̄b S̄ Petr de Burg   { m̄ ſimil .
x . bou træ ad gl̄d . Tra . iiii . car̄ . Ibi m̄ in dn̄io . i . car̄ . 7 ii . ſoch
de . ii . bou træ 7 dim . 7 v . uill 7 iii . bord hn̄tes . i . car̄ 7 dim .
7 ii . molin̄ . xx . ſolid . 7 i . waſtū . 7 dimid piſcar̄ . 7 xxx . ac̄ p̄ti.
T.R.E. ual . lx . ſol . m̄ . xl . ſol.

4 M. In CODDINGTON Leofric had 5 b. of land taxable. Land for 2
ploughs. Oudkell has ½ plough under the Bishop and
4 Freemen with 4 b. of this land and 3 smallholders
with ½ plough.
Meadow, 5 acres.
[Value....]

[In THURGARTON Wapentake]

5 M. In ROLLESTON Godwin had 2½ c. of land taxable, and the fourth
part of 1 b. Land for 6 ploughs. Losoard, the Bishop's man,
has 1 plough and
11 villagers and 9 smallholders who have 4½ ploughs.
1 mill, 27s; meadow, 68 acres.
Value before 1066 £8; now £4 10s.
To this manor belong 7 Freemen in Upton and Collingham.

[In BINGHAM Wapentake]

6 M. In SCREVETON Toti had 12 b. of land taxable. Land for 3 ploughs.
Hugh nephew of Herbert, the Bishop's man, has
5 Freemen, 4 villagers and 1 smallholder who have 3 ploughs
and 6 oxen.
Meadow, 12 acres.
Value before 1066, 20s; now 32s.

8]   LAND OF PETERBOROUGH [ABBEY]

[In NEWARK Wapentake]

1 M. In COLLINGHAM Peterborough had 4 c. and ½ b. of land taxable.
Land for 14 ploughs. Now in lordship 2 ploughs;
37 Freemen with 2 c. and 3 b. of this land; 8 villagers and
20 smallholders who have 14 ploughs.
A priest and 2 churches; 2 mills, 20s; meadow, 200 acres;
underwood, 2 furlongs long and 1 furlong wide.
Value before 1066 £9; now the same.

[In LYTHE Wapentake]

2 M. In NORTH MUSKHAM Peterborough had 10 b. of land taxable.
Land for 4 ploughs. Now in lordship 1 plough;
2 Freemen with 2½ b. of land; 5 villagers and 3 smallholders
who have 1½ ploughs.
2 mills, 20s; 1 wasteland; half a fishery; meadow, 30 acres.
Value before 1066, 60s; now 40s.

.VIII.   TERRA ROGERIJ DE BVSLI.

NEWERCA WAPENTAC

℗ In *ELVESTVNE*.ħƀ Oudenecar.ii.boū tre
ad glđ.Tra dim caŕ.Ibi Normann de Rogerio
de buſli ħ.v.uiłłos hñtes.v.boū in caŕ.T.R.E.

r   7 m̄ uał.x.ſoł.

℗ In *SCELTVNE* 7 *FLODBERGE* ħƀ Ælſi.vii.bō træ
7 dim ad glđ.Tra.ii.caŕ 7 dim.Ibi Roƀt hō Rog
ħ.i.caŕ.7 vi.uiłł 7 ii.borđ hñt.ii.caŕ.Ibi æccła
7 ſeđ.i.molini.7 xxx.ač p̃ti.T.R.E.uał xl.ſoł.

℗ In *CLISTONE*.ħƀ Oudgrim.vi.bou træ   ſ m̄.xxx.
ad glđ.Tra.iii.caŕ.Ibi Roger hō Rogerii ħ
.i.caŕ.7 i.ſocħ de.i.bou hui træ 7 vii.uiłł cū.iii.
caŕ.7 iiii.partē æcclæ.7 xxx.ačs p̃ti.Silua paſtił
ii.q̃ꝫ lḡ.7 dim lat̄.T.R.E.uał.xl.ſoł.m̄.xxx.

ſ In Spaldesforde.iiii.bou tre ad glđ.Tra.i.caŕ.SOCA
Ibi.ii.ſocħ hñt dim caŕ.7 xii.ačs p̃ti.

℗ In *BRODEHOLM* ħƀ Aluui.iii.bou træ
   vel CLIFIVNE
ad glđ.Tra.xii.boū.Ibi.iiii.ſocħ de.ii.bou hui
tre.7 iii.uiłł hñtes.iiii.caŕ.7 xii.ačs p̃ti Rog
de Buſli tenet.T.R.E.uał.xl.ſoł.m̄.xxx.

BERNESEDELAWE WAPENTAC.

℗ In *MARCHAM*.ħƀ Eduui.ix.bou træ ad glđ.Tra
.iiii.caŕ.Ibi Goisfrid hō Rogerii ħ.i.caŕ.7 ix.uiłł
7 v.borđ.hñt.iii.caŕ.Ibi æccła 7 i.moliñ.xvi.ſoliđ.

†   T.R.E.iii.liƀ.m̄.iiii.liƀ.

℗ Ibidē ħƀ Frane.iii.bou træ 7 dim ad glđ.Tra.ii.caŕ.
Ibi Turold hō Rog ħ.i.caŕ.7 i.uiłł cū.ii.bob in caŕ.
T.R.E.7 m̄ uał.xx.ſoł.

NEWARK Wapentake

1 M. In ELSTON Odincar had 2 b. of land taxable. Land for ½ plough.
From Roger of Bully Norman the priest has
    5 villagers who have 5 oxen in a plough.
Value before 1066 and now 10s.

2 M. In SHELTON and FLAWBOROUGH Alfsi had 7½ b. of land taxable.
Land for 2½ ploughs. Robert, Roger's man, has 1 plough.
    6 villagers and 2 smallholders have 2 ploughs.
    A church; 1 mill-site; meadow, 30 acres.
Value before 1066, 40s; now 30[s.]

3 M. In CLIFTON Oudgrim had 6 b. of land taxable. Land for 3 ploughs.
Roger, Roger's man, has 1 plough and
    1 Freeman with 1 b. of this land and 7 villagers
        with 3 ploughs.
    The fourth part of a church; meadow, 30 acres; woodland
        pasture 2 furlongs long and ½ wide.
Value before 1066, 40s; now 30[s.]

4 S. In SPALFORD 4 b. of land taxable. Land for 1 plough. Jurisdiction.
    2 Freemen have ½ plough.
    Meadow, 12 acres.

5 M. In BROADHOLME, or CLIFTON, Alfwy had 3 b. of land taxable.
Land for 12 oxen.
    4 Freemen with 2 b. of this land and 3 villagers who
        have 4 ploughs.
    Meadow, 12 acres.
    Roger of Bully holds it.
Value before 1066, 40s; now 30[s.]

BASSETLAW Wapentake

6 M. In (East) MARKHAM Edwy had 9 b. of land taxable.
Land for 4 ploughs. Geoffrey, Roger's man, has 1 plough.
    9 villagers and 5 smallholders have 3 ploughs.
    A church; 1 mill, 16s.
[Value] before 1066 £3; now £4.

†   *(9,7-9 are entered after 9,15, written across both columns at the foot of the page,*
     directed to their proper place by transposition signs.)

10 M. There also Fran had 3½ b. of land taxable. Land for 2 ploughs.
Thorold, Roger's man, has 1 plough and
    1 villager with 2 oxen in a plough.
Value before 1066 and now 20s.

ℳ Ibidē ħƀr Goduin̉ 7 Vlchel.vii.bou̇ træ 7 dim̃ ad glđ.

Tra̅.iii.car̅ 7 dim̃.Ibi Vlchel 7 iiii.ſoch 7 ii.borđ

.II. hn̅t.i.car̅ 7 dim̃.T.R.E.7 m̊ ual̃.xvi.ſoliđ.

ℳ In TVXFARNE ħƀr Eluui 7 Vlmær.xii.bou̇ træ ad

glđ.Tra̅.x.car̅.Ibi Rog̅ ħ̅.iiii.car̅.7 xxxii.uilł

7 ii.borđ hn̅tes.xiiii.car̅.7 i.molin̅.x.ſol 7 viii.den̉.

T.R.E.ual̃.x.liƀ.m̊ viii.liƀ　　　　　Soca h̅ ℳ̅

S In Schidrinton 7, Waleſbi.ii.bō træ ad gld.Tra̅.vi.bob̉.

Ibi.v.ſoch 7 i.borđ hn̅t.ii.car̅.

S In Agemuntone.i.bou̇ træ 7 dim̃ ad gld.Tra̅.i.car̅.

Ibi.i.ſoch 7 iii.uilł hn̅t.ii.car̅.Silua past̅.i.leu̇ lg̅

.III. 7 dim̃ leu̇ lat̉.

ℳ In AGEMVNTONE ħƀ Torchetel 7 Vlmer.iiii.bō

tre̥ 7 dim̃.7 iii.partē.i.bou ad gld.Tra̅.iii.car̅.

Ibi Rog̅ ħ̅.iiii.car̅.7 xiii.uilł.7 ix.borđ.hn̅tes.viii.car̅.

✝ ⌐ In Hedune.i.bō træ ad glđ.Tra̅.ii.boṵ.Soca in Marchā.

7 ii.ac̅ p̅ti.Ibi.i.ſoch ħ̅.ii.bou ⌐ In Vpetun.ii.bō træ 7 dim̃ ad gld.

Tra.ii.car̅.Soca ĩ mark.

Ibi.ix.ſoch.7 ii.borđ.hn̅t.iiii.car̅.7 vi.ac̅s p̅ti.

⌐ In Gameleſtune.i.ortṵ.7 i.ſoch p̅tin̅ ad Marchā.

7.i.ortṵ p̅tin̅ ad Etune.

✚ In Miſna.i.bou̇ træ ad glđ.Ad Ettone p̅tinet.

284 d

Ibi.ii.mol.xxx.ſoliđ.T.R.E.ual̃ iiii.liƀ.m̊ ſimil.

ℳ In BVCHETONE.ħƀ Æduui.iii.bou̇ træ ad glđ.

Tra̅.iii.car̅.Ibi m̊.i.car̅ in dn̅io.7 ii.uilł 7 i.borđ

cū.i.car̅.T.R.E.ual̃.xx.ſol.m̊.x.ſol.

ℳ In ALRETVN.ħƀ Aluuold.ii.bou̇ tre 7 dim̃

ad gld.Tra̅.i.car̅.Ibi m̊.v.ſochi 7 i.uilł hn̅t

11 $\frac{2}{M.}$ There also Godwin and Ulfkell had 7½ b. of land taxable.
Land for 3½ ploughs.
> Ulfkell, 4 Freemen and 2 smallholders have 1½ ploughs.
Value before 1066 and now 16s.

12 $\frac{2}{M.}$ In TUXFORD Alfwy and Wulfmer had 12 b. of land taxable.
Land for 10 ploughs. Roger has 4 ploughs and
> 32 villagers and 2 smallholders who have 14 ploughs.
1 mill, 10s 8d.
Value before 1066 £10; now £8.

Jurisdiction of this manor.

13 S. In KIRTON and WALESBY 2 b. of land taxable. Land for 6 oxen.
> 5 Freemen and 1 smallholder have 2 ploughs.

14 S. In EGMANTON 1½ b. of land taxable. Land for 1 plough.
> 1 Freeman and 3 villagers have 2 ploughs.
Woodland pasture 1 league long and ½ league wide.

15 $\frac{3}{M.}$ In EGMANTON Thorketel and Wulfmer had 4½ b. and the third
part of 1 b. of land taxable. Land for 3 ploughs.
Roger has 4 ploughs and
> 13 villagers and 9 smallholders who have 8 ploughs.

(9,15 is continued at the top of column 284 d, 9,7-9 and 9,21, entered at the foot of the page, are directed to their proper places by transposition signs.)

† 7 In HEADON 1 b. of land taxable. Land for 2 oxen. Jurisdiction
in Markham.
> Meadow, 2 acres.
1 Freeman has 2 oxen.

8 In UPTON 2½ b. of land taxable. Land for 2 ploughs. Jurisdiction
in Markham.
> 9 Freemen and 2 smallholders have 4 ploughs.
Meadow, 6 acres.

9 In GAMSTON 1 garden and 1 Freeman, which belong to Markham.
1 garden, which belongs to Eaton.

(9,21 entered at the foot of column 284 c, marked by transposition signs.)

†† 21 In MISSON 1 b. of land taxable. It belongs to Eaton.

(9,15 continued)
> 2 mills, 30s.
Value before 1066 £4; now the same.

284 d

16 M. In BOUGHTON Edwy had 3 b. of land taxable. Land for 3 ploughs.
Now in lordship 1 plough;
> 2 villagers and 1 smallholder with 1 plough.
Value before 1066, 20s; now 10s.

17 M. In OLLERTON Alfwold had 2½ b. of land taxable. Land for 1 plough.
> Now 5 Freemen and 1 villager have 2 ploughs.

II.car̄.7 I.moliñ.vi.foliđ 7 viii.denar.T.R.E.7 m̄

ꝏ In COTVNE. h̄b Hardulf.iiii.bou træ   ʃxx.foł.

ad głđ.Tra.ii.car̄.Ibi Fulco h̄o Rog h̄t.viii.

.iiii.uiłł cū.ii.car̄.T.R.E.7 m̄ uał.xvi.foł.

★ ꝏ In ORDESHALE h̄br Ofuuard Turftin Ordric

    7 Turftin.iiii.bou tre ad głđ.Tra.iiii.car̄.Ibi

    ii.h̄oes Rogerii h̄nt.iii.car̄.7 v.uiłł 7 ii.borđ

    h̄ntes.ii.car̄. Ibi xvi.ac̄ p̄ti.Silua paſt.i.q̄ʒ łg.

.x. 7 dim lat̄.T.R.E.uał.xxviii.foł.m̄ xxiiii.foł.

ꝏ In ÆTTVNE.h̄br x.taini quiſqʒ Aulā fuā.

Int eos.vi.bou træ 7 dim 7 vi.parte uni bou

ad głđ.Tra.iiii.car̄   Ibi Fulco

       or

h̄o Rog

h̄t.i.car̄·   7 xiiii.uiłł

               7 ix.borđ.

               h̄ntes.vii.car̄.

               7 ii.moliñ

.xx.foliđ.   7 lx.ac̄s p̄ti.Silua

✝ paſt.v.q̄ʒ łg.7 iii.lat̄.T.R.E.uał.vi.lib̄.m̄.iii.

ꝏ In GRAVE. h̄br Aluui 7 Ofmund.iiii.bou træ

    7 dim ad głđ.Tra.iii.car̄.Ibi Rob̄t h̄o Rog

In Ordeſ   h̄t.i.car̄ 7 dim.7 vi.uiłł 7 iii.borđ.7 i.foch h̄ntes

hale'.i.

b̄o 7 dim   ii.car̄ 7 dim.Ibi pb̄r 7 æccła.7 viii.ac̄ p̄ti.Silua

Tra.i.car

    paſt.i.lev łg.7 dim lat̄.T.R.E.uał.xl.foł.m̄ fimilit.

§ In Ranebi.ii.bou træ 7 dim ad głđ.Tra.i.car̄.Soc̄a in ⌐Graue

    in Graue.Waſta.ē.ʃIn Ranebi.i.bou ad gt.Soc̄a in ⌐Etunæ

ꝏ In HEDVNE.h̄br Godric 7 alii.vi.taini.qſqʒ hallā.

    Int eos.viii.bou træ.7 iii.parte.i.bou ad gld.Tra ⌐ciā

    v.car̄ 7 dim.Ibi Wiłłs h̄o Rog.ii.car̄.7 xiiii.foch

    7 ix.uiłł.7 vi.borđ h̄ntes xvi.car̄.Ibi.xx.vi.ac̄

1 mill, 6s 8d.
[Value] before 1066 and now 20s.

8   M. In COTTAM Hardwulf had 4 b. of land taxable. Land for 2 ploughs. Fulk, Roger's man, has
    8 villagers with 2 ploughs.
Value before 1066 and now 16s.

9 $\frac{4}{M.}$ In ORDSALL Osward, Thurstan, Ordric and Thurstan had 4 b. of land taxable. Land for 4 ploughs. Two of Roger's men have 3 ploughs and
    5 villagers and 2 smallholders who have 2 ploughs.
    Meadow, 16 acres, woodland pasture, 1 furlong long
      and ½ wide.
Value before 1066, 28s, now 24s.

0 $\frac{10}{M.}$ In EATON 10 thanes each had his hall. Between them, 6½ b. of land and the sixth part of 1 b. taxable. Land for 4 ploughs. Fulk, Roger's man , has 1 plough and
    14 villagers and 9 smallholders who have 7 ploughs.
    2 mills, 20s; meadow, 60 acres; woodland pasture 5
      furlongs long and 3 wide.
Value before 1066 £6; now [£] 3.

9,21, entered above, before 9,16, is directed here by transposition signs)

2   M. In GROVE Alfwy and Osmund had 4½ b. of land taxable.
    Land for 3 ploughs. Robert, Roger's man, has 1½ ploughs and
      6 villagers, 3 smallholders and 1 Freeman who have 2½
        ploughs.
    A priest and a church; meadow, 8 acres; woodland pasture
      1 league long and ½ wide.
    Value before 1066, 40s; now the same.
3   In ORDSALL 1½ b. Land for 1 plough.
4   S. In RANBY 2½ b. of land taxable. Land for 1 plough.
Jurisdiction in Grove. Waste.
5   In RANBY 1 b. taxable. Jurisdiction in Eaton.

5   M. In HEADON Godric and 6 other thanes each had a Hall. Between them 8 b. of land and the third part of 1 b. taxable. Land for 5½ ploughs. William, Roger's man, [has] 2 ploughs and
    14 Freemen, 9 villagers and 6 smallholders who have
      16 ploughs.

p̃ti.Silua past̕.v.q̃ɀ lḡ.7 iiii.lat̕.T.R.E.uaɫ.ii.liɓ.

§ In Vpetune dim̕ boū træ ad glɗ.Tra.ii.boū. ⌠m̃ ſimiɫ.
Ibi.|iii.ſocħ 7 ii.borɗ.cū.i.car̕.7 ii.ac̃ p̃ti.

ꝏ In WESTMARCHA̅.ħɓ Godric.iiii.boū træ ad glɗ.Tra
ii.car̕.Ibi ħ Rog̕.ii.car̕.7 iiii.uiɫɫ.7 ii.borɗ.ħntes
ii.car̕.7 xvi.ac̃ p̃ti.Silua past̕.v.q̃ɀ lḡ.7 iii.lat̕.
T.R.E.vaɫ xl.ſoɫ.m̃ ſimiɫ.Claron tenet.

285 a

§ In Weſtmarchā.vi.boū træ ad glɗ.Tra.iii.car̕.
Soca in Tuxfarne.Ibi.vi.ſocħ 7 v.uiɫɫ hn̄t.iiii.
car̕ 7 dim̕.Ibi.xvi.ac̃ p̃ti.

§ Ibidē.i.boū træ ad glɗ.Soca in Grᴈue.7 i.boū ad gɫ
Soca in Etune.7 i.bō aɗ gld.Soca in Draitone.
Tra dim̕ car̕.Ibi.iii.ſocħ hn̄t.ii.car̕.

ꝏ In DTRAITONE ħɓr Suen 7 Vlſtan.iiii.bou̕ træ
ad gld.Tra.ii.car̕.Ibi.ii.hōc̃s Rog̕ hn̄t.i.car̕.
7 viii.uiɫɫ 7 i.borɗ hn̄tes.ii.car̕.Ibi.iii.molini
l.ſoɫ redɗ.7 vii.ac̃ p̃ti.Silua past̕.iii.q̃ɀ lḡ.
.ii. 7 dim̕ q̃ɀ lat̕.T.R.E.uaɫ xxx.ſoɫ.m̃ xvii.ſoɫ 7 ii.d.

ꝏ In ELCHESLIE.ħɓr Locre 7 Vlchel.iiii.boū træ
ad glɗ.Tra.ii.car̕.Ibi Claron hɫ.i.car̕.7 iii.uiɫɫ
7 i.borɗ hn̄t.i.car̕ 7 dim̕.T.R.E.7 m̃.xxvi.ſoɫ.

ꝏ In BABVRDE.ħɓ Vlmar.ii.boū træ 7 dim̕ ad glɗ.
Tra.ii.car̕.Ibi Goisfriɗ hō Rog̕ hɫ.i.car̕.7 i.borɗ
cū dim̕ car̕.Silua past̕.ii.q̃ɀ lḡ.7 i.lat̕.T.R.E.
.ii. uaɫ.xl.ſoɫ.m̃.x.ſoɫ.

ꝏ In NORDERMORTVNE.ħɓr Asford 7 Luſchel.ii.boū
træ ad gld.Tra.ii.car̕.Waſta.ē.Silua past̕.i.q̃ɀ lḡ.
7 dim̕ q̃ɀ lat̕.T.R.E.uaɫ.xvi.ſoɫ.

Meadow, 26 acres; woodland pasture 5 furlongs long and
4 wide.

Value before 1066 £4; now the same.

27 S. In UPTON ½ b. of land taxable. Land for 2 oxen.
3 Freemen and 2 smallholders with 1 plough.
Meadow, 2 acres.

28 M. In WEST MARKHAM Godric had 4 b. of land taxable. Land
for 2 ploughs. Roger has 2 ploughs and
4 villagers and 2 smallholders who have 2 ploughs.
Meadow, 16 acres; woodland pasture 5 furlongs long
and 3 wide.

Value before 1066, 40s; now the same.
Claron holds it.

29 S. In WEST MARKHAM 6 b. of land taxable. Land for 3 ploughs.   285 a
Jurisdiction in Tuxford.
6 Frenchmen and 5 villagers have 4½ ploughs.
Meadow, 16 acres.

30 S. There also 1 b. of land taxable; jurisdiction in Grove.
1 b. taxable; jurisdiction in Eaton. 1 b. taxable; jurisdiction
in (West) Drayton. Land for ½ plough.
3 Freemen have 2 ploughs.

31 $\frac{2}{M.}$ In (West) DRAYTON Swein and Wulfstan had 4 b. of land and 2
parts of 1 b. taxable. Land for 2 ploughs. Two of Roger's
men have 1 plough and
8 villagers and 1 smallholder who have 2 ploughs.
3 mills which pay 50s; meadow, 7 acres; woodland pasture 3
furlongs long and ½ furlong wide.

Value before 1066, 30s; now 17s 4d.

32 $\frac{2}{M.}$ In ELKESLEY Locar and Ulfkell had 4 b. of land taxable.
Land for 2 ploughs. Claron has 1 plough.
3 villagers and 1 smallholder have 1½ ploughs.
[Value] before 1066 and now 26s.

33 M. In BABWORTH Wulfmer had 2½ b. of land taxable.
Land for 2 ploughs. Geoffrey, Roger's man, has 1 plough and
1 smallholder with ½ plough.
Woodland pasture, 2 furlongs long and 1 wide.
Value before 1066, 40s; now 10s.

34 $\frac{2}{M.}$ In NORTH MORTON Asferth and Leofkell had 2 b. of land taxable.
Land for 2 ploughs. Waste.
Woodland pasture 1 furlong long and ½ furlong wide.
Value before 1066, 16s.

ⓜ In *CALDECOTES* . ħб Cafchin . 1 . boū træ ad gld . Tra

ɪɪɪɪ . boū . Wafta . ē . Ibi . vɪ . ac̃ p̃ti . 7 ɪɪ . mot . xx . fot.

.ɪɪ. T.R.E . uat . xxx . fot.

ⓜ In *CVCHENAI* . ħбr Alric 7 Vlfi . 1 . car̃ træ ad gld̃.

Tra . ɪɪ . car̃ . Ibi Goisfr̃ hõ Rog hт̃ . 1 . car̃ . 7 ɪx . uilt

hn̄tes . ɪɪɪ . car̃ . Silua paſt . ɪɪ . q̃ӡ lḡ . 7 ɪɪ . lat̃ . T.R.E.

.ɪɪ. uat xx . fot . m̊ . ɪɪ . fot min.

ⓜ In *TORP* . ħбr Turſtan 7 Vlmer . x . boū træ ad gld̃.

Tra . ɪɪɪ . car̃ . Ibi Ricard hõ Rogerii hт̃ . ɪɪɪɪ . car̃.

7 v . uilt . 7 ɪɪɪɪ . bord̃ hn̄tes . ɪɪ . car̃ 7 dim . 7 vɪɪ . ac̃s

p̃ti . Silua paſt q̃ӡ lḡ . 7 ɪɪɪɪ . lat̃ . T.R.E . uat xL.

fot . m̊ xxvɪ . fot.   Soca jbid.

ˢS In Gletorp . ɪɪɪɪ . boū træ.   ad gld̃.

Tra vɪ . boū . Ibi . ɪɪɪɪ . foċħ hn̄t . ɪɪ . car̃ . Silua paſt

.ɪɪ. ɪ . q̃ӡ lḡ . 7 ɪ . lat̃.

ⓜ In *CLIPESTVNE* . ħбr Osбn 7 Vlfi . ɪ . car̃ træ ad gld̃.

Tra . ɪɪ . car̃ . Ibi Rog in dñio hт̃ . ɪ . car̃ 7 dim . 7 xɪɪ . uilt

7 ɪɪɪ . bord̃ hn̄tes . ɪɪɪ . car̃ 7 dim . 7 ɪ . molin̄ . ɪɪɪ . fot . Silua

.ɪɪɪ. p loca paſtit . ɪ . lev lḡ . 7 ɪ . lat̃ . T.R.E . uat . Lx . fot . m̊ . xL.

ⓜ In *WARESOPE* ħбr Godric 7 Leuiet 7 Vlchel.

ɪɪɪ . car̃ træ ad gld̃ . Tra . vɪ . car̃ 7 dim . Ibi Roger

in dñio hт̃ . ɪɪɪ . car̃ 7 dim . 7 vɪ . foċħ de . ɪɪ . boū hui

træ . 7 xv . uilt . 7 xɪ . bord̃ . hn̄tes . ɪɪɪ . car̃ . Ibi p̃br

285 b

7 æccta . 7 ɪ . molend . xvɪ . den . 7 dim fed ṃolin̄i.

Silua paſt . v . q̃ӡ lḡ . 7 ɪɪɪɪ . lat̃ . T.R.E . Lxɪɪɪɪ . fot.

.ɪɪ. m̊ . ɪɪɪɪ . fot min.

ⓜ In *CLVNBRE* . ħбr Adeluuol 7 Vlchil . v . boū træ

ad gld̃ . Tra . ɪɪ . car̃ . pars . ē wafta . quā Fulco tenet.

In alia hт̃ Vlchel fub Rog . ɪ . car̃ . 7 ɪ . mot . xɪɪ.

den . Silua paſt . ɪɪ . q̃ӡ lḡ . 7 ɪ . lat̃ . T.R.E . uat . xx.

fot . m̊ . ɪɪɪɪ . fot.

35 M. In 'COLD COATES' Kaskin had 1 b. of land taxable.
        Land for 4 oxen. Waste.
            Meadow, 6 acres; 2 mills, 20s.
        Value before 1066, 30s.

36 2
    M. In CUCKNEY Alric and Wulfsi had 1 c. of land taxable.
        Land for 2 ploughs. Geoffrey, Roger's man, has 1 plough and
            9 villagers who have 3 ploughs.
            Woodland pasture 2 furlongs long and 2 wide.
        Value before 1066, 20s; now 2s less.

37 2
    M. In PERLETHORPE Thurstan and Wulfmer had 10 b. of land
        taxable. Land for 3 ploughs. Richard, Roger's man,
        has 4 ploughs and
            5 villagers and 4 smallholders who have 2½ ploughs.
            Meadow, 7 acres; woodland pasture ... furlongs long
                and 4 wide.
        Value before 1066, 40s; now 26s.

        Also Jurisdiction there.
38 S. In GLEADTHORPE 4b. of land taxable. Land for 6 oxen.
            4 Freemen have 2 ploughs.
            Woodland pasture 1 furlong long and 1 wide.

39 2
    M. In CLIPSTONE Osbern and Wulfsi had 1 c. of land taxable.
        Land for 2 ploughs. Roger has 1½ ploughs in lordship and
            12 villagers and 3 smallholders who have 3½ ploughs.
            1 mill, 3s; woodland pasture in places, 1 league
                long and 1 wide.
        Value before 1066, 60s; now 40[s.]

40 3
    M. In WARSOP Godric, Leofgeat and Ulfkell had 3 c. of land
        taxable. Land for 6½ ploughs. Roger has 3½ ploughs in
        lordship and
            6 Freemen with 2 b. of this land and 15 villagers and
                11 smallholders who have 3 ploughs.
            A priest and a church; 1 mill, 16d; half a mill-site;   285 b
                woodland pasture 5 furlongs long and 4 wide.
        [Value] before 1066, 64s; now 4s less.

41 2
    M. In CLUMBER Aethelwold and Ulfkell had 5 b. of land taxable.
        Land for 2 ploughs. Part of 2 b. which Fulk holds is waste;
        in the other (part) Ulfkell has 1 plough under Roger.
            1 mill, 12d; woodland pasture 2 furlongs long and 1 wide.
        Value before 1066, 20s; now 4s.

§ In Odeſtorp 7 Redford . i . boū trǽ 7 dim̄ ad gld . Tra . iiii . boů.
Soca in Clūbre . Waſta . ē.

ⓜ In *WERCHESOPE* . h̄b Elſi . iii . car trǽ ad gld . Tra
viii . car . Ibi h̄t Rog . i . car in dn̄io . 7 xxii . ſoch de
xii . boů hui tre . 7 xxiiii . uill 7 viii . bord hn̄tes . xxii.
car . 7 vii . acs p̄ti . Silua paſt . ii . lev lḡ . 7 iii . q̄z lat .
.II. T.R.E.ual . viii . lib̄ . m̄ . vii .

ⓜ In *ROLVETVNE* . h̄br Vlſi 7 Archil . i . car trǽ ad
gld . Tra . ii . car . Ibi Rog h̄o Rogerii h̄t . i . car . 7 iiii.
ſoch de . ii . boů hui trǽ . 7 i . bord cū . i . car . Ibi . ii . ac
p̄ti . Silua paſt . vi . q̄z lḡ . 7 iii . lat . T.R.E.ual . xx . ſol .
Ibid . i . boů trǽ ad gld . Soca Waſta . ē . ⌠ m̄ x . ſol .

ⓜ In *BILLEBI* . h̄b Grimchel . vi . boů trǽ ad gld . Tra
iii . car . Ibi Ingrann h̄o Rog h̄t . i . car . 7 ix . uill
7 i . bord . hn̄tes . iii . car . 7 vi . ac p̄ti . T.R.E.ual xl . ſol m̄ xx .

ⓜ In *ODESACH* . h̄b Vlſy . ii . car tre ad gld . Tra . iiii . car .
Ibi Turold h̄o Rog h̄t . ii . car . 7 iii . ſoch de . iiii . boů
hui trǽ . 7 xii . uill hn̄tes . ix . car . Ibi . ii . molini . xvi .
ſolid 7 iiii . denar . 7 viii . ac p̄ti . Silua paſt . i . lev lḡ .
7 dim lev lat . T.R.E. 7 m̄ . lx . ſol .   Soca h̄ ⓜ

§ In Blide . i . boů tre 7 iiii . pars . i . boů ad gld . Tra . i . car .
.VI. Ibi . iiii . uill 7 iiii . bord hn̄t . i . car . 7 i . ac p̄ti .

ⓜ In *CARELTVNE* . h̄br . vi . taini . q̄ſq̄ Aulā . Int om̄s . ii .
car trǽ ad gld . Tra . iiii . car . Ibi Turold h̄o Rog h̄t . ii . car .

Ibid . i . car tre ſoca ad gld .
de Mamesfeld regis ⓜ
Ibid . i . car tre ſoca ad
Bodmeſcel ⓜ re_is . 7 gld .

285 b

2 S. In 'ODSTHORPE' and RETFORD 1½ b. of land taxable.
Land for 4 oxen. Jurisdiction in Clumber. Waste.

3 M. In WORKSOP Alfsi had 3 c. of land taxable. Land for 8 ploughs.
Roger has 1 plough in lordship and
    22 Freemen with 12 b. of this land and 24 villagers and
        8 smallholders who have 22 ploughs.
    Meadow, 7 acres; woodland pasture 2 leagues long
        and 3 furlongs wide.
Value before 1066 £8; now [£] 7.

4 2
   M. In 'ROOLTON' Wulfsi and Arkell had 1 c. of land taxable.
Land for 2 ploughs. Roger, Roger's man, has 1 plough and
    4 Freemen with 2 b. of this land and 1 smallholder with
        1 plough.
    Meadow, 2 acres; woodland pasture 6 furlongs long and
        3 wide.
Value before 1066, 20s; now 10s.
There also 1 b. of land taxable. Jurisdiction. Waste.

   M. In BILBY Grimkell had 6 b. of land taxable. Land for 3 ploughs.
Ingran, Roger's man, has 1 plough and
    9 villagers and 1 smallholder who have 3 ploughs.
    Meadow, 6 acres.
Value before 1066, 40s; now 20[s.]

46 M. In HODSOCK Wulfsi had 2 c. of land taxable. Land for 4 ploughs.
Thorold, Roger's man, has 2 ploughs and
    3 Freemen with 4 b. of this land and 12 villagers who
        have 9 ploughs.
    2 mills, 16s 4d; meadow, 8 acres; woodland pasture 1
        league long and ½ league wide.
Value before 1066 and now 60s.

   Jurisdiction of this manor.
There also 1 c. of land taxable. Jurisdiction of the King's manor
of Mansfield.
There also 1 c. of land. Jurisdiction in the King's manor
of Bothamsall; taxable.

   S. In BLYTH 1 b. of land and the fourth part of 1 b. taxable.
Land for 1 plough.
    4 villagers and 4 smallholders have 1 plough.
    Meadow, 1 acre.

   6
   M. In CARLTON (-in-Lindrick) 6 thanes each had a hall. Between
them 2 c. of land taxable. Land for 4 ploughs.
Thorold, Roger's man, has 2 ploughs and

7 ii.ſocħ.7 xvi.uiłł 7 iii.borđ hñtes.iiii.caꝛ.Ibi æccła.

7 ii.moliñ.xxi.ſoliđ.7 xx.aꝺ ꝓti.Silua paſt.i.lev 7 dim

łg.7 dim lev łaꝛ.T.R.E.uał.iiii.liƀ.m̂.iii.

℧In *Lvnd*.ħƀ Vlchel.ii.bou træ.7 ii.partes.i.bou ad glđ

Tra.i.caꝛ.Ibi in dñio.i.caꝛ.7 vi.uiłł cu.ii.caꝛ 7 v.

aꝺ ꝓti.Silua paſt.vi.q̨̈ łg.7 ii.łaꝛ.T.R.E.uał.xx.ſoł.m̂.x.

℧In *Serlebi*.ħƀ Aluric.i.bou træ 7 dim ad gld.Tra

.iiii.bou.Ibi Giſłeƀt hᷓ Rog ħꝛ.i.caꝛ.7 v.uiłł 7 viii.

.ii.borđ cu.iii.caꝛ.7 i.moliñ.iii.ſoliđ.T.R.E.7 m̂ uał.xx.ſoł.

℧In *Tvrdeworde* ħƀr Brixi 7 Caſchi.vi.bou tre ad glđ.

Tra.ii.caꝛ.I   Aᵖᵇʳzo de Rog ħꝛ 7 waſta.e͞.Silua paſt

.i.lev łg.7 i.q̨̈ łaꝛ.T.R.E.uał.xx.ſoł.m̂.iii.ſoł.

285 c

꒐꒙In *Barnebi*.hƀr Turuerd 7 Sorte.i.bou træ

7 dim ad glđ.Tra.iiii.bou.Waſta.e͞.Ibi.i.aꝺ ꝓti.

.iii.Silua paſt.i.q̨̈ łg.7 dim q̨̈ łaꝛ.T.R.E.uał x.ſoł.

℧In *Hareworde*.hƀr Wade.Vlſiet   ⌠m̂ xii.den.

7 Vlſtan.i.caꝛ træ ad glđ.Tra.ii.caꝛ.Ibi Fulco

hᷓ Rog in dñio.i.caꝛ.7 viii.uiłł 7.i.borđ cu.iii.caꝛ.

Ibi.æccła÷.Silua paſt.i.lev łg.7 i.łaꝛ.T.R.E.

.uał.xl.ſoł.m̂.xxx.ſoł.   Soca ibiđ.

Ƨ In Martune.i.caꝛ træ ad glđ.Tra.ii.caꝛ.Ibi.x.uiłł

.iii.hut.v.caꝛ.Silua paſt.i.lev łg.7 dim lev łaꝛ.

℧In *Estirape* ħƀr Leuing Torchil 7 Leuric.vii.

bou tre ad glđ.Tra.iiii.caꝛ.Ibi Bernard hᷓ Rog

ħꝛ.i.caꝛ.7 ix.ſocħ.7 vii.uiłł.7 v.borđ hñtes.iii.

caꝛ 7 dimid.Ibi.vi.aꝺ ꝓti.7 x.aꝺ ſiluæ paſt.T.R.E.

uał.l.ſoł.m̂.xxv.ſoliđ.

Ibid.i.bou træ ad glđ.Soca.e͞.Waſta.e͞

2 Freemen, 16 villagers and 3 smallholders who have 4 ploughs.
A church; 2 mills, 21s; meadow, 20 acres; woodland pasture
1½ leagues long and ½ league wide.
Value before 1066 £4; now [£] 3.

51 M. In LOUND Ulfkell had 2 b. of land and 2 parts of 1 b. taxable.
Land for 1 plough. In lordship 1 plough;
6 villagers with 2 ploughs.
Meadow, 5 acres; woodland pasture 6 furlongs long and 2 wide.
Value before 1066, 20s; now 10[s.]

52 M. In SERLBY Aelfric had 1½ b. of land taxable. Land for 4 oxen.
Gilbert, Roger's man, has 1 plough and
5 villagers and 8 smallholders with 3 ploughs.
1 mill, 3s.
Value before 1066 and now 20s.

53 2
    M. In TORWORTH Brictsi and Kaskin had 6 b. of land taxable.
Land for 2 ploughs. Azor the priest has it from Roger. Waste.
Woodland pasture 1 league long and 1 furlong wide.
Value before 1066, 20s; now 3s.

54 2
    M. In BARNBY (Moor) Thorferth and Swarti had 1½ b. of land taxable.   285 c
Land for 4 oxen. Waste.
Meadow, 1 acre; woodland pasture 1 furlong long
and ½ furlong wide.
Value before 1066, 10s; now 12d.

55 3
    M. In HARWORTH Wada, Wulfgeat and Wulfstan had 1 c. of land
taxable. Land for 2 ploughs. Fulk, Roger's man, [has] 1 plough
in lordship and
8 villagers and 1 smallholder with 3 ploughs.
A church; woodland pasture, 1 league long and 1 wide.
Value before 1066, 40s; now 30s.

Also Jurisdiction there.
56 S. In MARTIN 1 c. of land taxable. Land for 2 ploughs.
10 villagers have 5 ploughs.
Woodland pasture 1 league long and ½ league wide.

57 3
    M. In STYRRUP Leofing, Thorkell and Leofric had 7 b. of land
taxable. Land for 4 ploughs. Bernard, Roger's man,
has 1 plough and
9 Freemen with ½ c. of this land and 7 villagers and
5 smallholders who have 3½ ploughs.
Meadow, 6 acres; woodland pasture, 10 acres.
Value before 1066, 50s; now 25s.

58   There also 1 b. of land taxable. Jurisdiction. Waste.

Ⓜ In *CALVN* ħƀr Turchil 7 Godric . x . boũ træ. 7 iii . part . i . boũ ad glđ . Tra . iii . car . Ibi Turold hõ Rog ħt . i . car. 7 vii . foch de v . boũ hui træ. 7 iii . uiħ 7 iii . borđ . ħntes . ii . car 7 dim . Ibi . xxii . ac ꝑti . Silua min xvi . q̃ꝫ l̄g. 7 lxx.iiii . uirg lat̄ . T.R.E. ual̄ . lx . fol̄ . m̃

Ⓜ In *HOCRETONE* . ħƀr Vlfi 7 Turchil . i . car xxviii . fol̄ . træ ad glđ . Tra . ii . car 7 dim . Ibi Rog ħt in dñio . ii . car̄ . 7 xi . uiħ 7 iiii . borđ . ħntes . iiii . car̄ . Ibi . xxx.vi . ac ꝑti . Ibi æccɫa . Silua paſt . i . lev l̄g. 7 iiii . q̃ꝫ 7 iiii . uirg lat̄ . T.R.E. ual̄ . iiii . liƀ . m̃ . iii .

.II. In Carletun . ħt Rog . xii . acs ꝑti .

Ⓜ In *GRESTORP* . ħƀr Dunning 7 Grim . vi . bõ træ 7 dim̃. 7 iiii . part̄ . i . boũ ad glđ . Tra . ii . car̄ . Ibi Rog hõ Rogerii ħt . ii . car. 7 iiii . foch. 7 xii . uiħ 7 i . borđ ħntes . v . car̄ . Ibi . iii . molini . xx . folid. 7 xii . ac ꝑti . 7 iiii . ac filuæ paſt . T.R.E. 7 m̃ ual̄ . iii . liƀ .

Ṣ II. In Sudtone . i . boũ træ ad gld . SocA . Waſta . ē . Ibi . vi . ac ꝑti .

Ⓜ In *MARNEHA* . ħƀr Aluric 7 Dane . vi . boũ træ 7 dim̃ 7 iiii . part uni boũ ad glđ . Tra . ii . car̄ . Ibi Fulo hõ Rog ħt . i . car. 7 ibi . i . fochs ħt xii . acs tre. 7 x . uiħ 7 iiii . borđ ħntes . iiii . car̄ 7 dimiđ . Ibi xl . ac ꝑti . T.R.E. ual̄ . xl . fol̄ . m̃ xx .

Ⓜ In alia *MARNEHA* . ħƀ Vlfi . ii . car træ ad gld . Tra iiii . car̄ . Ibi ħt Rog in dñio . iiii . car. 7 ii . foch. 7 xx . de xl . acs fræ. uiħ ħntes . vii . car̄ . 7 i . molin̄ . iiii . folid. 7 i . pifcariã . 7 xxiiii . acs ꝑti . Silua minuta dim̃ lev l̄g. 7 tntđ lat̄ . T.R.E. ual̄ . iiii . liƀ . m̃ . iii . liƀ .

In LYTHE Wapentake

9 M. In KELHAM Thorkell and Godric had 10 b. of land and the
third part of 1 b. taxable. Land for 3 ploughs. Thorold,
Roger's man, has 1 plough and
7 Freemen with 5 b. of this land and 3 villagers and
3 smallholders who have 2½ ploughs.
Meadow, 22 acres; underwood 16 furlongs long and 74
virgates wide.
Value before 1066, 60s; now 28s.

50 M. In HOCKERTON Wulfsi and Thorkell had 1 c. of land taxable.
Land for 2½ ploughs. Roger has 2 ploughs in lordship and
11 villagers and 4 smallholders who have 4 ploughs.
Meadow, 36 acres; a church; woodland pasture 1 league
long and 4 furlongs and 4 virgates wide.
Value before 1066 £4; now [£] 3.

51 In CARLTON (-on-Trent) Roger has 12 acres of meadow.

52 2̸M. In GRASSTHORPE Dunning and Grim had 6½ b. of land and
the fourth part of 1 b. taxable. Land for 2 ploughs.
Roger, Roger's man, has 2 ploughs and
4 Freemen, 12 villagers and 1 smallholder who have
5 ploughs.
3 mills, 20s; meadow, 12 acres; woodland pasture, 4 acres.
Value before 1066 and now £3.

53 S. In SUTTON (-on-Trent) 1 b. of land taxable.
Jurisdiction. Waste. Meadow, 6 acres.

54 2̸M. In (High) MARNHAM Aelfric and Dena had 6½ b. of land and
the fourth part of 1 b. of land taxable. Land for 2 ploughs.
Fulk, Roger's man, has 1 plough.
1 Freeman has 12 acres of land; 10 villagers and 4
smallholders who have 4½ ploughs.
Meadow, 40 acres.
Value before 1066, 40s; now 20[s.]

55 M. In the other (Low) MARNHAM Wulfsi had 2 c. of land
taxable. Land for 4 ploughs. Roger has 4 ploughs in
lordship and
2 Freemen with 40 acres of land and 20 villagers who
have 7 ploughs.
1 mill, 4s; 1 fishery; meadow, 24 acres; underwood ½
league long and as wide.
Value before 1066 £4; now £3.

ꝏ In *SCACHEBI*. ħᵬr Aluuold 7 Vlchet . ɪ . caƀ́ træ

ad glđ . Tᷓra . ɪɪ . caƀ́ 7 dim . Ibi duo hões Rog̃ hn̄t

in dñio . ɪɪɪ . caƀ́ . 7 vɪɪ . uiłł 7 ɪɪ . borđ . hn̄tes . ɪɪɪ . caƀ́.

Ibi . xvɪ . ac̃ p̃ti . Silua past dim leu̇ lg̃ . 7 ɪɪɪ . q̃ᷝ laƀ́.

T.R.E. uał xlvɪɪɪ . fol . m̊ . xl . fol . Soca 𝄄 ħƀ . ɪ . caƀ́.

§ In Sudtone . ɪ . bou̇ træ ad glđ . Tᷓra dim caƀ́ . Ibi . ɪ . foctis

§ In Normentune . dim bou̇ tᷓre ad glđ . Ibi . ɪɪ . uiłti.

.v. 7 ɪɪ . borđ hn̄t . ɪ . caƀ́.

ꝏ In *NORMENTVNE* . ħᵬr . v . taini . Juſtan . Aseloc. ^(Durand.)

Eluuard . Vlmar . Aseloc . qſqᷓ aulā fuā . 7 unꝗ́ſqᷓ

ɪ . bou̇ træ 7 v . parƀ́ . ɪ . bou̇ ad glđ . Tᷓra xɪɪ . bou̇.

Ibi Rog̃ hõ Rog̃ ħƀ . ɪx . foct . 7 ɪɪɪɪ . borđ hn̄tes

.vɪ. ɪɪɪ . caƀ́ . 7 xɪɪ . ac̃s p̃ti . T.R.E. uał . x . fol . m̊ . vɪ . fol.

ꝏ In *WESTONE* . ħᵬr Elmer . Eluui . Osᵬn . Grim.

Edric . Stenulf . quiſqᷓ Aulā fuā . |7 ^(inƀ̃ oms . vɪ . bouatis) unꝗ́sqᷓ . ɪ . bõ tre

7 dim ad glđ . Tᷓra . ɪɪɪɪ . caƀ́ . Ibi Fulco Roᵬtus

7 Turold hões Rog̃ hn̄t . ɪɪɪɪ . caƀ́ 7 dim . 7 ɪ . foct

7 xɪɪɪɪ . uiłł 7 ɪɪɪ . borđ . hn̄tes . ɪɪɪ . caƀ́ 7 dim . Ibi æccła.

7 ɪ . moliñ . 7 xxx . ac̃ p̃ti . Silua past dim leu̇ lg̃ . 7 tntđ

laƀ́ . T.R.E. uał . ʟxx . fol . m̊ . ʟ . fol .   Soca ɪbɪᴅ. ^(or)

§ In Odeſtorp 7 Redford dim bou̇ . træ ad glđ . Tᷓra . ɪɪɪɪ . bou̇. ^(or)

Ibi . ē uñ uiłł . 7 ɪɪɪɪ . parˢ . ɪ . molini . 7 ɪɪɪɪ . ac̃ p̃ti. ^(ta)

In *TORGARTONE WAPENTAC*.

ꝏ In *GHELLINGE* . ħᵬ Dunſtan . ɪx . bou̇ træ 7 dim

7 ɪɪɪ . parƀ́ uni̇ bou̇ ad glđ . Tᷓra . ɪɪ . caƀ́ . Ibi ħƀ Rog̃

ɪɪ . caƀ́ . 7 ɪx . uiłł 7 ɪ . borđ hn̄tes . ɪɪ . caƀ́ . 7 x . ac̃s p̃ti.

Silua past . ɪɪ . q̃ᷝ lg̃ . 7 ɪ . q̃ᷝ laƀ́ . T.R.E. uał xxxɪɪ.

fol . m̊ xl . fol.

6 M. In SKEGBY Alfwold and Ulfketel had 1 c. of land taxable.　　285 d
　　Land for 2½ ploughs. Two of Roger's men have 3 ploughs
　　in lordship and
　　　　7 villagers and 2 smallholders who have 3 ploughs.
　　　　Meadow, 16 acres; woodland pasture ½ league long and
　　　　　　3 furlongs wide.
　　Value before 1066, 48s; now 40s.

　　Jurisdiction.

57 S. In SUTTON (-on-Trent) 1 b. of land taxable. Land for ½ plough.
　　　　1 Freeman has 1 plough.

8 S. In NORMANTON (-on-Trent) ½ b. of land taxable.
　　　　2 villagers and 2 smallholders have 1 plough.

9 5 In NORMANTON (-on-Trent) 5 thanes, Justan, Durand, Alfward,
　M. Wulfmer, Aslac each had his hall, and each 1 b. of land and the
　　fifth part of one b. taxable. Land for 12 oxen. Roger, Roger's
　　man, has
　　　　9 Freemen and 4 smallholders who have 3 ploughs.
　　　　Meadow, 12 acres.
　　Value before 1066, 10s; now 6s.

0 6 In WESTON Aelmer, Alfwy, Osbern, Grim, Edric, Steinulf each
　M. had his hall. Between them 6½ b. (? 6 b.) Land for 4 ploughs.
　　Fulk, Robert and Thorold, Roger's men, have 4½ ploughs and
　　　　1 Freeman, 14 villagers and 3 smallholders who have 3½ ploughs.
　　　　A church; 1 mill; meadow, 30 acres; woodland pasture
　　　　　　½ league long and as wide.
　　Value before 1066, 70s; now 50s.

　　Also Jurisdiction there.

1 S. In 'ODSTHORPE' and RETFORD ½ b. of land taxable. Land for 4 oxen.
　　　　1 villager.
　　　　The fourth part of 1 mill; meadow, 4 acres.

　　In THURGARTON Wapentake
2 M. In GEDLING Dunstan had 9½ b. of land and the third part of 1 b.
　　taxable. Land for 2 ploughs. Roger has 2 ploughs and
　　　　9 villagers and 1 smallholder who have 2 ploughs.
　　　　Meadow, 10 acres; woodland pasture 2 furlongs long
　　　　　　and 1 furlong wide.
　　Value before 1066, 32s; now 40s.

ꝏ In *EPRESTONE* 7 *VDESBVRG*. ħƀ Vluiet dim car̾
tr̾æ ad glđ. Tra xii. bou. Ibi Rog ħ̾. i. car̾. 7 ii.
focħ de una bou hui̾ tr̾æ. 7 iii. uiłł hn̄tes. i. car̾ 7 dim.
Ibi. i. moliñ. v. foliđ 7 iiii. den̾. 7 iii. ac̄s p̄ti. T.R.E.
uał. v. foł. m̊. i. mark argenti.

ꝏ In *GVLNETORP*. ħƀ Morcar. iii. car̾ tr̾æ 7 iii.
bou ad glđ. Tra. vi. car̾. Ibi Roger in dn̄io. ħ̄. iiii.
car̾. 7 v. focħ de. i. bou 7 dim huj̾ tr̾æ. 7 xl. uiłł
7 vii. borđ. hn̄tes xvi. car̾. Ibi theloneu 7 nauis
redđ. xxx foł 7 viii. den̾. 7 ii. pifcariæ. xxv. foliđ.
7 c 7 q̄t x̄x̄ ac̄ p̄ti. Silua paſt̾. vi. q̊₂ lg̾. 7 v. łat̾.
T.R.E. uał xv. liƀ. m̊. x. liƀ. Tailla. xxx. foł.

Ꝣ In Bertune 7 Ludħa xii. bou tr̾æ ad glđ. Tra. i. car̾.
.ii. Soca in Gūnetorp. Ibi. iiii. focħ 7 ii. uiłł. hn̄t. i. car̾.

ꝏ In *OSTONE* ħƀr Turſtan 7 Odincarle ⌐Ibi. ii̾. ac̄ p̄ti.
.i. car̾ tr̾æ ad glđ. Tra. ii. car̾ 7 dim. Ibi Rog ħ̄

286 a

ii. car̾ 7 v. uiłł 7 vi. borđ hn̄tes. ii. car̾. 7 i. moliñ
v. foliđ 7 iiii. denar̾. T.R.E. uał xl. foł. m̊ lx. foł.

IN RISECLIVE WAPENTAC.

ꝏ In *STANFORD*. ħƀ Elfi. x. bou tr̾æ ad gld. Tra
ii. car̾. Ibi Rog ħ̾. i. car̾. 7 v. focħ 7 iii. uiłł
7 ii. borđ hn̄tes. ii. car̾. Ibi dim moliñ. vi. foliđ 7 viii̾.
den̾. 7 xi. ac̄ p̄ti. T.R.E. uał xxx. foł. m̊ xl. foł.

Ꝣ In Normantone. iii. bou tr̾æ ad glđ. Tra. i. car̾.
Soca. Waſta. ē. Ibi. iiii. ac̄ p̄ti. T.R.E. 7 m̊. uał. iiii. foł.

ꝏ In *TVRMODESTVN*. ħƀr Leuuin 7 Elnod. vii. bou tr̾æ
ad glđ. Tra. ii. car̾. Ibi Rog ħ̾. i. car̾. 7 iii. focħ. 7 ii. uiłł
7 ii. borđ hn̄tes. i. car̾ 7 dim. T.R.E. uał. xl. foł. m̊. x̄x̄.

73 M. In **EPPERSTONE** and **WOODBOROUGH** Wulfgeat had ½ c. of land
    taxable. Land for 12 oxen. Roger has 1 plough and
      2 Freemen with 1 b. of this land and 3 villagers
        who have 1½ ploughs.
      1 mill, 5s 4d; meadow, 3 acres.
    Value before 1066, 5s; now 1 silver mark.

74 M. In **GUNTHORPE** Morcar had 3 c. of land and 3 b. taxable.
    Land for 6 ploughs. Roger has 4 ploughs in lordship and
      5 Freemen with 1½ b. of this land and 40 villagers
        and 7 smallholders who have 16 ploughs.
      Tolls and a ship which pay 30s 8d; 2 fisheries, 25s;
        meadow, 180 acres; woodland pasture 6 furlongs
        long and 5 wide.
    Value before 1066 £15; now £10; exactions, 30s.

75 S. In **BURTON** (Joyce) and **LOWDHAM** 12 b. of land taxable.
    Land for 1 plough. Jurisdiction in Gunthorpe.
      4 Freemen and 2 villagers have 1 plough.
      Meadow, 4 acres.

76 2 M. In **OXTON** Thurstan and Odincar had 1 c. of land taxable.
    Land for 2½ ploughs. Roger has 2 ploughs and
      5 villagers and 6 smallholders who have 2 ploughs.
      1 mill, 5s 4d.
    Value before 1066, 40s; now 60s.

      286 a

    In RUSHCLIFFE Wapentake

77 M. In **STANFORD** (-on-Soar) Alfsi had 10 b. of land taxable.
    Land for 2 ploughs. Roger has 1 plough and
      5 Freemen, 3 villagers and 2 smallholders who have
        2 ploughs.
      ½ mill, 6s 8d; meadow, 11 acres.
    Value before 1066, 30s; now 40s.

78 S. In **NORMANTON** (-on-Soar) 3 b. of land taxable.
    Land for 1 plough. Jurisdiction. Waste.
      Meadow, 4 acres.
    Value before 1066 and now 4s.

79 M. In **THRUMPTON** Leofwin and Alnoth had 7 b. of land
    taxable. Land for 2 ploughs. Roger has 1 plough and
      3 Freemen, 2 villagers and 2 smallholders who have 1½
        ploughs.
    Value before 1066, 40s; now 20s.

M̄ In *HOLMO* hb̄ Toret . XII . bou̓ træ ad gld̄ . Tra . III . car̄.
Ibi hr̄ Roger . II . car̄ . 7 XIIII . uill̄ . 7 II . bord̄ . hn̄tes . v.
+ .II. car̄ . 7 I . molin̄ . v . solid̄ . 7 qt xx . ac̄ p̄ti . T.R.E . 7 m̄ uat
M̄ In *PLVNTRE* . hb̄ Vlfac 7 Godric   VI . lib̄.
de XII . bou̓ træ ad gld̄ . Tra . III . car̄ . Ibi hr̄ Rogerus
in dn̄io . III . car̄ . 7 XXX . III . uill̄ hn̄tes . v . car̄ . Ibi eccl̄a.
7 XX . III . ac̄ p̄ti . T.R.E . 7 m̄ uat . LX . sol̄.   SOCA IBID.
S In Roddintone . x . bou̓ træ . 7 II . part̄ uni bou̓ ad
gld . Tra . II . car̄ . Ibi XVIII . soch̄ hn̄t . III . car̄ . 7 XXXIII.
M̄ In *NORMANTONE* . hb̄ Vnfac . VI . bou̓ træ   ac̄ p̄ti.
ad gld̄ . Tra . III . car̄ . Ibi Rog hr̄ . in dn̄io . II . car̄ . 7 VI.
uill̄ 7 III . bord̄ . 7 IIII . soch̄ cu̇ . III . car̄ . T.R.E . uat . XL . sol̄.
B IBIDĒ . IIII . bou̓ tre 7 dim̄ ad gld . Tra dim̄ car̄ .   m̄ XXX.
Ibi . II . uill̄ 7 I . bord̄ hn̄t dim̄ car̄ . In Pluntre iacet.
S In Stantune . dim̄ bou̓ tre ad gld̄ . Ibi . I . uill̄s hr̄ . v.
bou̓ in car̄ . Ad pluntre p̄tinet.   car̄ Ad Plunt̄ p̄tin̄.
S In Cauorde . II . bou̓ tre ad gld . Ibi . II . uill̄ hn̄t dim̄
.III. M̄ In *CAWORDE* . hb̄r Harold Ricard 7 Frane . VI . bou̓
træ . 7 II . part̄ uni bou̓ ad gld̄ . Tra . II . car̄ . Ibi Rog
hr̄ . II . soch̄ 7 III . uill̄ 7 II . bord̄ hn̄tes . III . car̄ . Ibi
XVI . ac̄ p̄ti . T.R.E . uat . XXX . sol̄ . m̄ XVII . sol̄.
M̄ In *LECHE* hb̄ Godric . II . bou̓ træ 7 III . part̄ uni bou̓
ad gld̄ . Tra . IIII . bou̓ . Ernulf hō Rog hr̄ . II . car̄.

0   M. In HOLME (Pierrepont) Thored has 12 b. of land taxable.
Land for 3 ploughs. Roger has 2 ploughs and
    14 villagers and 2 smallholders who have 5 ploughs.
    1 mill, 5s; meadow, 80 acres.
Value before 1066 and now £6.

9,81 is entered at the foot of column 286 b, after 9,106)

2 2 In PLUMTREE Wulfheah and Godric had....with 12 b. of land
  M. taxable. Land for 3 ploughs. Roger has in lordship 3 ploughs and
    33 villagers who have 5 ploughs.
    A church; meadow, 23 acres.
Value before 1066 and now 60s.

    Also Jurisdiction there.

3   S. In RUDDINGTON 10 b. of land and two parts of 1 b. taxable.
Land for 2 ploughs.
    18 Freemen have 3 ploughs.
    Meadow, 33 acres.

4   M. In NORMANTON (-on-the-Wolds) Wulfheah had 6 b. of land taxable.
Land for 3 ploughs. Roger has in lordship 2 ploughs and
    6 villagers, 3 smallholders and 4 Freemen with 3 ploughs.
Value before 1066, 40s; now 30[s.]

5   B. There also 4½ b. of land taxable. Land for ½ plough.
    2 villagers and 1 smallholder have ½ plough.
It lies in Plumtree (lands).

6   S. In STANTON (-on-the-Wolds) ½ b. of land taxable.
    1 villager has 5 oxen in a plough.
It belongs to Plumtree.

7   S. In KEYWORTH 2 b. of land taxable. 2 villagers have ½ plough.
It belongs to Plumtree.

8 3 In KEYWORTH Harold, Richard and Fran had 6 b. of land
  M. and two parts of 1 b. taxable. Land for 2 ploughs. Roger has
    4 Freemen, 3 villagers and 2 smallholders who have
      3 ploughs.
    Meadow, 16 acres.
Value before 1066, 30s; now 17s.

9   M. In LEAKE Godric had 2 b. of land and the third part of 1 b.
taxable. Land for 4 oxen. Ernulf, Roger's man has 2
ploughs and

7 ii . uiłł . cũ dim car̄ . 7 viii . acs p̃ti . T.R.E. uał xl . foł

IN BROLVESTOV WAPENTAC. ⌐ m̃ . x . foł.

.iii.
ⵣ In *WISOC* ħr Eſtan . Ælſi Gladuin . iii . car træ

ad glđ . Tra . iii . ꞏcar̄ . Ibi Rog ħo Rog ħꞇ . iii . car

, in dñio . 7 xv . uiłł . 7 v . focħ de vi . bou hui træ . 7 i .

bord . ħntes . x . car̄ . Ibi æccła . T.R.E. xlv . foł . m̃ . xlviii .

ⵉ In *WILGEBI* . ħƀ Odincar . vi . bou træ ad glđ . ⌐ foł.

Tra . vi . bou . Ibi . ii . focħ de . i . bou hui træ . 7 iii . uiłł

7 xv . bord̄ . ħnꞇ . iiii . car̄ . 7 xiii . acs p̃ti . T.R.E. xx . foł .

ⵣ In Torp . vii . bō træ ad gld . p̃tiñ ad Wiſoc Soca . ⌐ m̃ . x .
(Regis)

Waſta . ē . Ibi . vi . ac̃ p̃ti . 7 vał . ii . foł .

In Willebi . iiii (ta) . pars . i . bou træ ad glđ . Wast . ē .

286 b

.ii.
ⵣ In *COTINGESTOCHE* . ħr Godric 7 Algar xiii .
(7 Repeſtone.)

bou træ ad glđ . Tra . xiii . boū . Ibi ħꞇ Rog . ii . focħ

de . ii . bou hui tre . 7 iii . uiłł cũ . ii . car̄ . Vna car̄ hui

træ . ē waſta . Ibi . xxx . ac̃ p̃ti . T.R.E. uał xl . foł .

m̃ . xii . foł . *IN BINGAMESHOV WAPENTAC.*

ⵣ In *ROCLAVESTVNE* ħƀ Ælſi . ii . car̄ tre ad glđ .

Tra . iiii . car̄ . Ibi Rog in dñio ħꞇ . i . car̄ 7 dim .

7 xi . uiłł 7 i . bord̄ . ħntes . iii . car̄ . 7 viii . focħ cũ

iii . car̄ 7 dimid . 7 ii . moliñ . iii . folid . Ibi æccła . 7 xxx.

.ii. ac̃ p̃ti . T.R.E. uał xl . foł . m̃ . lx .

ⵣ In *LANBECOTE* . ħƀ Frane 7 Odincar . vii . bou træ

7 dim 7 iii (cũ) . parte i . bou ad glđ . Tra . i . car̄ . Ibi Rog

ħꞇ . i . car̄ 7 dim . 7 i . uiłł . 7 ii . acs p̃ti . T.R.E. 7 m̃ uał . xv . foł .

2 villagers with ½ plough.
Meadow, 8 acres.
Value before 1066, 40s; now 10s.

In BROXTOW Wapentake

)0 ³ꜰₘ. In WYSALL Alstan, Alfsi and Gladwin had 3 c. of land taxable.
Land for 3 ploughs. Roger, Roger's man, has 3 ploughs
in lordship and
15 villagers and 5 Freemen with 6 b. of this land
and 1 smallholder who have 10 ploughs.
A church.
[Value] before 1066, 45s; now 48s.

9,91 is entered after 9,92, with transposition signs)

)2 M. In WILLOUGHBY (-on-the-Wolds) Odincar had 6 b. of land
taxable. Land for 6 oxen.
2 Freemen with 1 b. of this land and 3 villagers
and 15 smallholders have 4 ploughs.
Meadow, 13 acres.
[Value] before 1066, 20s; now 10[s.]

)1 In the King's THORPE (-in-the-Glebe) 7 b. of land taxable, which
belong to Wysall. Jurisdiction. Waste.
Meadow, 6 acres.
Value 2s.

)3 In WILLOUGHBY the fourth part of 1 b. of land taxable. Waste.

)4 ²ₘ. In COSTOCK and REMPSTONE Godric and Algar had 13 b. of land   286 b
taxable. Land for 13 oxen. Roger has
2 Freemen with 2 b. of this land and 3 villagers
with 2 ploughs. 1 c. of this land is waste.
Meadow, 30 acres.
Value before 1066, 40s; now 12s.

In BINGHAM Wapentake

)5 M. In TOLLERTON Alfsi had 2 c. of land taxable. Land for 4 ploughs.
Roger has in lordship 1½ ploughs and
11 villagers and 1 smallholder who have 3 ploughs;
8 Freemen with 3½ ploughs.
2 mills, 3s. A church; meadow, 30 acres.
Value before 1066, 40s; now 60[s.]

)6 ²ₘ. In LAMCOTE Fran and Odincar had 7½ b. of land and the third
part of 1 b. taxable. Land for 1 plough. Roger has 1½ ploughs and
1 villager.
Meadow, 2 acres.
Value before 1066 and now 15s.

Ⓜ In *Bingheha̅* . h̅b Tofti . iii . car̅ tre . 7 ii . bou̅ 7 di̅m
ad gl̅d . T̅ra . v . car̅ . Ibi Roger in dn̅io h̅t . iiii . car̅.
7 xxvi . uil̅t . 7 v . bor̅d 7 xiiii . foch h̅ntes xii . car̅
7 di̅m . Silua paſt . i . lev l̅g . 7 viii . q̅z̅ la̅t . T.R.E.

.ii. 7 m̊ ual̅ . x . lib̅.   In Niuuetune . iii . bou̅ ad gl̅d.

Ⓜ I̅bide̅ . h̅b̅r Hoga 7 Helga . v . b̅o trǽ 7 ii . part . i . bou̅
ad gl̅d . T̅ra . i . car̅ . Ibi . i . foch 7 viii . uil̅t 7 i . bor̅d
h̅ntes . i . car̅ . 7 xxiiii . ac̅ p̅ti . T.R.E. ual̅ xx . fol̅ . m̊ . xiii.

S̅ In Scelforde . iii . bou̅ trǽ ad gl̅d . T̅ra . i . car̅ . Soca in
Bingheha̅ . Ibi . iii . foch h̅t . i . car̅.

Ⓜ In *Brvgeford* . h̅b Odincar . iiii . car̅ trǽ ad gl̅d.
T̅ra . vi . car̅ . Ibi Roger in dn̅io h̅t . iii . car̅ . 7 xx . foch
de . x . bou̅ hui̅ tre . 7 xv . uil̅t 7 iii . bor̅d . h̅ntes . xi . car̅.

.iii. Ibi p̅br 7 ǽccl̅a . 7 xii . ac̅ p̅ti . T.R.E. ual̅ . iii . lib̅ . m̊ . v . lib̅.

Ⓜ I̅bide̅ h̅b̅r Tu|ſtan 7 Rofchet 7 Juſtan . vi . b̅o trǽ ad gl̅d.
T̅ra . i . car̅ . Ibi . iii . ac̅ p̅ti . Tra n̅ colit . T.R.E. ual̅ . viii . fol̅.

Ⓜ In *Chenivetone* . h̅b Vluiet . v . bou̅ trǽ   ꟻ m̊ . iii . fol̅.
7 iii . part uni bou̅ ad gl̅d . T̅ra . i . car̅ . Ibi Rog h̅t

.ii. .i . car̅ . 7 ii . uil̅t cu̅ . i . car̅ . 7 iiii . ac̅ p̅ti . T.R.E. 7 m̊ ual̅ . x . fol̅.

Ⓜ In *Saxeden* . h̅b̅r Vluiet 7 Vnfpac . xii . bou̅ trǽ
ad gl̅d . T̅ra . iiii . car̅ . Ibi Rog in dn̅io h̅t . ii . car̅.
7 v . foch . 7 v . uil̅t . 7 iii . bor̅d h̅ntes . ii . car̅ . Ibi ǽccl̅a
7 i . ac̅ p̅ti . T.R.E. 7 m̊ ual̅ . xxv . fol̅.

Ⓜ In *Clipestvne* . h̅b Vluiet . iii . car̅ trǽ ad gl̅d . T̅ra
iii . car̅ . Ibi Rog in dn̅io h̅t . ii . car̅ . 7 iii . foch 7 xii .
uil̅t 7 i . bor̅d . h̅ntes . vi . car̅ . Ibi . xx . ac̅ p̅ti . T.R.E.
ual̅ lx . fol̅ . m̊ . xl.

7   M. In BINGHAM Tosti had 3 c. of land and 2½ b. taxable.
Land for 5 ploughs. Roger has in lordship 4 ploughs and
    26 villagers, 5 smallholders and 14 Freemen who
       have 12½ ploughs.
Woodland pasture 1 league long and 8 furlongs wide.
Value before 1066 and now £10.
    In Newton 3 b. taxable.

8   $\frac{2}{M.}$ There also Hoga and Helgi had 5 b. of land and two parts of 1 b.
taxable. Land for 1 plough.
    1 Freeman, 8 villagers and 1 smallholder who have 1 plough.
    Meadow, 24 acres.
Value before 1066, 20s; now 13[s.]

9   S. In SHELFORD 3 b. of land taxable. Land for 1 plough.
Jurisdiction in Bingham.
    3 Freemen have 1 plough.

0   M. In (East) BRIDGFORD Odincar had 4 c. of land taxable.
Land for 6 ploughs. Roger has in lordship 3 ploughs and
    20 Freemen with 10 b. of this land; 15 villagers
    and 3 smallholders who have 11 ploughs.
    A priest and a church; meadow, 12 acres.
Value before 1066 £3; now £5.

1   $\frac{3}{M.}$ There also Thurstan, Roskell and Justan had 6 b. of land
taxable. Land for 1 plough.
    Meadow, 3 acres; the land is not cultivated.
Value before 1066, 8s; now 3s.

2   M. In KNEETON Wulfgeat had 5 b. of land and the third part of 1 b.
taxable. Land for 1 plough. Roger has 1 plough and
    2 villagers with 1 plough.
    Meadow, 4 acres.
Value before 1066 and now 10s.

3   $\frac{2}{M.}$ In SAXONDALE Wulfgeat and Ospak had 12 b. of land taxable.
Land for 4 ploughs. Roger has in lordship 2 ploughs and
    5 Freemen, 5 villagers and 3 smallholders who have 2 ploughs.
    A church; meadow, 1 acre.
Value before 1066 and now 25s.

4   M. In CLIPSTON Wulfgeat had 3 c. of land taxable.
Land for 3 ploughs. Roger has in lordship 2 ploughs and
    3 Freemen, 12 villagers and 1 smallholder who have
      6 ploughs.
    Meadow, 20 acres.
Value before 1066, 60s; now 40[s.]

ⓂIn *WAREBERG* . ħɓ Godric xii . bou træ ad glđ . Tra

xii . bou . Wasta . ē . Ibi . x . aē p̄ti . T.R.E . ual xx . fol . m̄ . v . fol.

ⓂIn *ESCREVENTONE* . ħɓ Odincar . v . bou træ ad glđ.

Tra . i . caɼ . Ibi . i . foch cū . i . borđ hɼ . i . caɼ . T.R.E . ual . v . fol

✠ In Bafinfelt . x . bou træ ad glđ . 7 ii . part uni bou . Tra . ii . caɼ ⌐ m̄ . viii . s̄
Soca de Holmo . Ibi viii . foch hn̄t . iii . caɼ . 7 xv . aē p̄ti.

286 c

ⓂIn *COLESTONE* ħɓ Vluiet . vi . bou træ 7 i . aē
ad glđ . Tra . v . caɼ . Ibi Rog hō Rogerii hɼ . ii.
caɼ in dn̄io . 7 xiii . foch 7 iii . uilł 7 vii . borđ hn̄tes
viii . caɼ . Ibi . xvii . aē p̄ti . T.R.E . ual xxx . fol . m̄ xl.

ⓂIn *FLINTHA* . ħɓ Odincar . vi . bou tre ad glđ . Tra
ii . caɼ . Ibi Rog hō Rog hɼ . i . caɼ . 7 ii . foch 7 iii.
uilł 7 iiii . borđ . hn̄tes . ii . caɼ . T.R.E . 7 m̄ ual xx . fol.

s̄ Iɓɪdē . i . bou tre 7 dim ad glđ . Tra . iiii . bou . SOCA in
Cheniuetone . Ernuin hɼ de Rog Ibi . ii . foch 7 i . borđ.
hn̄t . i . caɼ . Ibi . viii . aē p̄ti.

ⓂIn Ailetone . ħɓ Morcar . vii . bou træ ad glđ . Tra . iiii.
caɼ . Ibi Radulf hō Rogerii hɼ . iii . caɼ . 7 iii . foch 7 xi.
uilł hn̄tes . vi . caɼ . Ibi æccła 7 xii . aē p̄ti . T.R.E . 7 m̄

ⓂIn *OVETORP* . ħɓ Helge dim car træ   ⌐iiii . liɓ.
ad glđ . Tra . iii . caɼ . Ibi Wilłs hō Rogerii hɼ . i . caɼ.
7 iiii . foch 7 viii . uilł hn̄tes . iii . caɼ . Ibi xii . aē p̄ti.
T.R.E . 7 m̄ ual . xxx . fol.

5 M. In 'WARBOROUGH' Godric had 12 b. of land taxable. Land
for 12 oxen. Waste.
Meadow, 10 acres.
Value before 1066, 20s; now 5s.

6 M. In SCREVETON Odincar had 5 b. of land taxable. Land
for 1 plough.
1 Freeman with 1 smallholder has 1 plough.
Value before 1066, 5s; now 8s.

(directed to its proper place by transposition signs.)
In BASSINGFIELD 10 b. of land taxable and two parts of 1 b.
Land for 2 ploughs. A jurisdiction of Holme (Pierrepont).
8 Freemen have 3 ploughs.
Meadow, 15 acres.

7 M. In (Car) COLSTON Wulfgeat had 6 b. of land and 1 acre taxable.   286 c
Land for 5 ploughs. Roger, Roger's man, has 2 ploughs in
lordship and
13 Freemen, 3 villagers and 7 smallholders who have
8 ploughs.
Meadow, 17 acres.
Value before 1066, 30s; now 40[s].

8 M. In FLINTHAM Odincar had 6 b. of land taxable. Land for 2 ploughs.
Roger, Roger's man, has 1 plough and
2 Freemen, 3 villagers and 4 smallholders who have 2 ploughs.
Value before 1066 and now 20s.

9 S. There also 1½ b. of land taxable. Land for 4 oxen.
Jurisdiction in Kneeton. Ernwin the priest has it from Roger.
2 Freemen and 1 smallholder have 1 plough.
Meadow, 8 acres.

0 M. In ELTON Morcar had 7 b. of land taxable. Land for 4 ploughs.
Ralph, Roger's man, has 3 ploughs and
3 Freemen and 11 villagers who have 6 ploughs.
A church; meadow, 12 acres.
[Value] before 1066 and now £4.

M. In OWTHORPE Helgi had ½ c. of land taxable. Land for 3
ploughs. William, Roger's man, has 1 plough and
4 Freemen and 8 villagers who have 3 ploughs.
Meadow, 12 acres.
Value before 1066 and now 30s.

Ꝑ In *Fentone* . ħƀr Vlfac 7 Leuric 7 Grim . ı . bou træ 7 ııı . parte . ı . bou ad glđ . Tra Wasta . ē p̃t uñ bord . Ibi xxx . ac̃ siłue past . T.R.E. uał . v . soł.

Ibidē ħƀ Sperauoc . ıı . bou træ 7 ıı . part uni bou ad glđ . Tra . ı . car . cũ saca 7 soca sine Aula . Wasta . ē.

.u. Ibi . ɪx . ac̃ siłuæ past . T.R.E. 7 m̃ uał . x . soł 7 vııı . den.

Ꝑ In *Estretone* ħƀ Sperhauoc 7 Archil . ıııı . bou tre 7 dim ad glđ . Tra . ıı . car 7 dim . Ibi m̃ . ıı . uiłłi 7 ıı . socħ 7 ıı . bord hñtes vıı . bou in car . 7 vııı . ac̃ p̃ti . Silua past vı . q̃ɫ̨ lḡ . 7 ııı . q̃ɫ̨ 7 dim lat̃ . T.R.E.

.v. uał . ıı . Marchas argenti . m̃ similit̃.

Ꝑ In *Wateleia* ħƀr . v . taini . ıx . bou træ ad glđ. Tra . vııı . car . Ibi Rog in dñio ħt . ıııı . car . 7 ıııı . socħ 7 xxv . uiłł hñtes xıı . car 7 dim . 7 v . ac̃ p̃ti . Silua miñ ı . lev lḡ . 7 ı . q̃ɫ̨ lat̃ . T.R.E. 7 m̃ uał . vııı . liƀ.

Ꝑ In *Bvrtone* . ħƀ Sperhauoc . vı . bou træ ad glđ. Tra . ıı . car . Ibi Goisfr hõ Roger ħt . ı . car . 7 ı . socħ 7 ı . uiłł 7 ıı . bord . hñt . ı . car 7 dim . Ibi . ı . piscaria cc . Anguiłł . Silua miñ . ı . q̃ɫ̨ lḡ . 7 ı . lat̃ . T.R.E. uał . xx . soł . m̃ xL.   Soca ıbıd.

Ş In Euretone 7 Hereuuelle . ıı . bou træ . 7 ııı . partes uni bou ad glđ . Tra . ı . car . Ibi . ı . socħ ħt dim car. 7 ı . ac̃ p̃ti 7 dim . Silua past . ı . q̃ɫ̨ lḡ . 7 ı . lat̃.

Ꝑ In *Bolyn*. ħƀ Turuert . vıı . bou træ ad glđ . Tra ıı . car . Ibi m̃ . ıııı . socħ 7 ıııı . bord hñt . ııı . car. Huic Ꝑ adiacent vı . bou træ ad glđ . De qbɂ . ē

In OSWALDBECK Wapentake

12 ³/M. In FENTON Wulfheah, Leofric and Grim had 1 b. of land and the third part of 1 b. taxable.
Waste, except for 1 smallholder.
Woodland pasture, 30 acres.
Value before 1066, 5s.

13 There also Sparrowhawk had 2 b. of land and two parts of 1 b. taxable. Land for 1 plough, with full jurisdiction, without a hall. Waste.
Woodland pasture, 60 acres.
Value before 1066 and now 10s 8d.

14 ²/M. In STURTON (-le-Steeple) Sparrowhawk and Arkell had 4½ b. of land taxable. Land for 2½ ploughs.
Now 2 villagers, 2 Freemen and 2 smallholders who have 7 oxen in a plough.
Meadow, 8 acres; woodland pasture 6 furlongs long and 3½ furlongs wide.
Value before 1066, 2 silver marks; now the same.

15 ⁵/M. In WHEATLEY 5 thanes had 9 b. of land taxable. Land for 8 ploughs. Roger has 4 ploughs in lordship and 4 Freemen and 25 villagers who have 12½ ploughs.
Meadow, 5 acres; underwood 1 league long and 1 furlong wide.
Value before 1066 and now £8.

16 M. In (West) BURTON Sparrowhawk had 6 b. of land taxable. Land for 2 ploughs. Geoffrey, Roger's man, has 1 plough.
1 Freeman, 1 villager and 2 smallholders have 1½ ploughs.
1 fishery of 200 eels; underwood 1 furlong long and 1 wide.
Value before 1066, 20s; now 40[s.]

Also Jurisdiction there.

17 S. In EVERTON and HARWELL 2 b. of land and three parts of 1 b. taxable. Land for 1 plough.
1 Freeman has ½ plough.
Meadow, 1½ acres; woodland pasture 1 furlong long and 1 wide.

18 M. In BOLE Thorferth had 7 b. of land taxable. Land for 2 ploughs.
Now 4 Freemen and 4 smallholders have 3 ploughs.
To this manor are attached 6 b. of land taxable whose

ſoca in Sandebi.Ťra.ɪɪ.caŕ.Ibi Gaufrid hō

Rogerii hŧ.ɪ.caŕ.7 ɪɪ.ſocħ 7 ɪɪɪɪ.uiłt 7 ɪɪɪ.borđ

hn̄tes.ɪ.caŕ 7 dimiđ.Ƥtū.vɪɪɪ.q̇꜠ lḡ.7 ɪ꞉.lať.

Silua paſt.ɪ.lev lḡ.7 ɪɪɪ.q̇꜠ lať.T.R.E.ual xʟ.ſoł.

꟩ Iɴ *Bechingehā̄*.ħƀ Osƀn.ɪɪɪ.bou ⎰ m̊.ʟ.ſoł.

træ ad glđ.Ťra.ɪ.caŕ.Ibi Goisfr hō Roǵ hŧ.ɪ.

caŕ.7 xv.ac̅s p̊ti.Silua paſt.vɪɪ.q̇꜠ lḡ.7 ɪ.lať.

T.R.E.ual.x.ſoł.m̊.xvɪ.ſoł.

꟩ Iɴ *Wacheringehā̄* ħƀ Adeſtan.x.bou træ

7 dim̄ ad glđ.Ibi Roǵ hō Rogerii hŧ.ɪɪɪɪ.ſocħ.

7 ɪ.uiłt 7 v.borđ hn̄tes.ɪɪ.caŕ.Ƥtū.ɪɪ.q̇꜠ lḡ.

7 ɪ.lať.Silua.ɪɪɪɪ.q̇꜠ lḡ.7 ɪ.lať.T.R.E.ual

.v. xx.ſoł.m̊ xv.ſoł.

.꟩.Iɴ *Ministretone* ħƀr.v.taini xɪɪɪ.bou

træ 7 dim̄ ad glđ.Ťra.ɪɪ.caŕ 7 dim̄.Ibi Roǵer

hŧ.vɪɪɪ.uiłt.7 v.borđ.hn̄tes ɪɪ.caŕ 7 dimiđ.

Ibi æccła 7 ɪɪɪ.q̇꜠ lḡ p̊tū.7 ɪ.q̇꜠ 7 dim̄ lať.

Silua paſt xɪɪ.q̇꜠ 7 dim̄ lḡ.7 ɪɪ.q̇꜠ lať.T.R.E.

.vɪɪ. ual.xx.ſoł.m̊.ɪɪ.ſoł plus.

꟩ Iɴ *Gringeleia*.ħƀr.vɪɪ.taini.ɪɪɪ.caŕ træ

ad glđ.Ťra.vɪɪɪ.caŕ.Ibi Roǵ hō Roǵ hŧ.ɪɪɪ.

caŕ.7 x.uiłt.7 vɪ.borđ.hn̄tes.vɪɪɪ.caŕ.Ibi æccła

7 ɪ.piſcaŕ mille anguiłt.7 xʟ.ac̅ p̊ti.Silua paſt

ɪ.lev lḡ.7 ɪɪɪ.q̇꜠ lať.T.R.E.ual x.liƀ.m̊.ɪɪɪɪ.liƀ.

§ Iɴ Miniſtretone.vɪɪ.bou tre 7 dim̄ ad glđ.Soca Iʙɪᴅ.

Ťra.xɪɪ.bou.Ibi.v.ſocħ 7 ɪ.uiłt 7 v.borđ.hn̄t.ɪ.

caŕ 7 dim̄.p̊tū.ɪɪɪɪ.q̇꜠ lḡ.7 dim̄ lať.Silua paſt.ɪɪɪɪ.

q̇꜠ lḡ.7 ɪ.q̇꜠ 7 dim̄ lať.

§ Iɴ Hereuuelle 7 Euretone.ɪɪɪ.bou træ 7 ɪɪɪ.parte

uni bou ad glđ.Ťra.ɪ.caŕ.Ibi.ɪ.ſocħ 7 ɪ.uiłt hn̄t

dim̄ caŕ.7 ɪɪɪ.ac̅s p̊ti.Silua paſt.v.q̇꜠ lḡ.7 ɪɪ.lať.

jurisdiction is in Saundby. Land for 2 ploughs.
Geoffrey, Roger's man, has 1 plough and
2 Freemen, 4 villagers and 3 smallholders who have 1½ ploughs.
Meadow 8 furlongs long and 2 wide; woodland pasture
1 league long and 3 furlongs wide.
Value before 1066, 40s; now 50s.

M. In BECKINGHAM Osbern had 3 b. of land taxable.
Land for 1 plough. Geoffrey, Roger's man, has 1 plough.
Meadow, 15 acres; woodland pasture 7 furlongs long
and 1 wide.
Value before 1066, 10s; now 16s.

M. In WALKERINGHAM Athelstan had 10½ b. of land taxable.
Roger, Roger's man, has
4 Freemen, 1 villager and 5 smallholders who have 2 ploughs.
Meadow 2 furlongs long and 1 wide; woodland 4 furlongs
long and 1 wide.
Value before 1066, 20s; now 15s.

5
M. In MISTERTON 5 thanes had 13½ b. of land taxable.
Land for 2½ ploughs. Roger has
8 villagers and 5 smallholders who have 2½ ploughs.
A church; meadow 3 furlongs long and 1½ furlongs wide;
woodland pasture 12½ furlongs long and 2 furlongs wide.
Value before 1066, 20s; now 2s more.

7
M. In GRINGLEY (-on-the-Hill) 7 thanes had 3 c. of land taxable.
Land for 8 ploughs. Roger, Roger's man, has 3 ploughs and
10 villagers and 6 smallholders who have 8 ploughs.
A church; 1 fishery, 1,000 eels; meadow, 40 acres;
woodland pasture 1 league long and 3 furlongs wide.
Value before 1066 £10; now £4.
Also Jurisdiction there.

S. In MISTERTON 7½ b. of land taxable. Land for 12 oxen.
5 Freemen, 1 villager and 5 smallholders have 1½ ploughs.
Meadow 4 furlongs long and ½ wide; woodland pasture
4 furlongs long and 1½ furlongs wide.

S. In HARWELL and EVERTON 3 b. of land and three parts of 1 b.
taxable. Land for 1 plough.
1 Freeman and 1 villager have ½ plough.
Meadow, 3 acres; woodland pasture 5 furlongs long
and 2 wide.

⊕ In *BOLVN*.ħƀ Vlmer.ɪ.boú trǽ �7 dim̄ ad glđ.

Tra.ɪ.car̄.Ibi Roǵ ħ̄.ɪ.car̄.�7 ɪɪɪɪ.parté ǽcclǽ.

᷇7 ɪɪ.molin̄ xxxɪɪ.folid.᷇7 x.acs̄ p̄ti.T.R.E.ual̄

xʟ.fol.m̄ fimilit́

⊕ In *CLAVORDE*.ħƀ Grinchil.ɪɪ.boú trǽ ad glđ.

Tra.ɪɪɪɪ.boū.Ibi Fulco ħō Roǵ ħ̄.ɪɪɪ.foch́.᷇7 ɪɪɪ.

borđ.cū.ɪɪɪ.car̄ ᷇7 diḿ.P̄tū.ɪɪ.q̂ẕ ᷇7 dim̄ lḡ.

᷇7 xvɪɪɪ.pticas lat̄.Silua past́ ɪɪɪ.q̂ẕ ᷇7 x.ptíc

lḡ.᷇7 tntđ lat́.T.R.E.ual̄.ɪɪɪɪ.fol.m̄.v.fol.

⊕ In *CLAVREBVRG*.ħƀ Ragenald.ɪɪ.boú trǽ ad

glđ.Tra.ɪɪ.car̄.Ibi Fulco ħō Roǵ ħ̄ dim̄ car̄.

᷇7 vɪɪɪ.uil̄.᷇7 ɪ.borđ.cū.ɪ.car̄ ᷇7 diḿ.᷇7 vɪɪ.acs̄ p̄ti.

Silua past́.ɪɪɪɪ.q̂ẕ lḡ.᷇7 ɪɪ.lat̄.T.R.E.ual̄.vɪ.fol.

287 a   ⨏.m̄ xx.fol.

Ibidḗ ħƀ Vlchil dim̄ boú trǽ ad glđ cū faca

᷇7 foca.Tra.ɪɪ.bob⁹.Idem ipfe Vlchil tenet de Ro

gero ᷇7 ħ̄ ibi.ɪɪ.borđ.cū ɪɪ.bob⁹.᷇7 ɪ.acra p̄ti.

Silua past́.ɪɪ.q̂ẕ lḡ.᷇7 ɪ.lat̄.T.R.E.᷇7 m̄ ual̄.xvɪ.

⊕ In *TIRESWELLE*.ħƀ Godric.vɪ.boú trǽ ⨏ den.

᷇7 ɪɪɪ.parté ᷇7 q̇ṅdecimā́ part́.ɪ.boú ad glđ.Tra

ɪɪɪɪ.car̄.Ibi Roǵ ħō Roǵ ħ̄.ɪɪ.car̄.᷇7 xɪɪɪɪ.uil̄

᷇7 v.borđ ħntes.v.car̄.p̄tū.ɪɪɪɪ.q̂ẕ lḡ.᷇7 ɪ.q̂ẕ lat̄.

Silua past́.ɪɪɪɪ.q̂ẕ lḡ.᷇7 ɪ.q̂ẕ ᷇7 dim̄ lat̄.T.R.E.

᷇7 m̄ ual̄.ʟ.folid.

In Cledretone.ɪɪɪ.boú trǽ ᷇7 diḿ.᷇7 medietaté

q̇ntǽ partis uni boú ad glđ.Hanc trā ħ̄ Roǵ.

᷇7 ibi ħ̄.vɪ̇ uil̄.ħntes.ɪ.car̄.᷇7 dim̄.Ibi dim̄ eccl̇a.

Ibi.ḗ filua past́.ɪ.q̂ẕ ᷇7 dim̄ lḡ.᷇7 ɪ.q̂ẕ lat̄.

᷇7 p̄tū.ɪ.q̂ẕ ᷇7 dim̄ lḡ.᷇7 ɪ.q̂ẕ lat̄.Huj filuǽ ᷇7 p̄ti

medietaté ħ̄ Roger̄.Valet.x.fol.Tra.ɪ.car̄.

9

5   M.   In BOLE Wulfmer had 1½ b. of land taxable. Land for 1 plough.
        Roger has 1 plough and
            the fourth part of a church; 2 mills, 32s; meadow, 10 acres.
        Value before 1066, 40s; now the same.

5   M.   In CLAYWORTH Grimkell had 2 b. of land taxable.
        Land for 4 oxen. Fulk, Roger's man, has
            3 Freemen and 3 smallholders with 3½ ploughs.
            Meadow 2½ furlongs and 18 perches wide; woodland
                pasture 3 furlongs and 10 perches long and as wide.
        Value before 1066, 4s; now 5s.

7   M.   In CLARBOROUGH Reginald had 2 b. of land taxable.
        Land for 2 ploughs. Fulk, Roger's man, has ½ plough and
            8 villagers and 1 smallholder with 1½ ploughs.
            Meadow, 7 acres; woodland pasture 4 furlongs long
                and 2 wide.
        Value before 1066, 6s; now 20s.

8   There also Ulfkell had ½ b. of land taxable, with full   287 a
        jurisdiction. Land for 2 oxen. Ulfkell holds from Roger; he has
            2 smallholders with 2 oxen.
            Meadow, 1 acre; woodland pasture 2 furlongs long and
                1 wide.
        Value before 1066 and now 16d.

9   M.   In TRESWELL Godric had 6 b. of land and the third part and
        the fifteenth part of 1 b. taxable. Land for 4 ploughs.
        Roger, Roger's man, has 2 ploughs and
            14 villagers and 5 smallholders who have 5 ploughs.
            Meadow 4 furlongs long and 1 furlong wide; woodland
                pasture 4 furlongs long and 1½ furlongs wide.
        Value before 1066 and now 50s.

0   In LEVERTON 3½ b. of land and a half of the fifth
        part of 1 b. taxable. Roger has this land; he has
            7 villagers who have 1½ ploughs.
            Half a church; woodland pasture 1½ furlongs long and
                1 furlong wide; meadow 1½ furlongs long and 1 furlong
                wide; Roger has half of this woodland and meadow.
        Value 10s.
            Land for 1 plough.

Ꝧ In *RAMETONE* hɓr.vii.taini.ii.car̄ tre.7 iii.

bou 7 v.parte uni bou ad glđ.Tra.vii.car̄ 7 dim.

Ibi Rog de bufli cū fuis.iiii.hōibʒ hr̄.iii.car̄.

7 xi.focħ 7 viii.uiłł 7 vi.borđ.hn̄tes.v.car̄ 7 dim.

Ibi æccła.7 iii.pifcar̄ 7 dim.iii.fot 7 vi.denar̄.

Ibi.lxv.ac̄ p̄ti.T.R.E.uał.liiii.fot.m̄.iiii.fot

S In Madreffei.i.bou tre ad glđ.Soc A.   min.

Ibi.i.focħ 7 ii;ac̄ p̄ti.

.IX. TERRA WILLI PEVREL.

Ꝧ In *COLEWIC*.ħɓ Godric.vii.bō træ ad glđ.

Tra.i.car̄.Ibi hr̄ Wiłłs peurel.i.car̄ in

dn̄io.7 vii.uiłł 7 vi.borđ hn̄tes.iii.car̄.Ibi p̄ɓr

7 æccła.7 ii.ferui.7 i.molin̄.v.folid.7 dimiđ pifcar̄.

7 xxx.ac̄ p̄ti.7 xv.ac̄ filuæ minutæ.T.R.E.uał

.ii. xx.fot.m̄.xl.Walann tenet.

Ꝧ In *SIBETORP*.ħɓr Leuuine 7 Turber.iiii.bou træ

ad glđ.Tra.xiii.bou.Ibi Roɓt hō Wiłłi hr̄.i.car̄.

7 v.uiłł cū.i.car̄.7 i.molin̄.xx.denar̄.7 xvii.

ac̄ p̄ti.T.R.E.uał.xl.fot.m̄ xx.iiii.fot.

Ꝧ In *GVNNVLVESTVNE* 7 Miletune ħɓ Vlsi.ii.car̄

træ 7 ii.bou 7 ii.part uni bou ad glđ.Tra.iii.car̄.

Ibi Wiłłs in dn̄io hr̄.i.car̄.7 ii.focħ de.iii.bou

huj træ.7 vii.uiłł 7 ii.borđ.7 ii.cenfor hn̄tes.iii.car̄.

7 ii.molin̄.xl.folid.7 x.ac̄ p̄ti.Silua paſt.v.q̄ʒ

lḡ.7 iii.łat.T.R.E.uał.iiii.liɓ.m̄.lx.fot.

Ꝧ In *TVRMODESTVN*.ħɓ Stapleuuin.iii.bou træ

7 iii.part.i.bou ad glđ.Tra.i.car̄.Ibi iiii.focħi

hn̄t.i.car̄.7 v.ac̄s p̄ti.T.R.E 7 m̄ uał.v.fot 7 iiii.den.

31 7 M. In RAMPTON 7 thanes had 2 c. of land and 3 b. and the fifth part of 1 b. taxable. Land for 7½ ploughs. Roger of Bully with 4 of his men has 3 ploughs and
  11 Freemen, 8 villagers and 6 smallholders who
    have 5½ ploughs.
  A church; 3½ fisheries, 3s 6d; meadow, 65 acres.
Value before 1066, 54s; now 4s less.
  Jurisdiction.

32 S. In MATTERSEY 1 b. of land taxable.
  1 Freeman.
  Meadow, 2 acres.

[10]   **LAND OF WILLIAM PEVEREL**   287 b

[THURGARTON Wapentake]
1 M. In COLWICK Godric had 7 b. of land taxable. Land for 1 plough.
  William Peverel has 1 plough in lordship and
    7 villagers and 6 smallholders who have 3 ploughs.
  A priest and a church; 2 slaves; 1 mill, 5s; half a
    fishery; meadow, 30 acres; underwood, 15 acres.
Value before 1066, 20s; now 40[s].
  Waland holds it.

[NEWARK Wapentake]
2 2 M. In SIBTHORPE Leofwin and Thorbern had 4 b. of land taxable.
  Land for 13 oxen. Robert, William's man, has 1 plough and
    5 villagers with 1 plough.
  1 mill, 20d; meadow, 17 acres.
Value before 1066, 40s; now 24s.

[THURGARTON Wapentake]
3 M. In GONALSTON and MILTON Young Wulfsi had 2 c. of land, 2 b.
  and two parts of 1 b. taxable. Land for 3 ploughs.
  William has in lordship 1 plough and
    2 Freemen with 3 b. of this land; 7 villagers,
      2 smallholders and 2 tributaries who have 3 ploughs.
  2 mills, 40s; meadow, 10 acres; woodland pasture 5 furlongs
    long and 3 wide.
Value before 1066 £4; now 60s.

[RUSHCLIFFE Wapentake]
4 M. In THRUMPTON Staplewin had 3 b. of land and 3 parts of 1 b. taxable.
  Land for 1 plough.
    4 Freemen have 1 plough.
    Meadow, 5 acres.
Value before 1066 and now 5s 4d.

ᛗ In *CLIFTVN* . ħħ Gode . ıı . car̄ tre 7 dim ad glđ .

Tra . v . car̄ . Ibi ħ Wiłłs . ıı . car̄ in dñio . 7 ıııı . focħ

7 xıx . uiłł 7 vııı . borđ . hn̄tes . ıx . car̄ . Ibi pƀr 7 æccła .

7 ı . molin̄ xıı . den̄ . 7 xıı . ac̄ p̄ti . T . R . E . uał . xvı . liƀ .

m̊ . ıx . liƀ .   ⌜ 7 ı . ac̄ p̄ti .

~~Ibid ħħ 7 ħ Vlchel . ı . bou tre ad glđ . 7 ı . uiłł cū . ıı . bob .~~

Ṡ In Wilesforde Soc᷎ᴀ . ııı . car̄ træ ad glđ . Tra . vı . car̄.   In *B᷎ᴀʀ᷎ᴛᴏɴᴇ* . ıı . bouat᷎æ ⫶
                                                                  7 tcia pars . ı . bou ad glđ .
Ibi . xxııı . focħ hn̄t . vıı . car̄ . Ibi pƀr 7 xvııı . ac̄ p̄ti .   Ṫra . ı . car̄ . Ibi . xıx . focħ ⫶

7 dim pifcar̄ .   hn̄t . ıı . car̄ . 7 ııı . ac̄ p̄ti .

Ṡ In Brigeforde Soc᷎ᴀ . xıı . bou træ ad glđ . Tra . ııı . car̄ .

Ibi Wiłłs ħ dim car̄ in dñio . 7 ııı . focħ 7 ıııı . uiłł . 7 ıı .

borđ hn̄tes . ıııı . car̄ 7 dim 7 xıı . ac̄s p̄ti .

Ṡ In Normantun . In Cauorde . In Willebi . In Stantun
      . ı . bŏ 7 dim̄.   tcia pars . ı . bŏ   . ıı . bŏ 7 dim᷎   ıı . bŏ

7 ıııı . pars uni bou ad glđ . Tra . ıı . car̄ . Soc᷎ᴀ in Cliftune᷎

Ibi . ıııı . focħ . 7 ı . uiłł 7 ı . borđ . hn̄tes . ııı . car̄ . Ibi Wiłłs
                            In Stantun.
in dñio ħ . ı . car̄ . 7 ıı . ac̄s p̄ti .

Ṡ In Cotingeftoche . ı . bou træ ad glđ . Ibi . ı . focħ ħ . ı . car̄ .

7 ıı . ac̄s p̄ti . Tra . ı . bou . In Alboltune . vı . bou . ad glđ .

Ṡ In Bafingfelt . v . bou træ . 7 ııı . part . ı . bou ad glđ . Tra . ı . car̄ .

Ibi . ıı . focħ 7 ıı . borđ hn̄t . ı . car̄ . 7 v . ac̄s p̄ti .

Ṡ In Gameleftune . vı . bou træ ad glđ . Tra . ı . car̄ . Ibi . ıı .

focħ hn̄t . ı . car̄ . 7 vıı . ac̄s p̄ti .

ᛗ In *REDEFORD* . ħħ Aluric . ııı . car̄ tre ad glđ . Tra . ııı . car̄ .

Ibi Wiłłs in dñio ħ . ıı . car̄ . 7 xı . uiłł 7 ıııı . borđ hn̄tes
                                                    or
                                      ⌜ ıııı . car̄ .

5 M. In CLIFTON Countess Gytha had 2½ c. of land taxable.
Land for 5 ploughs. William has 2 ploughs in lordship and
4 Freemen, 19 villagers and 8 smallholders who have 9 ploughs.
A priest and a church; 1 mill, 12d; meadow, 12 acres.
Value before 1066 £16; now £9.

6 *There also, Ulfkell had and has 1 b. of land taxable and
1 villager with 2 oxen. Meadow, 1 acre.*

7 In BARTON (-in-Fabis) 2 b. and the third part of 1 b. taxable.
Land for 1 plough.
3 Freemen have 2 ploughs.
Meadow, 3 acres.

8 S. In WILFORD, jurisdiction. 3 c. of land taxable. Land for 6 ploughs.
23 Freemen have 7 ploughs.
A priest; meadow, 18 acres; half a fishery.

9 S. In (West) BRIDGFORD, jurisdiction. 12 b. of land taxable.
Land for 3 ploughs. William has ½ plough in lordship and
3 Freemen, 4 villagers and 2 smallholders who have 4½ ploughs.
Meadow, 12 acres.

0 S. In NORMANTON (-on-the-Wolds) 1½ b. In KEYWORTH the third part
of 1 b. In WILLOUGHBY 2½ b. In STANTON 2 b. and the fourth
part of 1 b. taxable. Land for 2 ploughs. Jurisdiction in Clifton.
4 Freemen, 1 villager and 1 smallholder who have 3 ploughs.
William has in lordship 1 plough, in Stanton.
Meadow, 2 acres.

1 S. In COSTOCK 1 b. of land taxable.
1 Freeman has 1 plough.
Meadow, 2 acres. Land for 1 ox.

2 In ADBOLTON 6 b. taxable.

3 S. In BASSINGFIELD 5 b. of land and 3 parts of 1 b. taxable.
Land for 1 plough.
2 Freemen and 2 smallholders have 1 plough.
Meadow, 5 acres.

4 S. In GAMSTON 6 b. of land taxable. Land for 1 plough.
2 Freemen have 1 plough.
Meadow, 7 acres.

[BROXTOW Wapentake]

5 M. In RADFORD Aelfric had 3 c. of land taxable.
Land for 3 ploughs. William has in lordship 2 ploughs and
11 villagers and 4 smallholders who have 4 ploughs.

Ibi . iiii . molini . iii . lib̃ . 7 xxx ac̃ p̃ti . 7 iii . ac̃ filuæ min.

7 dimid piſcar̃ . T.R.E . 7 m̃ ual . iiii . lib̃.

.iiii. De ead̃ tra tenet Vlnod . i . bõ in Tainlande.

ⰁⰊ In *STAPLEFORD* hb Vl̃ſi 7 Stapleuin 7 Goduin.

7 Gladuin . ii . car̃ træ 7 vi . bou ad gld̃ . Tra iii . car.

Ibi Wil̃ts Rob̃t tenet de eo. ht̃ in dñio . iii . car̃ . 7 vi . uil̃t 7 ii . ſeruos.

Ibi p̃br 7 æccla . 7 lviii . ac̃ p̃ti . T.R.E . ual lx . ſol . m̃ . xl

ⰁⰊ In *MORTVNE* . hb Boui . i . car̃ tre 7 dim ad gld̃ . Tra

xii . bou . Ibi Wil̃ts ht̃ . i . car̃ 7 dim̃ . 7 v . ſoch de . iii.

bou huj tre . 7 xii . uil̃t 7 i . bord hñtes . ix . car̃ 7 dim.

T.R.E . 7 m̃ ual . xx . ſol.

ⰁⰊ In *NEVBOLD* . hb Morcar . xii . bou træ ad gl Tra . ii.

car̃ . Ibi Wil̃ts in dñio ht̃ . i . car̃ 7 dim̃ . 7 ix . uil̃t hñtes

.iii . car̃ . 7 xl . ac̃s p̃ti . T.R.E . 7 m̃ ual . lx . ſol.

Ƨ In Lentune . ii . car̃ tre ad gld . Soca in Neubold . Tra

.iii. ii . car̃ . Ibi . iiii . ſoch 7 iiii . bord hñt . ii . car̃ 7 i . moliñ.

ⰁⰊ In *LIDEBI* . tres fr̃s habuer̃ . i . car̃ tre 7 dim ad gld̃.

Tra . ii . car̃ . Ibi Wil̃ts ht̃ . iii . car̃ . 7 xii . uil̃t 7 ii . bord

hñtes . v . car̃ . Ibi p̃br . 7 i . moliñ x . ſolid . Silua paſt

i . lev l̃g . 7 i . lev lat . T.R.E . ual xxvi . ſol 7 viii . den.

m̃ . xl . ſol.

In Papleuuic . v . bou træ adjacen̄ huic Manerio.

ⰁⰊ In *BASEFORD* hb Aluuin . x . bou træ ad gld̃ . Tra

xii . bou . Ibi Safrid hõ Wil̃ti ht̃ . i . car̃ . 7 ii . uil̃t

7 . v . bord . 7 i . ſoch hñtes . ii . car̃ 7 dim . Ibi p̃br 7 i . ac̃

p̃ti . 7 i . ac̃ filuæ . T.R.E . 7 m̃ ual . xx . ſol.

ⰁⰊ ~~IBIDE hb Eſcul i bou træ ad gld̃ . m̃ eſt in cuſtodia Wil̃i.~~

ⰁⰊ In *LENTVNE* . hb Vnlof . iiii . bou træ ad gld̃ . Tra

dim car̃ . Modo in cuſtodia Wil̃i . Ibi iſd Vlnod

ht̃ . i . car̃ . 7 i . uil̃t 7 i . bord hñtes . i . car̃ . 7 i . moliñ

4 mills, £3, meadow, 30 acres; underwood, 3 acres;   287 c
    half a fishery.
    Value before 1066 and now £4.
    Wulfnoth holds 1 b. of this land in thane-land.

16 ⁴/M. In STAPLEFORD Young Wulfsi, Staplewin, Godwin and Gladwin
had 2 c. of land and 6 b. taxable. Land for 3 ploughs.
William has in lordship, and Robert holds from him, 3
ploughs and
    6 villagers with 6 ploughs; 2 slaves.
    A priest and a church; meadow, 58 acres.
Value before 1066, 60s; now 40[s].

17 M. In MORTON Bovi had 1½ c. of land taxable. Land for 12 oxen.
William has 1½ ploughs and
    5 Freemen with 3 b. of this land and 12 villagers and
        1 smallholder who have 9½ ploughs.
Value before 1066 and now 20s.

18 M. In NEWBOUND Morcar has 12 b. of land taxable. Land for 2 ploughs.
William has in lordship 1½ ploughs and
    9 villagers who have 3 ploughs.
    Meadow, 40 acres.
Value before 1066 and now 60s.

19 S. In LENTON 2 c. of land taxable. Jurisdiction in Newbound.
Land for 2 ploughs.
    4 Freemen and 4 smallholders have 2 ploughs.
    1 mill.

20 ³/M. In LINBY three brothers had 1½ c. of land taxable.
Land for 2 ploughs. William has 3 ploughs and
    12 villagers and 2 smallholders who have 5 ploughs.
    A priest; 1 mill, 10s; woodland pasture 1 league long
        and 1 league wide.
Value before 1066, 26s 8d; now 40s.

21 In PAPPLEWICK 5 b. of land are attached to this manor.

22 M. In BASFORD Alwin had 10 b. of land taxable. Land for 12 oxen.
Saxfrid, William's man, has 1 plough and
    2 villagers, 5 smallholders and 1 Freeman who have 2½ ploughs.
    A priest; meadow, 1 acre; woodland, 1 acre.
Value before 1066 and now 20s.

23 M. *There also Aswulf had 1 b. of land taxable; it is now
in William's charge.*

24 M. In LENTON Wulfnoth had 4 b. of land taxable. Land for ½ plough.
Now in William's charge. Wulfnoth has 1 plough and
    1 villager and 1 smallholder who have 1 plough.

x . ſolid .7. x . ac̃ p̃ti .7 x acs ſiluæ mĩn . T.R.E. uat

x . ſot . m̃ xv.

℥ In *TOVETVNE* h̃b Aldene . iii . car̃ tre ad gld̃.

Tra . iii . car̃ 7 dim̃ . Ibi Warner hõ Witti h̃t . iii.

car̃ .7 iiii . ſoch de . iii . bou huj træ .7 xvi . uitt 7 iii.

bord . hñtes . vi . car̃ . Ibi dim̃ æcta 7 p̃br .7 ii . moliñ

viii . ſolid .7 c . ac̃ p̃ti .7 paruũ ſalictũ . T.R.E.7 m̃

uat . lx . ſot.

S In Chideuuelle . v̈ . bou træ ad gld̃ . Sóca huj ℧.

℥ In *STRALEIA* . h̃b Godric . vi . boũ tre ad gld̃ . Tra . vi.

bob . Ibi Góduin de Witto . h̃t . i . car̃ .7 iii . uitt .7 ii . bord.

hñtes . ii . car̃ . T.R.E.7 m̃ vat . x . ſot.

℥ IBIDĒ h̃b Brun . iii . bou træ ad gld̃ . Ambroſius m̃ de

Witto tenet . T.R.E. uat . iii . ſot . m̃ . xii . denar̃.

287 d

℥ In *GRISELEIA* h̃b Vlſÿ . iiii . bou træ ad gld̃.

Tra . i . car̃ . Ibi Witts h̃t . i . car̃ .7 v . uitt 7 ii . bord.

hñtes . iii . car̃ . Ibi p̃br 7 æccta . Silua paſt . ix . q̃ʒ lḡ.

7 . vi . q̃ʒ lat̃ . T.R.E. uat . xvi . ſot . m̃ . x . ſot.

℥ IBIDĒ h̃b Vlſi . iiii . bou træ ad gld̃ . Tra . i . car̃.

Waſta . ē . Ailric tenet de Witto

℥ In *BRVNESLEIA* h̃b Brun . iiii . bou tre ad gld̃ . Tra

dim car̃ . Ibi Ailric ſub Witto h̃t . i . car̃ .7 i . uitt

hñtes . i . car̃ .7 ii . acs p̃ti . Silua paſt . vi . q̃ʒ lḡ .7 iii.

q̃ʒ 7 dim lat̃ . T.R.E. uat . vi . ſot 7 viii . den . m̃ . iiii . ſot.

℥ In *ESTEWIC* h̃b Vlfchetel . iiii . boũ træ ad gld̃ . Tra

Waſta . ē . Witts cuſtodit . Silua paſt . iii . q̃ʒ lḡ .7 iii . lat̃.

T.R.E. uat . v . ſot.

℥ In *NEVTORP* . h̃b Grinchel . v̈ . bou træ ad gld . Tra dim

.iii.car̃ . Waſta . ē . T.R.E. uat . v . ſot . m̃ . ii . ſot.

℥ In *BESTVNE* . h̃br Ælfag Aluuine 7 Vlchel . iii.

car̃ træ ad gld̃ . Tra . iiii . car̃ . Ibi Witts in dñio h̃t

287 c, d

1 mill, 10s; meadow, 10 acres; underwood, 10 acres.
Value before 1066, 10s; now 15[s].

25 M. In TOTON Haldane had 3 c. of land taxable. Land for 3½ ploughs.
Warner, William's man, has 3 ploughs and
 4 Freemen with 3 b. of this land and 16 villagers
 and 3 smallholders who have 6 ploughs.
 Half a church and a priest; 2 mills, 8s; meadow, 100
 acres; a small willow bed.
Value before 1066 and now 60s.

 Jurisdiction of this manor.

26 S. In CHILWELL 8 b. of land taxable.

27 M. In STRELLEY Godric had 6 b. of land taxable. Land for 6 oxen.
Godwin the priest has 1 plough from William and
 3 villagers and 2 smallholders who have 2 ploughs.
Value before 1066 and now 10s.

28 M. There also Brown had 3 b. of land taxable. Now Ambrose
holds from William.
Value before 1066, 3s; now 12d.

29 M. In GREASLEY Wulfsi had 4 b. of land taxable.   287 d
Land for 1 plough. William has 1 plough and
 5 villagers and 2 smallholders who have 3 ploughs.
 A priest and a church; woodland pasture 9 furlongs
  long and 6 furlongs wide.
Value before 1066, 16s; now 10s.

30 M. There also Wulfsi had 4 b. of land taxable. Land for 1 plough.
Waste. Alric holds from William.

31 M. In BRINSLEY Brown had 4 b. of land taxable.
Land for ½ plough. Alric has 1 plough under William and
 1 villager who has 1 plough.
 Meadow, 2 acres; woodland pasture 6 furlongs and
  3½ furlongs wide.
Value before 1066, 6s 8d; now 4s.

32 M. In EASTWOOD Ulfketel had 4 b. of land taxable. Land
[for...ploughs]. Waste. William has charge.
 Woodland pasture 3 furlongs long and 3 wide.
Value before 1066, 5s.

33 M. In NEWTHORPE Grimkell had 7 b. of land taxable.
Land for ½ plough. Waste.
Value before 1066, 5s; now 2s.

34 3/M In BEESTON Alfheah, Alwin and Ulfkell had 3 c. of land
taxable. Land for 4 ploughs. William has in lordship 2
ploughs and

II . car̄ . 7 XVII . uilł 7 I . focħ hn̄tes VIIII . car̄ . Ibi   xx^{ti}

7 IIII . ac̄ p̄ti . T.R.E . 7 m̄ uał . xxx . fol.

꭪ In OLAVESTONE . ħb Vlfi^{cilt} . I . car̄ 7 dim ad glđ.

Tra . XII . bou . Ibi Warner̄ ho⁹ Witłi ħt . I . car̄ . 7 VII.

focħ 7 IIII . uilł hn̄tes . IIII . car̄ . Silua min̄ . I . lev lḡ.

7 I . q̊₂ lat̄ . T.R.E . uał . c . fol . m̄ . LX . fol.

꭪ In COTESHALE BEREUU . VI . bou træ ad glđ . Tra . VI.

bob . Ibi in dn̄io . I . car̄ . 7 II . uilł . 7 I . ac̄ p̄ti . Siluæ paſt

IIII . q̊₂ lḡ . 7 II . lat̄.

꭪ In Brunecote SOCA . VI . bou træ ad glđ . Waſta . e̅.

꭪ In Sudtune SOCA . XII . bou træ ad glđ . Tra . III . car̄ . Waſta . e̅.

꭪ In BILEBVRG . ħbr Æilric 7 Vlfi . Suen . VII . bou træ

ad glđ . Tra totid bob . Ibi Ambrofius^{ho Witłi} ħt . I . car̄ . 7 II . focħ

7 III . uilł 7 IIII . feru cū . I . car̄ . Ibi . VIII . ac̄ p̄ti . 7 filua

minuta . T.R.E . uał . xxx . fol . m̄ xx . fol.

꭪ In NVTEHALE . ħb Aldene . IIII . bo^{tre} 7 dim ad glđ . Tra

totid bob . Ibi Witłs ħt . I . car̄ 7 dim . 7 III . uilł 7 II^{II} . bord.

hn̄tes . I . car̄ . Silua min̄ . v . q̊₂ lḡ . 7 I . lat̄ . T.R.E . 7 m̄ uał . x . fol.

In Brocheleſtou adjacent . v . acræ.

꭪ In Watenot SOCA . II . bou træ ad glđ.

꭪ In WATENOT . ħb Grinchel . I . car tre ad glđ . Tra . I . car̄.

Ibi Witłs ħt . III . car̄ jn dn̄io . Silua paſt . v . q̊₂ lḡ . 7 II . lat̄.

꭪ In WATENOT . ħb Siuuart . II . bou tre ad glđ.

꭪ Ibid Grim . II . bou tre ad glđ . SOCA in Watenot

꭪ Ibid Ælmær . II . bou træ ad glđ . SOCA in Buleuuelle.

Tra . I . car̄ . Ibi in dn̄io . I . car̄ . 7 I . focħ 7 II . uilł 7 II . bord.

hn̄t . II . car̄ . Silua paſt . v . q̊₂ lḡ . 7 III . q̊₂ lat̄ . T.R.E.

288 a

uał . xL . fol . m̄ fimilit̄ . Gozelin⁹ 7 Grichel teneɴ.

꭪ In CHINEMARELIE . ħb Azor . IIII . bou træ ad glđ.

7 Grichitel . IIII . bo̅ tre ad glđ . Tra . I . car̄ . Ibi . II . focħ . 7 I.

17 villagers and 1 Freeman who have 9 ploughs.
Meadow, 24 acres.
Value before 1066 and now 30s.

5 M. In WOLLATON Young Wulfsi had 1½ ploughs taxable.
Land for 12 oxen. Warner, William's man, has 1 plough and
7 Freemen and 4 villagers who have 4 ploughs.
Underwood 1 league long and 1 furlong wide.
Value before 1066, 100s; now 60s.

6 B. In COSSALL , an outlier, 6 b. of land taxable. Land for 6 oxen.
In lordship 1 plough;
2 villagers.
Meadow, 1 acre; woodland pasture 4 furlongs long and 2 wide.

7 S. In BRAMCOTE, jurisdiction. 6 b. of land taxable. Waste.

8 S. In SUTTON (Passeys), jurisdiction. 12 b. of land taxable.
Land for 3 ploughs. Waste.

9 2 M. In BILBOROUGH Alric and Wulfsi [son of?] Swein had 7 b. of
land taxable. Land for as many oxen. Ambrose, William's man,
has 1 plough and
2 Freemen, 3 villagers and 4 slaves with 1 plough.
Meadow, 8 acres; underwood.
Value before 1066, 30s; now 20s.

0 M. In NUTHALL Haldane had 4½ b. of land taxable. Land for as
many oxen. William has 1½ ploughs and
3 villagers and 4 smallholders who have 1 plough.
Underwood 5 furlongs long and 1 wide.
Value before 1066 and now 10s.

1 In BROXTOW 5 acres are attached.

2 S. In WATNALL, jurisdiction. 2 b. of land taxable.

3 M. In WATNALL Grimkell had 1 c. of land taxable.
Land for 1 plough. William has 3 ploughs in lordship.
Woodland pasture 5 furlongs long and 2 wide.

4 M. In WATNALL Siward had 2 b. of land taxable.

5 S. There also Grim, 2 b. of land taxable. Jurisdiction in Watnall.

6 S. There also Aelmer, 2 b. of land taxable. Jurisdiction in
Bulwell. Land for 1 plough. In lordship 1 plough.
1 Freeman, 2 villagers and 2 smallholders have 2 ploughs.
Woodland pasture 5 furlongs long and 3 furlongs wide.
Value before 1066, 40s; now the same.   288 a
Jocelyn and Grimkell hold it.

7 M. In KIMBERLEY Azor had 4 b. of land taxable and Grimketel 4 b.
of land taxable. Land for 1 plough.

uilł.7 v.borđ hñt.iii.car 7 dim.Silua min.iiii.q̴ łg

7 ii.lat.T.R.E.7 m̄ uał.x.soł.   ſcuſtodit.

ᛒ In *ELDEVRDE*
BIDĒ h̄b Aluuin.iiii.bou tre ad głđ.Waſta.ē Wiłłs

ᛒ In *HOCHENALE* duo frs h̄br iiii.bou træ ad głđ.Tra

dim car.Ibi.iii.uiłł hñt.i.car.T.R.E.uał.viii.soł.m̄.ii.

Ŝ In hameſſel.vi.bou tre 7 dim ad głđ.Tra.i.car.

Ibi.ii.ſocħ 7 ii.uiłł 7 ii.borđ.hñt.ii.car.7 iiii.ac̃s

ii.ſiluæ min.H̄ Soca jacet in Buleuuelle 7 Watenot

ᛒ In *BASEFORD* h̄br Alfag 7 Algod.ii.car træ 7 iii.bou

ad głđ.Tra totid car 7 bob.Ibi Pagen hōes Wiłłi hñt

i.car.7 ii.uiłł 7 v.borđ hñtes.ii.car.7 iii.moliñ xxv.

ſolid.7 iiii.den.7 vi.ac̃s p̃ti.7 ſilua minuta.T.R.E.

uał.xl.ſoł.m̄ ſimilit.Ibid.i.bou ad gld.Eſcul tenuit.

ᛒ In *CORTINGESTOCHES*.h̄b Fredghis.ii.bou træ ad głđ

Tra.ii.bou.Ibi Goduin ſub Wiłło h̄.i.car.7 ii.uiłłi

.i.car.7 iii.ac̃s p̃ti.T.R.E.uał.x.ſoł.m̄.v.ſoł 7 iiii.den.

ᛒ In *RAMPESTVNE*.h̄b Fredgis vi.bou tre ad gld.Tra

vi.bou.Ibi.v.uiłłi hñt.i.car.7 xv.ac̃s p̃ti.T.R.E.uał

ii.x.ſoł.m̄.v.ſoł 7 iiii.den.

ᛒ In *RADECLIVE* h̄b Fredgis.i.car træ 7 dim ad głđ.

Tra.iii.car.Modo Fredgis 7 Vluiet ſub Wiłło hñt ibi

ii.car.7 xv.uiłł 7 vi.borđ hñtes.iiii.car.7 xviii.ac̃s

p̃ti.7 ſeđ piſcar dimidiæ.7 tciā part uni piſcar.T.R.E.

uał.lx.ſoł.m̄ xxx.ii.ſolid.

ᛒ In *ALBOLTVNE*.h̄b Goduin.vi.bou træ ad głđ.Tra

.i.car.Ibi Wiłłs in dñio h̄.i.car.7 vi.uiłł 7 i.borđ.hñtes

ii.car.Ibi æccła.7 vii.ac̃s p̃ti.T.R.E.uał.x.ſoł.m̄.xx.

ᛒ In *TIEDEBI*.h̄b Vluric.iiii.bou træ 7 tres partes uni

bou ad głđ.Tra.i.car.Nc̃ Fredgis ſub Wiłło tenet.Ibi

.i.ſocħ 7 v.uiłł 7 iiii.borđ hñt.ii.car 7 dim.7 xx.ac̃s

2 Freemen, 1 villager and 5 smallholders have 3½ ploughs.
Underwood 4 furlongs long and 2 wide.
Value before 1066 and now 10s.

8 M. There also, in AWSWORTH, Alwin, 4 b. of land taxable.
Waste. William has charge.

9 M. In HUCKNALL (Torkard) two brothers had 4 b. of land taxable.
Land for ½ plough.
   3 villagers have 1 plough.
Value before 1066, 8s; now 4[s].

0 M. In HEMPSHILL 6½ b. of land taxable. Land for 1 plough.
   2 Freemen, 2 villagers and 2 smallholders have 2 ploughs.
   Underwood, 4 acres.
The jurisdiction lies in Bulwell and Watnall.

1 $\frac{2}{M.}$ In BASFORD Alfheah and Algot had 2 c. of land and 3 b. taxable.
Land for as many ploughs and oxen. Payne and Saxfrid,
William's men, have 1 plough and
   2 villagers and 5 smallholders who have 2 ploughs.
   3 mills, 25s 4d; meadow, 6 acres; underwood.
Value before 1066, 40s; now the same.

2 There also 1 b. taxable. Aswulf held it.

3 M. In COSTOCK Fredegis had 2 b. of land taxable. Land for 2 oxen.
Godwin has 1 plough under William and
   2 villagers [who have] 1 plough.
   Meadow, 3 acres.
Value before 1066, 10s; now 5s 4d.

4 M. In REMPSTONE Fredegis had 6 b. of land taxable. Land for 6 oxen.
   5 villagers have 1 plough.
   Meadow, 15 acres.
Value before 1066, 10s; now 5s 4d.

[BINGHAM Wapentake]

5 $\frac{2}{M.}$ In RADCLIFFE (-on-Trent) Fredegis had 1½ c. of land taxable.
Land for 3 ploughs. Now Fredegis and Wulfgeat have 2 ploughs
under William and
   15 villagers and 6 smallholders who have 4 ploughs.
   Meadow, 18 acres; the site of half a fishery and the third
      part of 1 fishery.
Value before 1066, 60s; now 32s.

6 M. In ADBOLTON Godwin the priest had 6 b. of land taxable.
Land for 1 plough. William has in lordship 1 plough and
   6 villagers and 1 smallholder who have 2 ploughs.
   A church; meadow, 7 acres.
Value before 1066, 10s; now 20[s].

7 M. In TITHBY Wulfric had 4 b. of land and 3 parts of 1 b. taxable.
Land for 1 plough. Now Fredegis holds it under William.
   1 Freeman, 5 villagers and 4 smallholders have 2½ ploughs.

p̃ti . T.R.E . ual . xx . ſol . m̃ x . ſol.

ꟽ In *WIVRETVN* . h̄b Vluric . 1 . boū tɾæ 7 111 . partes
uni⁹ bou ad glđ . Tra dim caɾ . Ibi . 111 . uiłł 7 1 . borđ
h̄nt . 1 . caɾ . 7 vi . ac̃s p̃ti . T.R.E . 7 m̃ ual . x . ſol.

ꟽ In *LANGARE* . h̄b Godric . 11 . caɾ tɾæ 7 1111 . boū 7 dim
ad glđ . Tra . vi . caɾ . Ibi Wiłłs in dño h̃ . 111 . caɾ . 7 xv.
ſocħ de . vi . bou huj⁹ tɾæ . 7 xix . uiłł 7 vi . borđ h̄ntes
xi . caɾ . 7 11 . molin . v . ſolid . 7 L . ac̃s p̃ti . Ibi . 1 . franc⁹
h̃ō h̃ . 1 . caɾ . T.R.E . ual . c . ſol . m̃ x . liɓ.

Š In Wiuretune SocA . 111 . bou tɾæ 7 dim ad glđ . Tra
1 . caɾ . Ibi . vii . ſocħ 7 1 . borđ . h̄nt . 111 . caɾ . 7 11 . boū . 7 viii.

ſ ac̃s p̃ti.

ꟽ In *BERNESTVNE* . h̄b Godric 7 Azor q̃ſq̃ aulā.
7 unq̃ſq̃ . 1111 . bou tɾæ 7 vii⁏ . partes . 1 . bou ad glđ . Tra
1111 . caɾ . Ibi Wiłłs in dño h̃ . 111 . caɾ . 7 vii . ſocħ
de . 1111 . bou huj⁹ tre . 7 vii . uiłł 7 vi . borđ h̄ntes . 1111.
caɾ 7 dim . Ibi . xxx . vi . ac̃ p̃ti . T.R.E . ual x . ſol . m̃ . ii . liɓ.

ꟽ In *NEVTORP* . h̄b Grinchel . v . bou tɾæ ad glđ . Tra dim caɾ.
B Ibidē . 11 . bou tre ad glđ . Tra . 11 . boū . BEREẆ in Chine
mareleie . Waſta utraq̃.

★ In *MENNETVNE* Eluuin 7 Vluiet . 1 . caɾ ad glđ ᵽ . 11 . ꟽ.
Tra . 11 . caɾ . Ibi ſt̃ . 111 . ſocħi . cū . 111 . caɾ . Valuit 7 ual . x . ſol.

In *SALESTVNE* . habueɾ Vlmer Gladuin 7 Vluric . 111.
bou tɾæ ᵽ . 111 . ꟽ . Tra . ē . 1 . caɾ . Ibi . 1111 . uiłłi 7 11 . borđ
h̄nt . 11 . caɾ . Ibi æccła 7 111 . ac̃ p̃ti . Ołi . viii . ſol . M ual . x . ſol.

In *BVLVVELLE* . habuit Godric . 11 . caɾ tɾæ ᵽ . ꟽ . Tra
11 . caɾ . Ibi . ē . 1 . caɾ 7 1 . uiłłs 7 1 . borđ . 7 11 . ac̃ p̃ti.
Ołi . xii . ſol . Modo ual . v . ſolid.

10

Meadow, 20 acres.
Value before 1066, 20s; now 10s.

M. In WIVERTON Wulfric had 1 b. of land and 3 parts of 1 b.
taxable. Land for ½ plough.
3 villagers and 1 smallholder have 1 plough.
Meadow, 6 acres.
Value before 1066 and now 10s.

M. In LANGAR Godric had 2 c. of land and 4½ b. taxable.
Land for 6 ploughs. William has in lordship 3 ploughs and
15 Freemen with 6 b. of this land and 19 villagers
and 6 smallholders who have 11 ploughs.
2 mills, 5s; meadow, 50 acres.
1 freeman has 1 plough.
Value before 1066, 100s; now £10.

S. In WIVERTON, jurisdiction. 3½ b. of land taxable.
Land for 1 plough.
7 Freemen and 1 smallholder have 3 ploughs and 2 oxen.
Meadow, 8 acres.

M. In BARNSTONE Godric and Azor each had a hall and each   288 b
had 4 b. of land and 7 parts of 1 b. taxable.
Land for 4 ploughs. William has in lordship 3 ploughs and
7 Freemen with 4 b. of this land and 7 villagers and
6 smallholders who have 4½ ploughs.
Meadow, 36 acres.
Value before 1066, 10s; now £4.

[BROXTOW Wapentake]

M. In NEWTHORPE Grimkell had 5 b. of land taxable.
Land for ½ plough.

B. There also 2 b. of land taxable. Land for 2 oxen.
An outlier in Kimberley. Both waste.

[BASSETLAW Wapentake]

In MANTON Alwin and Wulfgeat [had] 1 c. taxable as 2 manors.
Land for 2 ploughs.
3 Freemen with 3 ploughs.
The value was and is 10s.

[BROXTOW Wapentake]

In SELSTON Wulfmer, Gladwin and Wulfric had 3 b. of land
as 3 manors. Land for 1 plough.
4 villagers and 2 smallholders have 2 ploughs.
A church; meadow, 3 acres.
Formerly 8s; value now 10s.

In BULWELL Godric had 2 c. of land as a manor.
Land for 2 ploughs. 1 plough there.
1 villager and 1 smallholder.
Meadow, 2 acres.
Formerly 12s; value now 5s.

.X. TERRA WALTERIJ DE AINCVRT.

In *FLODBERGA* hb Vluric . II . bou træ ad glđ .
Tra . I . car . Ibi Walter de Aincurt ht . I . car .
7 IIII . uilt cū . I . car . T.R.E. 7 m̄ uat . xx . fot .

In *STANTVNE* . hb Tori x . bou tre ad glđ . Tra
III . car . Ibi m̄ . III . car in dnĩo . 7 IIII . focħ de . I . bou
7 dim̄ huj træ . 7 xI . uilt 7 II . bord . hn̄tes . II . car . Ibi
pbr 7 æccl̃a . 7 I . molin̄ . v . folid 7 IIII . den . 7 q̄t xx . ac̄s
p̄ti . T.R.E. uat . IIII . liħ . m̄ . c . fot .   SOCA H⁹MAN .

In Aluretun 7 Flodberge 7 Dallintune . vI . bou træ ad
glđ . Tra . II . car . Ibi . xII . focħ hn̄t . III . car . 7 c . ac̄s
.II. p̄ti . Malger tenet .

In *COTES* hbr Suen 7 Tori . Ix . bou træ ad glđ . Tra
vI . car . Ibi Walt in dnĩo ht . I . car . 7 x . uilt 7 vIII .
bord hn̄tes . III . car . Ibi pbr 7 æccl̃a . 7 Lx . ac̄ p̄ti .
T.R.E. uat . c . fot . m̄ . vI . liħ .   SOCA

In Flodberge . I . bou tre 7 dim̄ ad glđ . Tra . I . car . Ibi
xx.IIII . ac̄ p̄ti . Ibi . v . focħ hn̄t . I . car 7 dim̄ . 7 xx.II . ac̄s p̄ti .

In *STOCHES* . hb Tori . vI . bou tre ad glđ . Tra . II . car .
Ibi in dnĩo . I . car . 7 III . uilt 7 v . bord hn̄tes dim̄ car .
7 Lx . ac̄s p̄ti . T.R.E. uat . Lx . fot . m̄ xL .   Osbt tenet .

In Houtune . II . bou tre ad glđ . Tra . I . car . Ibi . vI . focħ
hn̄t . II . car . 7 xx . ac̄s p̄ti .

In *HOCRETVNE* hb Tori . III . bou tre ad glđ . Tra . I . car .
Ibi Walter ht . I . car . 7 v . uilt 7 v . bord hn̄tes dim̄
car . 7 xvI . ac̄s p̄ti . Silua paʃt . I . lev lḡ . 7 I . q̄z
7 dim̄ lat . T.R.E. uat xx . fot . m̄ xv .

]

M. In FLAWBOROUGH Wulfric had 2 b. of land taxable.
Land for 1 plough. Walter of Aincourt has 1 plough and
4 villagers with 1 plough.
Value before 1066 and now 20s.

M. In STAUNTON Thori had 10 b. of land taxable. Land for 3 ploughs.
Now 3 ploughs in lordship;
4 Freemen with 1½ b. of this land and 11 villagers
and 2 smallholders who have 2 ploughs.
A priest and a church; 1 mill, 5s 4d; meadow, 80 acres.
Value before 1066 £4; now 100s.
Jurisdiction of this manor.

S. In ALVERTON, FLAWBOROUGH and 'DALLINGTON' 6 b. of land taxable.
Land for 2 ploughs.
12 Freemen have 3 ploughs.
Meadow, 100 acres.
Mauger holds it.

2
M. In COTHAM Swein and Thori had 9 b. of land taxable.
Land for 6 ploughs. Walter has in lordship 1 plough and
10 villagers and 8 smallholders who have 3 ploughs.
A priest and a church; meadow, 60 acres.
Value before 1066, 100s; now £6.
Jurisdiction.

S. In FLAWBOROUGH 1½ b. of land taxable. Land for 1 plough.
Meadow, 24 acres.
5 Freemen have 1½ ploughs and 24 acres of meadow.

M. In (East) STOKE Thori had 6 b. of land taxable.
Land for 2 ploughs. In lordship 1 plough;
3 villagers and 5 smallholders who have ½ plough.
Meadow, 60 acres.
Value before 1066, 60s; now 40[s].
Osbert holds it.

S. In HAWTON 2 b. of land taxable. Land for 1 plough.
6 Freemen have 2 ploughs.
Meadow, 20 acres.

[LYTHE Wapentake]

M. In HOCKERTON Thori had 3 b. of land taxable. Land
for 1 plough. Walter has 1 plough and
5 villagers and 5 smallholders who have ½ plough.
Meadow, 16 acres; woodland pasture 1 league long
and 1½ furlongs wide.
Value before 1066, 20s. now 15[s].

ᴍ In *CHENAPETORP*. ħɓ Tori . IIII . boū tre 7 dimiđ
ad glđ . Tra . I . caɍ . Ibi in dn̄io . I . caɍ . 7 v . uiłł 7 III . borđ
hn̄tes . I . caɍ 7 dim̄ . 7 II . aȼ p̄ti . Silua paſt . VIII . q̄ʒ
lḡ . 7 II . laɍ . T.R.E . 7 m̄ . xx . ſoł.

ᴍ In *BVLECOTE*. ħɓ Suen . II . caɍ tre 7 II . boū ad glđ .
7 Ibidē xv . boū tre 7 dim̄ ad glđ . Soca ejđ man .
Tra . v . caɍ 7 dim̄ . Ibi in dn̄io . I . caɍ . 7 VIII . ſocħ .
7 XI . uiłł 7 XII . borđ . 7 II . ſerū cū̄ . III . caɍ . Ibi LXX
VI . aȼ p̄ti . Silua paſtił p loca . I . lev lḡ . 7 VIII . q̄ʒ
laɍ . T.R.E . 7 m̄ uał . IIII . liɓ .

ᴍ In *OXETVNE*. ħɓ Tori . IIII . boū træ ad glđ . Tra XII . boɓ .
Ibi . I . ſocħ de . III . parte . I . boū huj træ cū̄ . I . borđ
hn̄s đ . caɍ . 7 IIII . aȼs p̄ti . T.R.E . uał . xvi . ſoł . m̄ . v . ſoł

ᴍ In *TVRGARSTVNE* 7 in Horſpol . ħɓ Suain ⦊ 7 II . den .
III . caɍ træ 7 III . boū ad glđ . Tra . vi . caɍ . Ibi ħɍ
Walter in dn̄io . II . caɍ . 7 x . ſocħ de . IX . boū huj træ .
In Tiedeɓi . II . boū ad glđ .

288 d

7 XII . uiłł 7 II . borđ . hn̄tes . VI . caɍ . Ibi pɓr 7 æccła .
· 7 XL . aȼ p̄ti . Silua paſt . I . lev lḡ . 7 dim̄ lat .
. T.R.E . uał . III . liɓ . m̄ . IIII . liɓ .

ᴍ In *HORINGEHA*. ħɓ Suain . II . caɍ tre 7 II . boū
ad glđ . Tra . IIII . caɍ . Ibi Walt ħɍ in dn̄io . II . caɍ .
7 VI . ſocħ de . III . boū 7 tcia parte . I . boū huj træ .
7 IX . uiłł 7 III . borđ hn̄tes . IIII . caɍ . Ibi pɓr 7 æccła
7 II . molin̄ . XL . ſolid . 7 II . piſcaɍ . VIII . ſoł . 7 XL . aȼ
p̄ti . T.R.E . uał . IIII . liɓ . m̄ ſimił 7 x . ſoł plus .

Ꞩ In Fiſcartune ħɍ Walt dim̄ caɍ træ ad glđ . Vnde
Soca p̄tin̄ ad Sudwelle . Ibi ħɍ ipſe . I . caɍ . 7 III . uiłł cū̄ . I . caɍ .

Ꞩ In Mortune ħɍ Walt dim̄ caɍ træ ad glđ . De qua Soca
p̄tin̄ ad Sudwelle . Ibi ipſe . I . caɍ . 7 III . uiłł hn̄t . I . caɍ .

288 c, d

9   M.   In KNAPTHORPE Thori had 4½ b. of land taxable.
        Land for 1 plough. In lordship 1 plough;
           5 villagers and 3 smallholders who have 1½ ploughs.
           Meadow, 2 acres; woodland pasture 8 furlongs long
             and 2 wide.
        Value before 1066 and now 20s.

        [THURGARTON Wapentake]

0   M.   In BULCOTE Young Swein had 2 c. of land and 2 b. taxable;
        there also 15½ b. of land taxable, jurisdiction of this manor.
        Land for 5½ ploughs. In lordship 1 plough;
           8 Freemen, 11 villagers, 12 smallholders and 2 slaves
             with 3 ploughs.
           Meadow, 76 acres; woodland pasture in places 1 league
             long and 8 furlongs wide.
        Value before 1066 and now £4.

1   M.   In OXTON Thori had 4 b. of land taxable. Land for 12 oxen.
           1 Freeman with a third part of 1 b. of this land,
             with 1 smallholder who has ½ plough.
           Meadow, 4 acres.
        Value before 1066, 16s; now 5s 4d.

2   M.   In THURGARTON and in HORSEPOOL Swein had 3 c. of land and 3 b.
        taxable. Land for 6 ploughs. Walter has in lordship 2 ploughs and
           10 Freemen with 9 b. of this land and

3   In TITHBY 2 b. taxable.

2)   12 villagers and 2 smallholders who have 6 ploughs.   288 d
           A priest and a church   meadow, 40 acres; woodland
             pasture 1 league long and ½ wide.
        Value before 1066 £3; now £4.

14   M.   In HOVERINGHAM Swein had 2 c. of land and 2 b. taxable.
        Land for 4 ploughs. Walter has in lordship 2 ploughs and
           6 Freemen with 3 b. and the third part of 1 b.
           of this land; 9 villagers and 3 smallholders who
             have 4 ploughs.
           A priest and a church; 2 mills, 40s; 2 fisheries, 8s;
             meadow, 40 acres.
        Value before 1066 £4; now the same and 10s more.

15   S.   In FISKERTON Walter has ½ c. of land taxable; its jurisdiction
        belongs to Southwell. He has 1 plough himself and
           3 villagers with 1 plough.

16   S.   In MORTON Walter has ½ c. of land taxable, whose
        jurisdiction belongs to Southwell. [He has] 1 plough himself.
           3 villagers have 1 plough.

Ŝ In Farnesfeld hͨ Walt˄.11.bou̇ træ̇ ad glͩ˄.Vna eſt
in Soca de Sudwelle.7 alia regis.fʒ tam̃ ad hunͩ
de Sudwelle ꝑtinet.Ibi.1.car̃ in dn̄io.T.R.E.uaͭ
v.ſoͭ.m̃.ᵗᵒviii.ſoͭ.

ᔬ In *ROLDESTVN*.h̄b Tori xi.bou̇ træ̇ 7 iiii.partẽ
uni⁹ bou̇˄ ad glͩ˄.Tra.ii.car̃.Ibi.1.car̃ in dn̄io.7 viii.
uiͭ 7 vi.borͩ.hn̄tes.iii.car̃ 7 iii.bou̇.Ibi pᷧr 7 æcclͣ.
7 xxx.ii.ac̃ ꝑti.Silua paſt˄.iiii.q̃ʒ lg̃.7 ii.laͭ.T.R.E.
uaͭ xl.ſoͭ.m̃ lx.   Soca hvi⁹ man̄.

Ŝ In Calun.ix.bou̇ træ̇ 7 iii.ᶜⁱᵃpars.1;bou̇ ad glͩ˄.Tra˄
ii.car̃ 7 dim̃.Ibi xviii.ſoch 7 iii.borͩ hn̄t vii.car̃
7 dim̃˄.7 xvi.ac̃s ꝑti.Silua miñ˄.ix.q̃ʒ lg̃.7 l.uirg˄

ᔬ In *FISCARTVNE*.h̄b Tori.ii.car̃ træ̇ 7 ii.bou̇ ⌐ laͭ.
ad glͩ˄.Tra˄.v.car̃.Ibi Walt˄ hͨ in dn̄io.1.car̃.7 xi.
uiͭ hn̄tes.iiii.car̃.Ibi.ii.molin̄.7 1.piſcar̃.7 1.paſ
ſagiu̇.xlvi.ſoͭ 7 viii.deñ˄.7 xlii.ac̃ ꝑti.Silua
paſt.ii.q̃ʒ lg̃.7 1.q̃ʒ laͭ.T.R.E.uaͭ.iii.lib̃.m̃.iiii.

Ŝ In iſta Fiſcartune hͨ Walt˄ vi.bou̇ træ̇.unde hͨ
archieꝑs ſoca̋.

ᔬ In *ASLACHETVNE*.h̄b Tori.1.car̃ tre ad glͩ˄.Tra˄
iii.car̃.Ibi Walchelin̄⁹ hō Walterij hͨ.ii.car̃.7 1.
ſoch de.1.bou̇ huj⁹træ̇.7 vi.uiͭ 7 ii.borͩ cu̇.1.car̃
7 dim̃˄.7 xx.iiii.ac̃ ꝑti.T.R.E.7 m̃ uaͭ xxx.ſoͭ.

Ŝ In Hocheſuorde.1.bou̇ tre ad glͩ˄.Tra˄.ii.bou̇.Soca.
Ibi.ii.ſoch 7 1.borͩ hn̄t.ii.boues in car̃.7 ii.ac̃s ꝑti.

ᔬ In *COLESTVNE* h̄b Tori.ii.bou̇ træ̇ 7 dim̃.7 una ac̃
træ̇ ad glͩ˄.Tra˄.1.car̃.Ibi.1.borͩ arat.1.boue.Ibi

17 S. In FARNSFIELD Walter has 2 b. of land taxable. One is in
the jurisdiction of Southwell and the other the King's,
but it nevertheless belongs to the Hundred of Southwell. 1
plough in lordship.
Value before 1066, 5s; now 8s.

18 M. In ROLLESTON Thori had 11 b. of land and the fourth part of 1 b.
taxable. Land for 2 ploughs. 1 plough in lordship;
8 villagers and 6 smallholders who have 3 ploughs and 3 oxen.
A priest and a church; meadow, 32 acres; woodland pasture
4 furlongs long and 2 wide.
Value before 1066, 40s; now 60 [s].
Jurisdiction of this manor.

19 S. In KELHAM 9 b. of land and the third part of 1 b. taxable.
Land for 2½ ploughs.
18 Freemen and 3 smallholders have 7½ ploughs.
Meadow, 16 acres; underwood 9 furlongs long
and 50 virgates wide.

20 M. In FISKERTON Thori had 2 c. of land and 2 b. taxable.
Land for 5 ploughs. Walter has in lordship 1 plough and
11 villagers who have 4 ploughs.
2 mills; 1 fishery; a ferry, 46s 8d; meadow, 42 acres;
woodland pasture 2 furlongs long and 1 furlong wide.
Value before 1066 £3; now [£] 4.

21 S. In FISKERTON Walter has 6 b. of land; the Archbishop has
its jurisdiction.

[BINGHAM Wapentake]

22 M. In ASLOCKTON Thori had 1 c. of land taxable. Land for 3
ploughs. Walkelin, Walter's man, has 2 ploughs and
1 Freeman with 1 b. of this land; 6 villagers and
2 smallholders with 1½ ploughs.
Meadow, 24 acres.
Value before 1066 and now 30s.

23 S. In HAWKSWORTH 1 b. of land taxable. Land for 2 oxen.
Jurisdiction.
2 Freemen and 1 smallholder have 2 oxen in a plough.
Meadow, 2 acres.

24 M. In (Car) COLSTON Thori had 2½ b. of land and 1 acre of
land taxable. Land for 1 plough.
1 smallholder ploughs with 1 ox.

.iii. aĉ p̃ti . T.R.E. ual̃ . x . ſol̃ . m̃ . v . ſol̃ . Walchel tenet.

ⓂIn FLINTEHÁ . ħƀ Tori . vi . boú tr̃æ ad gl̃d . Tra . ii . car̃.

Ibi . i . ſocħ 7 vii . uilt 7 i . bord hñt . ii . car̃ . 7 xxíi . aĉs

p̃ti . Raýnold ħõ Walt ħт̃ . i . car̃ . Silua minuta.

289 a

i . q̃ʒ lg̃ . 7 i . q̃ʒ lat̃ . T.R.E. 7 m̃ ual̃ . xx . ſol̃.

ⓂIn GRANEBI . ħƀ Haminc . i . car̃ tre 7 dim̃

ad gl̃d . Tra . xii . car̃ . Ibi Walteri in dñio

ħт̃ . iiii . car̃ . 7 xliiii . uilt 7 ix . bord hñtes . x .

car̃ . Ibi pƀr 7 æccla . 7 i . molin̄ . ii . ſol̃ . 7 cc . aĉ

p̃ti . T.R.E. ual̃ . xii . liƀ . m̃ . xx . liƀ . Soca нvi Ⓜ.

Š In Berneſtune dim̃ car̃ tr̃æ ad gl̃d . Tra . ii . car̃.

Ibi . v . ſocħ 7 i . bord hñt . ii . car̃ 7 ii . boú arant . 7 xi . aĉs

Š In Langare . iiii . boú tr̃æ 7 dim̃ ad gl̃d .   ⌠p̃ti.

Tra . ii . car̃ . Ibi viii . ſocħ hñt ii . car̃ . 7 vi . boú arant.

Ibi dimid æccla 7 xiii . aĉs p̃ti.

Š In Wiuretune . vi . boú tre 7 dim̃ ad gl̃d . Tra . i . car̃.

Ibi . v . ſocħ hñt . ii . car̃ 7 ii . boues arant . 7 xx . aĉs p̃ti.

Š In Hechelinge . ii . car̃ tr̃æ ad gl̃d . Tra . iiii . car̃.

Ibi . viii . ſocħ 7 i . uilt 7 x . bord hñt . v . car̃ . Ibi

molin̄ . xvi . ſolid . 7 q̃t xx . aĉ p̃ti.

Š In Chineltune . vii . boú tr̃æ ad gl̃d . Tra . ii . car̃ . Ibi

ix . ſocħ 7 iiii . bord hñtes . iii . car̃ . 7 vii . boues arant

Š In Crophille 7 Wiuretune . iiii . boú tr̃æ ⌠7 xx . aĉs p̃ti.

ad gl̃d . Tra . i . car̃ . Ibi . iiii . ſocħ 7 vii . bord hñt

.ii . car̃ . 7 xiii . aĉs p̃ti.

★ ⓂIn RADECLIVE . ħƀ Suain . i . car̃ tr̃æ 7 dim̃

ad gl̃d Tra . iii . car̃ . Ibi in dñio ſuɴ . ii . car̃.

7 xiiii . uilt 7 iii . bord hñtes . ii . car̃ . 7 xix . aĉs

p̃ti . T.R.E. 7 m̃ ual̃ . xl . ſol̃.

Meadow, 3 acres;
Value before 1066, 10s; now 5s.
Walkelin holds it.

25   M. In FLINTHAM Thori had 6 b. of land taxable. Land for 2 ploughs.
1 Freeman, 7 villagers and 1 smallholder have 2 ploughs
Meadow, 24 acres; Reginald, Walter's man, has 1 plough;
    underwood 1 furlong long and 1 furlong wide.   289 a
Value before 1066 and now 20s.

26   M. In GRANBY Heming had 1½ c. of land taxable. Land for 12
ploughs. Walter has in lordship 4 ploughs and
    44 villagers and 9 smallholders who have 10 ploughs.
    A priest and a church; 1 mill, 2s; meadow, 200 acres.
Value before 1066 £12; now £20.
   Jurisdiction of this manor.

27   S. In BARNSTONE ½ c. of land taxable. Land for 2 ploughs.
    5 Freemen and 1 smallholder have 2 ploughs and 2
      ploughing oxen.
Meadow, 11 acres.

28   S. In LANGAR 4½ b. of land taxable. Land for 2 ploughs.
    8 Freemen have 2 ploughs and 6 ploughing oxen.
Half a church; meadow, 13 acres.

29   S. In WIVERTON 6½ b. of land taxable. Land for 1 plough.
    5 Freemen have 2 ploughs and 2 ploughing oxen.
Meadow, 20 acres.

30   S. In HICKLING 2 c. of land taxable. Land for 4 ploughs.
    8 Freemen, 1 villager and 10 smallholders have 5 ploughs.
    A mill, 16s; meadow, 80 acres.

31   S. In KINOULTON 7 b. of land taxable. Land for 2 ploughs.
    9 Freemen and 4 smallholders who have 3 ploughs and
      7 ploughing oxen.
Meadow, 20 acres.

32   S. In CROPWELL (Butler) and WIVERTON 4 b. of land taxable.
Land for 1 plough.
    4 Freemen and 7 smallholders have 2 ploughs.
Meadow, 13 acres.

33   M. In RADCLIFFE (-on-Trent) Swein had 1½ c. of land taxable.
Land for 3 ploughs. In lordship 2 ploughs.
    14 villagers and 3 smallholders who have 2 ploughs.
    Meadow, 19 acres.
Value before 1066 and now 40s.

.XII. TERRA GOISFRIDI ALSELIN.

★ In *LAXINTVNE* . hb Tochi . III . car træ ad glð .

Tra . VI . caŕ . Ibi Walter hō Goisfridi Alselin

hŧ . I . caŕ . 7 XXII . uilł 7 VII . borð . hñtes . V . caŕ .

7 V . ſeru . 7 I . ancilł . 7 XL . aćs pti . Silua paſt . I . leў lḡ

7 dim laŧ . T.R.E. uał . IX . lib . m̂ VI . lib . SOCA HVI m̂ .

§ In Schidrinſtune . II . bou træ ad glð . Tra . IIII . bou . Ibi

III . ſoch hñt . I . caŕ . ⫽ In Wilgebi . e un ort ptinenſ ad Laxint .

§ In Waleſbi . II . bou træ ad glð . Tra . IIII . bou . Ibi . II . ſoch

§ hñt . I . caŕ . ⫽ In Echeringhe dim bou træ ad glð . Waſta . e .

§ In Almentune . II . bou træ ad glð . Waſta . e .

§ In Chenapetorp . I . bou træ ad glð . Waſta . e . Tra . II . bou .

§ In Calneſtune . VI . bou træ ad glð . Tra . III . caŕ . Ibi . VIII .

ſoch . 7 X . borð hñt . V . caŕ . Ibi . I . molin . II . ſol . 7 VIII .

aĉ pti . Silua paſt . I . leu lḡ . 7 IIII . q̃ʒ laŧ .

§ In Beſtorp . II . bou træ ad glð . Tra dim caŕ . Ibi . II . ſoch

7 I . borð hñt dim caŕ . 7 dim aĉ pti . Silua paſt . X . aĉs .

§ In Carletun . I . car tre ad glð . Tra . I . caŕ . Ibi . IIII . ſoch

hñt . II . caŕ . 7 XX . aĉs pti . Silua paſt . IIII . q̃ʒ lḡ . 7 IIII . laŧ .

m̂ In *NORDMVSCHA* hb Vluric . III . bou træ ad gld . Tra

. IIII . caŕ . Ibi in dn̄io . e . I . caŕ . 7 IIII . uilł 7 VII . borð hñtes

. I . caŕ 7 dim . Ibi . I . molin . X . ſolið 7 XII . aĉ pti . T.R.E.

uał . XL . ſol . m̂ . XXX .

§ Ibide . IIII . bou træ ad glð . Tra . I . caŕ . SOCA . Waſta . e .

Ibi . XII . aĉ pti .

§ In Carletun . I . bou træ ad glð . Ibi . II . ſoch ſuɲ nichil hñtes

Ibiđ . II . car træ
7 dim ad gld .
Tra . IIII . caŕ .
In dn̄io ſ . III . car .
7 XVI . ſochi . 7 V . uilli
7 II . borð cu . VI . caŕ .
Ibi . II . molini . XX . ſol .
7 XL . aĉ pti . 7 XL . aĉ ſiluæ .
Olĩ . c . ſol . M uał . II . lib .
Tochi tenuit ꝑ m̂ .

[BASSETLAW Wapentake]

1   In LAXTON Toki had 2 c. of land taxable. Land for 6 ploughs.
       Walter, Geoffrey Alselin's man, has 1 plough and
            22 villagers and 7 smallholders who have 5 ploughs;
            5 male slaves, 1 female slave; meadow, 40 acres;
                woodland pasture 1 league long and ½ wide.
       Value before 1066 £9; now £6.

       Jurisdiction of this manor.

2 S. In KIRTON 2 b. of land taxable. Land for 4 oxen.
            3 Freemen have 1 plough.
3   In WILLOUGHBY 1 garden which belongs to Laxton.
4 S. In WALESBY 2 b. of land taxable. Land for 4 oxen.
            2 Freemen have 1 plough.
5 S. In EAKRING ½ b. of land taxable. Waste.
6 S. In OMPTON 2 b. of land taxable. Waste.
7 S. In KNAPTHORPE 1 b. of land taxable. Waste. Land for 2 oxen.
8 S. In CAUNTON 6 b. of land taxable. Land for 3 ploughs.
            8 Freemen and 10 smallholders have 5 ploughs.
            1 mill, 2s; meadow, 8 acres; woodland pasture 1 league
            long and 4 furlongs wide.
9 S. In BESTHORPE 2 b. of land taxable. Land for ½ plough.
            2 Freemen and 1 smallholder have ½ plough.
            Meadow, ½ acre; woodland pasture, 10 acres.
10 S. In CARLTON (-on-Trent) 1 c. of land taxable. Land for 1 plough.
            4 Freemen have 2 ploughs.
            Meadow, 20 acres; woodland pasture 4 furlongs long
                and 4 wide.

       [LYTHE Wapentake]

11 M. In NORTH MUSKHAM Wulfric had 3 b. of land taxable.
       Land for 4 ploughs. In lordship 1 plough;
            4 villagers and 7 smallholders who have 1½ ploughs.
            1 mill, 10s; meadow, 12 acres.
       Value before 1066, 40s; now 30[s].
12   There also 2½ c. of land taxable. Land for 4 ploughs.
       In lordship 3 ploughs;
            16 Freemen, 5 villagers and 2 smallholders with 6 ploughs.
            2 mills, 20s; meadow, 40 acres; woodland, 40 acres.
       Formerly 100s; value now £4. Toki held it as a manor.
13 S. There also 4 b. of land taxable. Land for 1 plough. Jurisdiction.
       Waste. Meadow, 12 acres.
14 S. In CARLTON (-on-Trent) 1 b. of land taxable.
            2 Freemen who have nothing.

ꝳ In WILGEBI. ħɓ Tochi.ɪ.bou træ 7 dim ad glđ.Tra.ɪɪɪɪ.boɓ.
wafta.ē.Ibi dim molin 7 xɪɪ.ać p̃ti.

ꝳ In STOCHES 7 Ghellinge ħɓ Tochi.ɪɪɪ.car 7 ɪɪ.part
uni bou ad glđ.Tra.ɪɪɪɪ.car.Ibi in dñio Goisfrid ħ.ɪɪ.
car.7 xv.uiłł 7 xxɪ.borđ.hñtes.vɪɪɪ.car.Ibi p̃ɓr
7 æccła.7 ɪ.pifcar.7 ɪɪ.molin.xx.fol.7 xxx.ać p̃ti.Silua
paſt.ɪɪɪ.q̃ʒ lḡ.7 ɪɪɪ.q̃ʒ lat.T.R.E.ual.cx.fol.m̃.vɪ.liɓ.

ꝸ In Carentune 7 Ghellinge 7 Coleuin.xv.bou træ ad glđ.
Tra.ɪɪɪɪ.car.Ibi.xxx.foch hñt.x.car 7 dim̃.7 xx.ać p̃ti.
Silua miñ.ɪɪɪ.q̃ʒ lḡ.7 ɪ.lat.

ꝳ In BERTVNE.ħɓ Suen.ɪ.car træ 7 ɪɪɪɪ.part.ɪ.bou ad glđ.
Tra.ɪɪ.car.Ibi Goisfrid ħ.ɪ.foch de.v.acris træ.7 v.
uiłł.7 ɪ.borđ.7 ɪ.ferū.7 ɪ.anciłł.Simul hñt.ɪɪɪ.car.
Ibi æccła 7 p̃ɓr.7 xvɪ.ać p̃ti.Silua paſt.ɪɪ.q̃ʒ lḡ.
7 ɪ.lat.T.R.E.7 m̃ ual unā marħ argenti.

ꝳ In SCELFORD.ħɓ Tochi.ɪɪɪɪ.car træ ad glđ.Tra
.vɪɪɪ.car.Ibi m̃.xxxvɪ.uiłł 7 xɪɪ.borđ hñtes.ɪx.car.

289 c
7 ɪ.moliñ.ɪɪɪɪ.folid.7 ɪ.pifcar.Ibi p̃ɓr 7 æccła.T.R.E.
ual.vɪɪɪ.liɓ.m̃.ɪɪɪɪ.liɓ.   SOCA HVI ꝳ

ꝸ In Neutone.ɪx.bou træ ad glđ.Tra.ɪɪɪ.car.Ibi.ɪx.
fochi 7 нɪɪ.borđ hñtes.ɪɪɪɪ.car.7 ɪɪɪɪ.ać p̃ti.

In Obetorp.ħɓ Tochi.ɪ.car træ ad glđ.Nil ibi habet.

In CHENATORP dim bou ad glđ.Jacet in NORTWELLE.

In CARLENTVN.ɪɪ.bou træ ad glđ.Tra dim car.Ibi.ɪɪɪɪ.fochi
7 ɪɪɪ.ać p̃ti.Oli.vɪɪɪ.fol.modo.ɪɪɪ.folid.

.XIII.   TERRA RADVLFI FILIJ HVBERTI.

ꝳ In BARTONE ħɓ Leuric xɪɪɪ.bou tre ad glđ.Tra.ɪɪɪ.
car.Ibi Radulf fili Huɓti ħ.ɪɪ.car.7 xvɪɪɪ.uiłł 7 v.

15   M.   In WILLOUGHBY Toki had 1½ b. of land taxable.
Land for 4 oxen. Waste.
½ mill; meadow, 12 acres.

[THURGARTON Wapentake]

16   M.   In STOKE (Bardolph) and GEDLING Toki had 3 c. and 2 b. and
two parts of 1 b. taxable. Land for 4 ploughs. Geoffrey
has in lordship 2 ploughs and
15 villagers, 6 slaves and 21 smallholders who have 8 ploughs.
A priest and a church; 1 fishery; 2 mills, 20s; meadow,
30 acres; woodland pasture, 3 furlongs long and 3
furlongs wide.
Value before 1066, 110s; now £6.

17   S.   In CARLTON (by Nottingham), GEDLING and COLWICK 15 b. of
land taxable. Land for 4 ploughs.
30 Freemen have 10½ ploughs.
Meadow, 20 acres; underwood 3 furlongs long and 1 wide.

18   M.   In BURTON (Joyce) Swein had 1 c. of land and the fourth
part of 1 b. taxable. Land for 2 ploughs. Geoffrey has
1 Freeman with 5 acres of land; 5 villagers, 1 smallholder,
1 male and 1 female slave; together they have 2 ploughs.
A church and a priest; meadow, 16 acres; woodland
pasture 2 furlongs long and 1 wide.
Value before 1066 and now 1 silver mark.

[BINGHAM Wapentake]

19   M.   In SHELFORD Toki had 4 c. of land taxable. Land for 8 ploughs.
Now 36 villagers and 12 smallholders who have 9 ploughs.
1 mill, 4s; 1 fishery. A priest and a church.   289 c
Value before 1066 £8; now £4.
Jurisdiction of this manor.

20   S.   In NEWTON 9 b. of land taxable. Land for 3 ploughs.
9 Freemen and 4 smallholders who have 4 ploughs.
Meadow, 4 acres.

21   In OWTHORPE Toki had 1 c. of land taxable. Nothing is recorded.

22   In KNAPTHORPE ½ b. taxable. It lies in Norwell (lands).

23   In CARLTON (-on-Trent) 2 b. of land taxable. Land for ½ plough.
4 Freemen.
Meadow, 3 acres.
Formerly 8s; now 3s.

3   **LAND OF RALPH SON OF HUBERT**

[RUSHCLIFFE Wapentake]

1   M.   In BARTON (-in-Fabis) Leofric had 13 b. of land taxable.
Land for 3 ploughs. Ralph son of Hubert has 2 ploughs and

borđ.hñtes.v.caῤ 7 dim̅.Ibi.xlviii.a̅c p̅ti.Silua

minuta.ii.q̆ῤ lg̅.7 dim̅ q̆ῤ laῤ.T.R.E.ual.vi.liƀ.

m̅.c.fol.Cũ duaƀ ciluellis.in qƀῤ.vii.foch 7 dim̅ æccla.

Ⓜ I̅bide̅ hƀ Vluric.ii.boῡ tre ad glđ.Tra.i.caῤ.Ibi

Rad hῤ.i.caῤ.7 ii.uiłł 7 i.borđ.cũ.i.caῤ.T.R.E.7 m̅

ᴮIn Cliftune.ii.bou træ ad glđ.ad Bartone ⌐ual xx.fol.
ptineꝫ.

ˢIn Cilleuuelłe 7 Eftrecilleuelłe.iii.caῤ træ 7 iii.bou

ad glđ.Soca de Bart.Tra.iiii.caῤ 7 dim̅.Ibi Rađ hῤ

.i.caῤ.7 ii.foch.7 v.uiłł 7 xiii.borđ.hñtes vi.caῤ 7 ii

boues arant.Ibi.lxx.a̅c p̅ti.7 dim̅ æccla.7 iiii.a̅c filuæ

minutæ.7 iiii.a̅c falicti.In Ciduuelle.v.bou de foca ad glđ.
In Tolueftone.

★ Ⓜ I̅n Bonei.hƀ Leuenot.iii.caῤ træ ad glđ.Tra.vi.caῤ.

Ibi Rađ hῤ in dñio.ii.caῤ.7 xviii.uiłł.7 vii.foch.7 ii.

borđ hñtes.vii.caῤ.Ibi æccla 7 pƀr.7 i.moliñ.xii.den.

7 clx.a̅c p̅ti.7 filua min̅.x.q̆ῤ lg̅.7 i.laῤ.T.R.E.iiii.liƀ
or

Ⓜ I̅n Caworde.hƀ Frane.v.bo̅ tre ad glđ.Tra.i.⌐ m̅.lx.fol.

caῤ.Ibi hῤ Rađ.i.caῤ 7 dim̅.7 iii.a̅c p̅ti.T.R.E.xx.fol.

Ⓜ I̅n Tevreshalt.hƀ Leuric.vi.bou træ ad glđ.⌐ m̅ x.fol.

Tra.i.caῤ 7 dim̅.Ibi Rađ hῤ.ii.caῤ.7 i.foch de.i.bou

træ.7 ix.uiłł hñtes.iii.caῤ 7 dim̅.Ibi.i.moliñ xvi.den.

7 viii.a̅c p̅ti.7 filua min̅.i.lev lg̅.7 i.laῤ.T.R.E.ual

lx.fol.m̅.xxx.Goisfriđ tenet.

Ⓜ I̅n Chirchebi.hƀ Leuenot x.bou træ ad glđ.Tra

ii.caῤ.Ibi Rađ hῤ in dñio.iii.caῤ.7 i.foch de.i.bo̅ træ.

7 xx.uiłł 7 vi.borđ hñtes.xii.caῤ.Ibi æccla 7 pƀr.7 ii.mol

iii.fol.7 iii.a̅c p̅ti.Silua ꝑ loca past.ii.lev lg̅.7 i.laῤ.

T.R.E.ual.iiii.liƀ.m̅.iii.liƀ.

18 villagers and 5 smallholders who have 5½ ploughs.
Meadow, 48 acres; underwood 2 furlongs long and
½ furlong wide.
Value before 1066 £6; now 100s, with the two Chilwells,
in which there are
7 Freemen and half a church.

2 M. There also Wulfric had 2 b. of land taxable. Land for 1 plough.
Ralph has 1 plough and
2 villagers and 1 smallholder with 1 plough.
Value before 1066 and now 20s.

3 B. In CLIFTON 2 b. of land taxable which belong to Barton.

4 S. In CHILWELL and EAST CHILWELL 3 c. of land and 3 b. taxable.
Jurisdiction of Barton. Land for 4½ ploughs.
Ralph has 1 plough and
2 Freemen, 5 villagers and 13 smallholders who have 6
ploughs and 2 ploughing oxen.
Meadow, 70 acres; half a church; underwood, 4 acres;
willow-beds, 4 acres.

5 In CHILWELL 5 b. of the Jurisdiction taxable, in Toton.

6 M. In BUNNY Leofnoth had 2 c. of land taxable. Land for 6 ploughs.
Ralph has in lordship 2 ploughs and
18 villagers, 7 Freemen and 2 smallholders who have 7 ploughs.
A church and a priest; 1 mill, 12d; meadow, 160 acres;
underwood 10 furlongs long and 1 wide.
Value before 1066 £4; now 60s.

7 M. In KEYWORTH Fran had 5 b. of land taxable. Land for 1 plough.
Ralph has 1½ ploughs.
Meadow, 3 acres.
Value before 1066, 20s; now 10s.

[BROXTOW Wapentake]
8 M. In TEVERSAL Leofric had 6 b. of land taxable.
Land for 1½ ploughs. Ralph has 2 ploughs and
1 Freeman with 1 b. of land; 9 villagers who have 3½ ploughs.
1 mill, 16d; meadow, 8 acres; underwood 1 league long
and 1 wide.
Value before 1066, 60s; now 30[s].
Geoffrey holds it.

9 M. In KIRKBY (-in-Ashfield) Leofnoth had 10 b. of land taxable.
Land for 2 ploughs. Ralph has in lordship 3 ploughs and
1 Freeman with 1 b. of land; 20 villagers and 6
smallholders who have 12 ploughs.
A church and a priest; 2 mills, 3s; meadow, 3 acres;
woodland pasture in places 2 leagues long and 1 wide.
Value before 1066 £4; now £3.

ⓂIn *WANDDESLEI*.ħƀ Leuric.v.bou trǽ ad glđ.Tra
.I.car.Ibi Rad ħt dim car.7 IIII.uiłł 7 II.borđ.lbi
pƀr 7 ǽccła.7 IIII.ac͞ p̃ti.Silua past.IIꞁꞁ.q̃ꞇ l͞g.7 IIII.lat.
T.R.E.uał VIII.soł.m̃.x.soł.

ⓂIn *ANESLEI*.ħƀ Leuenot.I.car tre ad glđ.Tra
XII.bou.Ibi Rad ħt.I.car.7 XIX.uiłł 7 I.borđ.

289 d

hn͡tes.VII.car.7 III.ac͞s p̃ti.Silua past.I.leu l͞g.
7 I.lev lat.T.R.E.7 m̃ uał.XL.soł.Ricard tenet.
In *COTESHALE*.habuit Leuenot.VI.bo͞ trǽ
ad glđ.Tra totiđ bob.Ibi st.III.car cu͞.III.
uiłłis.7 v.ac͞ p̃ti.Oli.XVI.soł.m̃ uał.x.soliđ.
In *GIP,SMARE* 7 Mortun.I.car trǽ 7.III.bou ad glđ.⌐soł.
Soca de Sudwelle.Tra.III.car 7 dim.Valuit 7 uał.XXVIII.
In *WIMARSPOL*.I.bou trǽ ad glđ.7 iacet ad *BONEI*.

.XII. TERRA RADVLFI DE LIMESI.

ⓂIn *HOLTONE*.ħƀ Tored.IIII.bou tre 7 dim ad
glđ.Tra.II.car.Ibi Radulf de Limesi ħt.II.
car.7 IIII.soch de.II.bou 7 dim trǽ.7 v.uiłł 7 v.borđ
hn͡tes.III.car.Ibi pƀr 7 II.ǽcclǽ.7 I.moliñ.v.soliđ
.IIII.7 IIII.denar.

ⓂIBIDE͞ ħƀr Bugo.Rainald Toruet 7 Bugo.VI.bou
trǽ 7 dim ad glđ.Tra.II.car 7 dim.
§Ibide͞.v.bou trǽ ad glđ.Tra.II.car.   SOCA
In his tris sunt.XVIII.soch.7 II.uiłł.   7 x.borđ.
hn͡tes.VI.car.Hos.v.Ⓜ tenet Alured
de Radulfo.T.R.E.uał.c.soł.m̃.IIII.liƀ.   7 x.soł.
In Dordentorp.I.bou trǽ ad glđ.Tra.II.bo͞. SOCA
Ibi.v.soch 7 VI.borđ hn͡t.II.car.Ibi ǽccła 7 pƀr
cu͞.I.car.7 qt xx.ac͞ p̃ti.

M. In WANSLEY Leofric had 5 b. of land taxable.
  Land for 1 plough. Ralph has ½ plough and
    3 villagers and 2 smallholders.
      A priest and half a church; meadow, 4 acres;
        woodland pasture 4 furlongs long and 4 wide.
  Value before 1066, 8s; now 10s.

M. In ANNESLEY Leofnoth had 1 c. of land taxable.
  Land for 12 oxen. Ralph has 1 plough and
    19 villagers and 1 smallholder who have 7 ploughs.   289 d
    Meadow, 3 acres; woodland pasture 1 league long
      and 1 league wide.
  Value before 1066 and now 40s.
    Richard holds it.

In COSSALL Leofnoth had 6 b. of land taxable.
Land for as many oxen.
  3 ploughs with 3 villagers.
    Meadow, 5 acres.
Formerly 16s; value now 10s.

In GIBSMERE and MORTON (-in-Fiskerton) 1 c. of land and 3 b. taxable.
Jurisdiction of Southwell. Land for 3½ ploughs.
The value was and is 28s.

In WIDMERPOOL 1 b. of land taxable. It lies with Bunny.

LAND OF RALPH OF LIMESY

[NEWARK Wapentake]
M. In HAWTON Thored had 4½ b. of land taxable. Land for 2 ploughs.
  Ralph of Limesy has 2 ploughs and
    4 Freemen with 2½ b. of land; 5 villagers and 5
      smallholders who have 3 ploughs.
    A priest and 2 churches; 1 mill, 5s 4d.

4
M. There also Bugg, Reginald, Thorferth and Bugg had 6½ b.
  of land taxable. Land for 2½ ploughs.

S. There also 5 b. of land taxable. Land for 2 ploughs. Jurisdiction.
  In these lands are
    18 Freemen, 2 villagers and 10 smallholders who have 6 ploughs.
    Alfred holds these five manors from Ralph.
  Value before 1066, 100s; now £4 10s.

In DANETHORPE 1 b. of land taxable. Land for 2 oxen. Jurisdiction.
  5 Freemen and 6 smallholders have 2 ploughs.
    A church and a priest with 1 plough; meadow, 80 acres.

ꝰ In *EPSTONE* 7 Vdeburg ħɓ Vluric 7 Elſi . III . car ⁿ aulā

træ 7 IIII . boū ad glð . Tra . VI . car . Ibi Rad ħⁱ in dñio

III . car . 7 XIIII . ſocħ de VI . boū 7 ferding huj træ . .I.boū

7 XII . uiłł 7 X . borð hñtes . VI . car . Ibi æccła 7 pɓr .

7 IIII . moliñ . LXXVII . ſoł . 7 VIII . ac̄ pti . Silua paſt

II . lev lḡ . 7 .IX . q̃ꝥ łat . T.R.E . uał v . liɓ . m̄ . VII . liɓ .

In Gunnulueſtone ħⁱ Radulf . IIII . car træ⁷ ad glð . Limeſi 9 .v . boⁱ 7 ī cꝺ parē . I . boū .

ꝰ In *TORP* . ħɓ Vluric . VI . boū tre 7 dim ad glð . Tra . IIII .

car . Ibi Mainfrid hō Radulfi ħⁱ . I . car . 7 IX . uiłł . 7 V .

borð . hñtes . III . car . 7 LXXII . ac̄s pti .

S In Sceltun 7 Colingehā . V . boū tre 7 dim ad glð . Tra

.IIII . car . Ibi . VIII . ſocħ 7 V . uiłł hñtes . III . car . 7 LX . ac̄s p̄ti .

7 II . ac̄s 7 I . uirg ſiluæ n̄ paſt . T.R.E . uał . IIII . liɓ . m̄ . XL . ſoł .

290 a

.XV. TERRA RADVLFI *de Burun.* *BERNESEDELAV WAP*

ꝰ In *OSCHINTONE* . ħɓ Oſmund . VI . boū træ ad glð .

Tra . III . car . Ibi Radulf de burun ħⁱ . III . car .

7 IIII . ſocħ de dim boū huj træ . 7 XVI . uiłł 7 VI . borð .

hñtes . VI . car . 7 XXVIII . ac̄s p̄ti . Silua paſt . II . lev

lḡ . 7 I . lev łat . T.R.E . uał . LX . ſoł . m̄ XL .

In Almentun . III . boū træ ad glð . Tra . I . car . Ibi . II .

borð hñt . I . car .

ꝰ In *CALVN* . ħɓ Oſmund . II . boū træ 7 III . part uni tiā

bou ad glð . Ibi Wiłłs hō Radulfi ħⁱ . I . car . 7 III

borð cū . II . boɓ arant . 7 IX . ac̄s p̄ti . Silua min

VIII . q̃ꝥ lḡ . 7 XII . uirgatas łat . T.R.E . uał . XL . ſoł .

BROCOLVESTOV WAPENT . ƒ m̄ XVI . s

ꝰ In *HOCHEHALE* . ħɓ Vlchet . XII . boū træ ad glð .

289 d, 290 a

[THURGARTON Wapentake]

M. In EPPERSTONE and WOODBOROUGH Wulfric and Alfsi (who had)
no hall, had 3 c. and 4 b. of land taxable. Land for 6 ploughs.
Ralph has in lordship 3 ploughs and
14 Freemen with 6 b. and a quarter of 1 b. of this land;
12 villagers and 10 smallholders who have 6 ploughs.
A church and a priest; 4 mills, 77s; meadow, 8 acres;
woodland pasture 2 leagues long and 9 furlongs wide.
Value before 1066 £5; now £7.
In GONALSTON Ralph of Limesy has *4 c. of land,* 5 b. and
the third part of 1 b. taxable.

[NEWARK Wapentake]

M. In THORPE (-by-Newark) Wulfric had 6½ b. of land taxable.
Land for 4 ploughs. Manfred, Ralph's man, has 1 plough and
9 villagers and 5 smallholders who have 3 ploughs.
Meadow, 72 acres.

S. In SHELTON and COLLINGHAM 5½ b. of land taxable.
Land for 4 ploughs.
8 Freemen and 5 villagers who have 3 ploughs.
Meadow, 60 acres; woodland, not pasture, 2 acres and 1 virgate.
Value before 1066 £4; now 40s.

LAND OF RALPH OF BURON 290 a

BASSETLAW Wapentake

M. In OSSINGTON Osmund had 6 b. of land taxable. Land for 3 ploughs.
Ralph of Buron has 3 ploughs and
4 Freemen with ½ b. of this land; 16 villagers and
6 smallholders who have 6 ploughs.
Meadow, 28 acres; woodland pasture 2 leagues long
and 1 league wide.
Value before 1066, 60s; now 40[s].
In OMPTON 3 b. of land taxable. Land for 1 plough.
2 smallholders have 1 plough.

[LYTHE Wapentake]

M. In KELHAM Osmund had 2 b. of land and the third part of 1 b.
taxable. William, Ralph's man, has 1 plough and
3 smallholders with 2 ploughing oxen.
Meadow, 9 acres; underwood 8 furlongs long and 12
virgates wide.
Value before 1066, 40s; now 16s.

BROXTOW Wapentake

4 M. In HUCKNALL (Torkard) Ulfketel had 12 b. of land taxable.

Tŕa.ii.caŕ.Ibi Oſmund hő Rad hŕ.i.caŕ.7 v.

uilł hńtes.iii.caŕ 7 dim.Silua past.i.lev lḡ.

7 dim lat.T.R.E.uał.xxx.ſoł.m̂.xv.ſoł.

⑳ In CORTINGESTOCHE.ħɓ Seric 7 ii.frs ſui.xiiii.

boū tŕæ ad glđ.Tra xiiii.boū.Ibi Wilłs hő Rad

hŕ.iii.caŕ.7 i.ſoch de.ii.bou tŕæ.7 ix.uilł.7 iiii.

borđ hńtes.v.caŕ.Ibi.xxx.ac̄ ṕti.T.R.E.uał

xl.ſoł.m̂.xxx.ſoł.

⑳ In RAPESTONE.ħɓ Vlchetel vi.bou tŕæ ad glđ.

Tra vi.boū.Waſta.ē.T.R.E.uał x.ſoł.m̂.ii.ſoł.

Ibi.x.ac̄ ṕti.   BINGAMESHOV WAꝐ.

⑳ In LANBECOTE ħɓ Vlchet v.bou tŕæ ad glđ.

Ibi Oſmund hő Rad hŕ.i.caŕ.7 i.uilł 7 vi.ac̄s ṕti.

T.R.E.7 m̂ uał x.ſoł.

⑳ In GODEGRAVE.ħɓ Oghe.ii.caŕ tre ad glđ.Tŕa

iii.caŕ.Ibi.in dn̄io ſuꝝ.iii.caŕ.7 vii.ſoch 7 iiii.uilł

7 iiii.borđ hńtes.iiii.caŕ 7 dim.Ibi dim æccła.Silua

min̄.i.q̂ꝫ lḡ.7 i.q̂ꝫ lat.T.R.E.uał xl.ſoł.m̂ lx.

⑳ IBIDĒ ħɓ Turchil.i.caŕ tŕæ ad glđ.Tŕa.i.caŕ.

Ibi Gozeł hő Rad hŕ dim caŕ.7 v.uilł.7 i.borđ

hńtes.ii.caŕ.Ibi.xxx.ac̄ ṕti.Silua min̄ dim q̂ꝫ

lḡ.7 dim lat.T.R.E.7 m̂ uał.x.ſoł.

In Godegraue hŕ Warner.vi.bou de tŕa ejđ ꝏań.

.XVI.TERRA ROGERIJ PICTAꝞ. BERNESEDELAV WAꝐ

⑳ In GAMELESTVN.ħɓr Gamel 7 Suain.i.caŕ tre

ad glđ.Tŕa.viii.caŕ.Ibi Roger pictauenſis

hŕ in dn̄io.ii.caŕ.7 vii.ſoch de.ii.bou huj tŕæ.

7 iii.uilł 7 i.borđ hńtes.iii.caŕ 7 dim.Ibi.ii.moł

xl.ſolidoꝫ.7 xx ac̄ ṕti.7 xx.ac̄ ſiluæ min̄.T.R.E.

uał.iiii.liɓ.m̂ ſimilit.

Land for 2 ploughs. Osmund, Ralph's man, has 1 plough and
  5 villagers who have 3½ ploughs.
  Woodland pasture 1 league long and ½ wide.
Value before 1066, 30s; now 15s.

5 M. In COSTOCK Seric and his two brothers had 14 b. of land taxable.
  Land for 14 oxen. William, Ralph's man, has 3 ploughs and
    1 Freeman with 2 b. of land; 9 villagers
      and 4 smallholders who have 5 ploughs.
    Meadow, 30 acres.
  Value before 1066, 40s; now 30s.

6 M. In REMPSTONE Ulfketel had 6 b. of land taxable.
  Land for 6 oxen. Waste.
  Value before 1066, 10s; now 2s.
    Meadow, 10 acres.

  BINGHAM Wapentake
7 M. In LAMCOTE Ulfketel had 5 b. of land taxable. Osmund, Ralph's
  man, has 1 plough and
    1 villager.
    Meadow, 6 acres.
  Value before 1066 and now 10s.

8 M. In COTGRAVE Ogga had 2 c. of land taxable. Land for 3 ploughs.
  In lordship 3 ploughs;
    7 Freemen, 4 villagers and 4 smallholders who have 4½ ploughs.
    Half a church; underwood 1 furlong long and 1 furlong wide.
  Value before 1066, 40s; now 60[s].

9 M. There also Thorkell had 1 c. of land taxable. Land for 1 plough.
  Jocelyn, Ralph's man, has ½ plough and
    5 villagers and 1 smallholder who have 2 ploughs.
    Meadow, 30 acres; underwood ½ furlong long and ½ wide.
  Value before 1066 and now 10s.
10   In COTGRAVE Warner has 6 b. of the land of this manor.

16   **LAND OF ROGER OF POITOU**   290 b

  BASSETLAW Wapentake
1 2 In GAMSTON Gamel and Swein had 1 c. of land taxable.
   M. Land for 8 ploughs. Roger of Poitou has in lordship 2 ploughs and
      7 Freemen with 2 b. of this land; 3 villagers and 1
        smallholder who have 3½ ploughs.
      2 mills, 40s; meadow, 20 acres; underwood, 20 acres.
  Value before 1066 £4; now the same.

M Ibidē h̄b Chetelbern . i . bou tre ad gld̄ . Tra . i . car.
Idē Chetelbern h̄t de Rog . 7 ibi h̄t . i . car . 7 ii . borđ.
7 iii . ac̄s siluæ p loca past . T.R.E . uat xx . sot 7 viii . den.

Torgartone Wapent. m̄ x . sol.

M In *Calvretone* . h̄b Vluric . iii . bou træ ad gld̄ . Tra
. i . car . Ibi m̄ sunt . ii . uilli . 7 i . uirg p̄ti . T.R.E . uat . xx.
sol . m̄ . v . sol . 7 iiii . den.

Riseclive Wapent.

M In *Edvvoltone* h̄b Stepi . vi . bou træ ad gld̄ . Tra
xii . bou . Ibi in dn̄io m̄ . i . car . 7 i . uill . 7 xvi . ac̄ p̄ti.
T.R.E . uat xxx . sol . m̄ x . sol.

II. M In *Wilgebi* . h̄br Godric 7 Ernui . vi . bou træ 7 dim
7 ii . part . i . bou ad gld̄ . Tra . xii . bou . Ibi m̄ in dn̄io
i . car 7 dim . 7 ii . soch 7 vi . uill 7 ii . borđ h̄ntes . ii . car
7 dim . Ibi . ix . ac̄ p̄ti . T.R.E . uat . l . sol . m̄ . xxii . sol.

Bingameshov Wapent.

M In *Crophelle* . h̄b Vluric . ii . car 7 vi . bou træ ad gld̄.
Tra . vi . car . Ibi Rog h̄t . iii . car . 7 viii . soch . 7 xvii.
uill h̄ntes vi . car . Ibi . xx . ac̄ p̄ti . Silua past dim lev
lḡ . 7 iiii . q̄z lat . T.R.E . uat . viii . lib . m̄ . c . sol.

M In *Godegrave* . h̄b Vluric . iii . car tre ad gld̄ . Tra
iiii . car . Ibi Rog h̄t . i . car in dn̄io . 7 vi . soch . 7 x . uill.
7 i . borđ . h̄ntes . v . car . Ibi . xxx . ac̄ p̄ti . Silua min.
ii . q̄z lḡ . 7 i . lat . T.R.E . uat . iiii . lib . m̄ . xl . sol.

M In *Warberga* . h̄b Fredgis . xiii . bo træ 7 dim ad gld̄.
Tra . ii . car . Ibi Rog h̄t . i . car . 7 ii . soch . 7 i . borđ.
h̄ntes . i . car . 7 x . ac̄s p̄ti . T.R.E . uat . x . sol . m̄ xii . sol.

M In *Hoctvn* . h̄b Baldric . xii . bou træ ad gld̄ . Tra . iiii . car.
Wasta . ē . Ibi xvi . ac̄ p̄ti . 7 Silua past . i . q̄z lḡ . 7 viii . ptic
lat . T.R.E . uat . lx . sol . m̄ . xx . sol.

2 M. There also Ketelbern had 1 b. of land taxable. Land for 1 plough. Ketelbern also has it from Roger. He has 1 plough and
2 smallholders.
Woodland pasture in places, 3 acres.
Value before 1066, 20s 8d; now 10s.

THURGARTON Wapentake
3 M. In CALVERTON Wulfric had 3 b. of land taxable. Land for 1 plough.
Now 2 villagers.
Meadow, 1 virgate.
Value before 1066, 20s; now 5s 4d.

RUSHCLIFFE Wapentake
4 M. In EDWALTON Stepi had 6 b. of land taxable. Land for 12 oxen.
In lordship now 1 plough;
1 villager.
Meadow, 16 acres.
Value before 1066, 30s; now 10s.

5 2 In WILLOUGHBY (-on-the-Wolds) Godric and Ernwy had 6½ b. and
M. two parts of 1 b. of land taxable. Land for 12 oxen.
Now in lordship 1½ ploughs.
2 Freemen, 6 villagers and 2 smallholders who have 2½ ploughs.
Meadow, 9 acres.
Value before 1066, 50s; now 22s.

BINGHAM Wapentake
6 M. In CROPWELL (Butler) Wulfric had 2 c. and 6 b. of land taxable.
Land for 6 ploughs. Roger has 3 ploughs and
8 Freemen and 17 villagers who have 6 ploughs.
Meadow, 20 acres; woodland pasture ½ league long
and 4 furlongs wide.
Value before 1066 £8; now 100s.

7 M. In COTGRAVE Wulfric had 3 c. of land taxable. Land for 4 ploughs.
Roger has 1 plough in lordship and
6 Freemen, 10 villagers and 1 smallholder who have 5 ploughs.
Meadow, 30 acres; underwood 2 furlongs long and 1 wide.
Value before 1066 £4; now 40s.

8 M. In 'WARBOROUGH' Fredegis had 13½ b. of land taxable. Land for 2
ploughs. Roger has 1 plough and
2 Freemen and 1 smallholder who have 1 plough.
Meadow, 10 acres.
Value before 1066, 10s; now 12s.

[BASSETLAW Wapentake]
9 M. In HAUGHTON Baldric had 12 b. of land taxable. Land for 4 ploughs.
Waste.
Meadow, 16 acres; woodland pasture 1 furlong long and 8
perches wide.
Value before 1066, 60s; now 20s.

§ In Walefbi.dim bou͛ træ ad glđ.Tra.iiii.bou͛.Wafta.ē.Soca.

ⰏIn *DRAITVN*.ħɓ Suain.ii.bou͛ træ 7 iii͛ꞇᶜⁱᵃ.part uni bou⁹
ad glđ.Tra.i.car͛.Nc̄ Vlfi de Rogerio tenet.7 ibi ħ dim̄ car͛.
7 i.uiħ 7 i.borđ cū dim̄ car͛.Ibi.iii.ac̄ p̄ti.Silua paſt͛.
i.q̃ɀ lḡ.7 dim̄ q̃ɀ laꞇ.T.R.E.uaꞇ.x.foꞇ.m̄ v.foꞇ 7 iiii͛ᵒʳ.den͛.

In *WILGEBI*.habuit Ernui.v.bõ tre ꝑ Ⰿ.Tra totiđ bob.
Ibi ſꞇ.ii.car͛ cū.i.uiħo 7 vi.borđ.7 iiii.ac̄ p̄ti.Oli͛.xx.foꞇ
Ⲅ m̄ uaꞇ.x.foliđ.

290 c

TERRA GⷮSLEBERTI ᵈᵉ ᴳᵃⁿᵈ· *NEWERCE WAꝒ*

ⰏIn *BVCHETVN*.ħɓ Vlf   iii.bou͛ træ ad glđ.
Tra͛.iii.car͛.Ibi Gisleɓt de gand ħ.iii.uiħ 7 i.focħ
7 i.borđ hn̄tes.iii.car͛ 7 dim̄.Ibi.iiii.ac̄ p̄ti.Silua
paſt͛.iii.q̃ɀ lḡ.7 iii.laꞇ.T.R.E.uaꞇ xx.foꞇ.m̄.x.foꞇ.

ⰏIn *SCHIDRICTVNE*.ħɓ Ragenalt.ii.bou͛ træ ad glđ.
Tra͛ dim̄ car͛.Ibi.iiii.uiħ hn̄t.ii.car͛.Silua paſt͛.i.
q̃ɀ lḡ.7 i.laꞇ.T.R.E.uaꞇ.xx.foꞇ.m̄ x.foꞇ.

ⰏIn *ALRETVN*.ħɓ Wade.v.bou͛ træ 7 dim̄ ad glđ.
Tra͛.iii.car͛.Ibi Wiħs hõ Gisleɓti ħ.i.car͛.7 vi.focħ
de.ii.bou͛ træ.7 iii.uiħ hn̄tes.vi.car͛.Ibi.ii.moliñ
xvi.folidoɀ.Silua paſt͛.i.lev͛ lḡ.7 iiii.q̃ɀ laꞇ.T.R.E.uaꞇ
xL.foꞇ.m̄ xxx.foꞇ.

ⰏIn *RVGFORDE*.ħɓ Vlf xii.bou͛ træ ad glđ.Tra͛.iiii.
car͛.Ibi Gifleɓt in dn̄io ħ.i.car͛.7 x.uiħ hn̄tes
iii.car͛.Ibi.xx.ac̄ p̄ti.Silua paſt͛.i.lev͛ 7 dim̄ lḡ.
7 i.lev͛ laꞇ.T.R.E.uaꞇ.vi.liɓ.m̄.Lx.foꞇ.   Soca iɓiᴰ.

§ In Bildeſtorp.ii.car͛ tre ad glđ.Tra͛.vi.car͛.Ibi.xiii.
focħ 7 vi.borđ hn̄t.vi.car͛.7 iiii.ac̄s p̄ti.Silua paſt͛
.i.lev͛ lḡ.7 iiii.q̃ɀ laꞇ.

10 S. In WALESBY ½ b. of land taxable. Land for 4 oxen. Waste. Jurisdiction.

11 M. In (West) DRAYTON Swein had 2 b. of land and the third part of 1 b. taxable. Land for 1 plough. Now Wulfsi holds from Roger. He has ½ plough and
1 villager and 1 smallholder with ½ plough.
Meadow, 3 acres; woodland pasture 1 furlong long and ½ furlong wide.
Value before 1066, 10s; now 5s 4d.

12 In WILLOUGHBY (in Walesby) Ernwy had 5 b. of land as a manor. Land for as many oxen.
2 ploughs with 1 villager and 6 smallholders.
Meadow, 4 acres.
Formerly 20s; value now 10s.

17   LAND OF GILBERT OF GHENT   290 c

[BASSETLAW] Wapentake
1 M. In BOUGHTON Ulf had 3 b. of land taxable.
Land for 3 ploughs. Gilbert of Ghent has
3 villagers, 1 Freeman and 1 smallholder who have 3½ ploughs.
Meadow, 4 acres; woodland pasture 3 furlongs long and 3 wide.
Value before 1066, 20s; now 10s.

2 M. In KIRTON Reginald had 2 b. of land taxable. Land for ½ plough.
4 villagers have 2 ploughs.
Woodland pasture 1 furlong long and 1 wide.
Value before 1066, 20s; now 10s.

3 M. In OLLERTON Wada had 5½ b. of land taxable. Land for 3 ploughs.
William, Gilbert's man, has 1 plough and
6 Freemen with 2 b. of land; 3 villagers who have 6 ploughs.
2 mills, 16s; woodland pasture 1 league long and 4 furlongs wide.
Value before 1066, 40s; now 30s.

4 M. In RUFFORD Ulf had 12 b. of land taxable. Land for 4 ploughs.
Gilbert has in lordship 1 plough and
10 villagers who have 3 ploughs.
Meadow, 20 acres; woodland pasture 1½ leagues long and 1 league wide.
Value before 1066 £6; now 60s.

Also Jurisdiction there.
5 S. In BILSTHORPE 2 c. of land taxable. Land for 6 ploughs.
13 Freemen and 6 smallholders have 6 ploughs.
Meadow, 4 acres; woodland pasture 1 league long and 4 furlongs wide.

ᴮIn Wirchenefeld.ı.car̄ træ ad glđ.Bᴇʀ Wasta est.

ᴹIn ECHERINGHE ħƀ Ingolf.vı.bou̅ træ ad glđ.Tra
ıı.car̄.Ibi Witts ħō Gisleƀti ħť.ı.car̄.7 ııı.socħ
de.ııı.bou huj træ.7 ıı.uitt 7 ııı.borđ ħn̄tes.ıı.car̄.
Ibi pƀr 7 æccła.7 ııı.ac̄ p̄ti.Silua past.vı.q̊₂ lḡ.
7 ıııı.lat̄.T.R.E.ual.xx.soł.m̊ xvı.soł.

ᴹIʙɪᴅᴇ̄ ħƀ Echebrand.vı.bou træ ad glđ.Tra.ıı.car̄.
Idē Echebrand de Gisleƀto tenet.7 ħť ibi.ı.car̄.7 vı.
socħ de.ıııı.bou træ.7 ıı.uitt 7 ıı.borđ.ħn̄tes.ıı.car̄
7 dim.Ibi.ııı.ac̄ p̄ti.Silua past.vı.q̊₂ lḡ.7 ıııı.lat̄.
T.R.E.ual xx.soł.m̊ xvı.soł.

ᴹIn CHENESHALE 7 Cheruesħale ħƀ Vlf .xıı.bou træ
ad glđ.Tra.ıııı.car̄.Ibi Gisleƀt in dn̄io ħť.ııı.car̄.
7 vııı.socħ de.ııı.bou træ.7 xvı.uitt 7 ıııı.borđ ħn̄tes
xıı.car̄.Ibi.xxıı.ac̄ p̄ti.Silua past.ı.lev lḡ.7 dim
lat.T.R.E.ual.vııı.liƀ.m̊.vı.liƀ.   Sᴏᴄᴀ Iʙɪᴅᴇ̄.

ˢIn Almentun.ı.bou træ 7 dim ad glđ.Tra.ıı.bou.Ibi
ıı.socħ 7 ı.borđ ħn̄t.ıı.car̄.

ˢIn Mapleberg.xıııı.bou træ ad glđ.Tra.ıııı.car̄.Ibi ħť
Gisleƀt.ı.car̄.7 ıx.socħ de.x.bou 7 dim huj træ.7 v.
borđ ħn̄tes.ıııı.car̄.7 xxx.ac̄ p̄ti.Silua past.ı.lev lḡ.
7 ııı.q̊₂ lat̄.

ᴹIn Creilege ħƀ Vlf ıı.car̄ tre 7 dim ad glđ.Tra.ıııı.
car̄.Ibi Gisleƀt ħť.ıı.car̄.7 xxıı.uitt 7 ıı.borđ.ħn̄tes
ıx.car̄.7 xxvı.ac̄s p̄ti.Silua past dim lev lḡ.7 dim lat.
                              T.R.E.ual vı.liƀ.m̊.ııı.liƀ.

290 d

In Cherlinton ħƀ Vlf ıııı.bou tre 7 dim ad glđ.Tra
ıı.car̄.Sᴏᴄᴀ p̄tin ad Sudwelle ᴹ arcħ.Ibi Gisleƀt
ħť.ı.car̄.7 ıııı.uitt h ᵃˢıı.car̄.7 ı.moł.xvı.solidoᵣ.
T.R.E.ual.xʟ.soł.m̊.xxx.soł.

6 B. In INKERSALL 1 c. of land taxable. Outlier. Waste.

7 M. In EAKRING Ingulf had 6 b. of land taxable. Land for 2 ploughs.
William, Gilbert's man, has 1 plough and
    3 Freemen with 3 b. of this land; 2 villagers and 3
       smallholders who have 2 ploughs.
    A priest and a church; meadow, 3 acres; woodland pasture
       6 furlongs long and 4 wide.
Value before 1066, 20s; now 16s.

8 M. There also Erchenbrand had 6 b. of land taxable.
Land for 2 ploughs. Erchenbrand also holds from Gilbert;
he has 1 plough and
    6 Freemen with 4 b. of land; 2 villagers and 2 smallholders
      who have 2½ ploughs.
    Meadow, 3 acres; woodland pasture 6 furlongs long and 4 wide.
Value before 1066, 20s; now 16s.

9 M. In KNEESALL and KERSALL Ulf had 12 b. of land taxable.
Land for 4 ploughs. Gilbert has in lordship 3 ploughs and
    8 Freemen with 3 b. of land; 16 villagers and 4
      smallholders who have 12 ploughs.
    Meadow, 22 acres; woodland pasture 1 league long and ½ wide.
Value before 1066 £8; now £6.

   Also Jurisdiction there.

10 S. In OMPTON 1½ b. of land taxable. Land for 2 oxen.
    2 Freemen and 1 smallholder have 2 ploughs.

11 S. In MAPLEBECK 14 b. of land taxable. Land for 4 ploughs.
Gilbert has 1 plough and
    9 Freemen with 10½ b. of this land; 5 smallholders who
      have 4 ploughs.
    Meadow, 30 acres; woodland pasture 1 league long and
      3 furlongs wide.

12 M. In WELLOW Ulf had 2½ c. of land taxable. Land for 4 ploughs.
Gilbert has 2 ploughs and
    22 villagers and 2 smallholders who have 9 ploughs.
    Meadow, 26 acres; woodland pasture ½ league long and ½ wide.
Value before 1066 £6; now £3.

[THURGARTON Wapentake]   290 d

13   In KIRKLINGTON Ulf had 4½ b. of land taxable. Land for 2 ploughs.
The jurisdiction belongs to Southwell, a manor of the Archbishop's.
Gilbert has 1 plough.
    4 villagers have 2 ploughs.
    1 mill, 16s.
Value before 1066, 40s; now 30s.

In Normantun . ħɓ Vlf . iii . bou tre᷄ 7 dim᷄ ad glđ . Tra᷄
. i . car᷄ . Ibi ħt Gisleɓ . iiii . uiłt cũ . i . car᷄ . Soca i᷄ Sudw᷄ .
T.R.E . uał xvi . soł . m̊ . viii . soł .

Ꟁ In *RODDINTON* . ħɓ Vlf dim᷄ car᷄ tre ad glđ . Tra . i . car᷄
Ibi m̊ in dñio . i . car᷄ . 7 iiii . socħ . 7 v . uiłt 7 ii . borđ .
hñtes . iii . car᷄ . Ibi . xxx . ac̄ p̃ti . T.R.E . uał xx . soł . m̊ viii . soł .

BINGAMESHOV WAPENT᷄ .

Ꟁ In *WATONE* . ħɓ Vlf   ii . car᷄ tre 7 dim᷄ ad glđ .
Tra . ix . car᷄ . Ibi Roɓt h̊ Gisleɓti ħt . iii . car᷄ .
7 xxviii . uiłt 7 xii . borđ hñtes . ix . car᷄ . 7 i . moliñ . iiii .
solidoᷮ . 7 q̃t xx . ac̄ p̃ti . Ibi una molaria ubi molæ
fodiunt . de . iii . marꝃ argenti . T.R.E . uał . xx . liɓ .
m̊ xvi . liɓ .   Soca ejđ Ꟁ .

S In Hoches Holesuuorde . xiii . bou tre ad glđ . Tra . iii . car᷄ .
Ibi . xx . socħ 7 i . borđ hñt . iiii . car᷄ 7 dim᷄ . 7 xx . ac̄s p̃ti .
S In Haslacheſtone . dim᷄ car᷄ tre ad glđ . Tra . i . car᷄
7 dim᷄ . Ibi . ix . socħ hñt . iiii . car᷄ .

291 a
.XVIII.   ## TERRA GISLEBERTI TISON .

★ Ꟁ In *AIGRVN* . ħɓ Suain . iii . car᷄ træ ad glđ .
Tra . vi . car᷄ . Ibi Gisleɓt tison ħt in dñio . ii . car᷄ .
7 viii . socħ de . vi . bou træ . 7 xxi . uiłt 7 xxi . borđ
hñtes . xii . car᷄ . Ibi æccła 7 pɓr . 7 i . moliñ . v . solidoᷮ .
7 q̃t xx : ac̄ p̃ti . Silua min . viii . q̃ᷮ lḡ 7 iiii . lat . T.R.E .
uał . vi .   m̊ x . liɓ . 7 xii . den . Huic Ꟁ appenduᷧ
v . socħ in aliis hundret .
S In Crunuuelle . ii . bou træ ad glđ . Tra . iiii . boū . Ibi . ii .
socħ hñt . i . car᷄ .
Ꟁ In *FENIGLEI* . ħɓ Suain . vi . bou træ ad glđ . Tra . iii .
car᷄ . Ibi Gisleɓt ħt dim᷄ car᷄ . 7 xv . uiłt . 7 iiii . borđ .
hñtes . v . car᷄ 7 dim᷄ . Silua paſt᷄ . ii . leᷣ lḡ . 7 ii . lat .
T.R.E . uał xl . soł . m̊ xl . v . soł .

4   In NORMANTON (by Southwell) Ulf had 3½ b. of land taxable.
Land for 1 plough. Gilbert has
    4 villagers with 1 plough.
    Jurisdiction in Southwell.
Value before 1066, 16s; now 8s.

[RUSHCLIFFE Wapentake]

5   M. In RUDDINGTON Ulf had ½ c. of land taxable. Land for 1 plough.
   Now in lordship 1 plough and
    4 Freemen, 5 villagers and 2 smallholders who have 3 ploughs.
    Meadow, 33 acres.
Value before 1066, 20s; now 8s.

BINGHAM Wapentake

6   M. In WHATTON Ulf had 2½ c. of land taxable. Land for 9 ploughs.
   Robert, Gilbert's man, has 3 ploughs and
    28 villagers and 12 smallholders who have 9 ploughs.
    1 mill, 4s; meadow, 80 acres. A millstone quarry where
     millstones are dug, at 3 silver marks.
Value before 1066 £20; now £16.

Jurisdiction of this manor.

17   S. In HAWKSWORTH 13 b. of land taxable. Land for 3 ploughs.
    20 Freemen and 1 smallholder have 4½ ploughs.
    Meadow, 20 acres.

18   S. In ASLOCKTON ½ c. of land taxable. Land for 1½ ploughs.
    9 Freemen have 4 ploughs.

18   THE LAND OF GILBERT TISON   291 a

[LYTHE Wapentake]

1   M. In AVERHAM Swein had 3 c. of land taxable. Land for 6 ploughs.
   Gilbert Tison has in lordship 2 ploughs and
    8 Freemen with 6 b. of land; 21 villagers and 22 smallholders
     who have 12 ploughs.
    A church and a priest; 1 mill, 5s; meadow, 80 acres;
     underwood 8 furlongs long and 4 wide.
Value before 1066 [£] 6; now £10 and 12d.
   To this manor are attached 5 Freemen in other Hundreds.

2   S. In CROMWELL 2 b. of land taxable. Land for 4 oxen.
    2 Freemen have 1 plough.

[BASSETLAW Wapentake]

3   M. In FINNINGLEY Swein had 6 b. of land taxable. Land for 3 ploughs.
   Gilbert has ½ plough and
    15 villagers and 4 smallholders who have 5½ ploughs.
    Woodland pasture 2 leagues long and 2 wide.
Value before 1066, 40s; now 45s.

⅏ In *CALVN*. ħɓ Aluric . ɪɪ . bou træ ad glđ . Ťra . vɪ . bou.
Ibi . ɪ . foch 7 ɪ . borđ . cũ dĩɱ cař . 7 vɪ . ač p̃ti . Silua
mĩn . vɪɪɪ . q̃ɀ lǥ . 7 xɪɪɪɪ . uirg lat . T.R.E. ual xvɪ . fol.

⅏ In *WICHEBVRNE* ħɓ Suain . xɪɪ . bou træ ∫ m̃ . ɪɪɪ . fol.
ad glđ . Ťra . ɪɪɪ . cař . Ibi ħ̃ Gifleɓt . ɪɪ . cař . in dɴio.
7 xv . foch de . ɪɪɪɪ . bou tre . 7 vɪɪ . uiłł 7 v . borđ . hɴtes
vɪɪ . cař . Ibi æccła . 7 xvɪ . ač p̃ti . Silua past . ɪ . lev lǥ.
7 dĩɱ lev lať . T.R.E. ual . c . fol . m̃ . ʟx . fol.
Duas bou de hac ťra tenueř . v . taini . Vɴ eoɀ erat
fenior alioɀ . q̃ ɴ p̃tinuit ad Suain.

⅏ In *ALWOLDESTORP*. ħɓ Adeftan . ɪɪɪɪ . bou træ ad glđ.
Ťra . ɪ . cař . Ibi Gifleɓt ħ̃ . ɪ . cař in dɴio . 7 ɪɪɪɪ . borđ.
Ibi . x . ač p̃ti . T.R.E. ual . xx . fol . m̃ x . fol . *BLIDEVORDE*.

⅏ In *STARTORP*. ħɓ Suain . ɪx . bou træ ad glđ . Ťra . ɪɪ.
cař . Ibi Gifleɓt ħ̃ . ɪ . cař . 7 xɪɪ . uiłł 7 ɪɪɪɪ . borđ hɴtes
ɪɪɪɪ . cař 7 dĩɱ . 7 ɪ . molin . v . foliđ . 7 ʟx . ač p̃ti . T.R.E.
ual . ʟx . fol . m̃ fimilit.

.XIX. TERRA GOISFRIDI DE WIRCE.

⅏ In *LANDEFORDE*. ħɓ Leurie . ɪɪ . cař træ 7 ɪɪɪ . bou 7 v.
partẽ . ɪ . bou ad glđ . Ťra . vɪɪɪ . cař . Ibi Rannulfus
ħõ Goisfridi de Wirce ħ̃ . ɪɪ . cař . 7 dimiđ cař 7 xvɪ . foch . 7 xvɪɪ.
uiłł . 7 ɪɪɪɪ . borđ hɴtes . vɪɪ . cař . Ibi pɓr 7 æccła . 7 ɪɪ.
molin xɪɪ . folidoɀ . 7 ɪ . pifcaria . 7 c . ač p̃ti . T.R.E.
ual . ɪɪɪɪ . liɓ . m̃ fimilit 7 x . fol plus.

291 b

.XX. TERRA ILBERTI DE LACI.

⅏ In *SIBETORP* ħɓ Pileuuin . ɪɪ . bou træ 7 dĩɱ ad glđ.
Ťra . ɪ . cař . Modo Ilɓt de Laci ħ̃ . Arnegri de eo tenet.

[LYTHE Wapentake]

4 M. In KELHAM Aelfric had 2 b. of land taxable. Land for 6 oxen.
1 Freeman and 1 smallholder with ½ plough.
Meadow, 6 acres; underwood 8 furlongs long and 14 virgates wide.
Value before 1066, 16s; now 3s.

5 M. In WINKBURN Swein had 12 b. of land taxable. Land for 3 ploughs.
Gilbert has 2 ploughs in lordship and
15 Freemen with 4 b. of land; 7 villagers and 5
smallholders who have 7 ploughs.
A church; meadow, 16 acres; woodland pasture 1 league long
and ½ league wide.
Value before 1066, 100s; now 60s.
5 thanes held 2 b. of this land. One of them was the
senior of the others. It did not belong to Swein.

[THURGARTON Wapentake]

6 M. In *ALWOLDESTORP* Athelstan had 4 b. of land taxable.
Land for 1 plough. Gilbert has 1 plough in lordship and
4 smallholders.
Meadow, 10 acres.
Value before 1066, 20s; now 10s. BLIDWORTH Hundred.

7 M. In STAYTHORPE Swein had 9 b. of land taxable. Land for 2 ploughs.
Gilbert has 1 plough and
12 villagers and 4 smallholders who have 4½ ploughs.
1 mill, 5s; meadow, 60 acres.
Value before 1066, 60s; now the same.

19   THE LAND OF GEOFFREY OF LA GUERCHE

[NEWARK Wapentake]

1 M. In LANGFORD Leofric had 2 c. of land and 3 b. and the
fifth part of 1 b. taxable. Land for 8 ploughs. Ranulf,
Geoffrey of La Guerche's man, has 2½ ploughs and
16 Freemen, 17 villagers and 4 smallholders who have 7 ploughs.
A priest and a church; 2 mills, 12s; 1 fishery; meadow,
100 acres.
Value before 1066 £4; now the same, and 10s more.

20   LAND OF ILBERT OF LACY   291 b

[NEWARK Wapentake]

1 M. In SIBTHORPE Pilwin had 2½ b. of land taxable. Land for 1 plough.
Now Ilbert of Lacy has it. Arngrim holds from him.
1 plough in lordship.

Ibi . i . car̃ in dñio . 7 iii . soch de dim̃ bou træ . 7 xvi . borđ.

hñtes . iii . car̃ . 7 iii . part̃ . i . mol . x . denar̃ . 7 x . aĉs p̃ti.

Quarta pars huj tre p̃tiñ ad æcclam̃ ejđ m̃ . Ibi pbr̃.

T.R.E. 7 m̃ . xxx . sot.

§ In Sceltun 7 Aluriton 7 Cheluintun 7 Toruentun . Soca

iii . bou træ ad gld̃ . Tra . i . car̃ . Ibi . vi . uitt 7 i . borđ.

hñt . ii . car̃ . 7 xxx . aĉs p̃ti.

m̃ In Stoches h̃b Turchil . v . bou træ ad gld̃ . Tra

ii . car̃ . Mainfriđ de Ilbto tenet . 7 ibi h̃t dim̃ car̃ . 7 iii.

soch 7 v . borđ . hñtes . i . car̃ 7 ii . bou arant . 7 lxii . aĉs p̃ti.

T.R.E. uat xx . sot . m̃ . xv.

In Elueſtune h̃t Ilbt . iii . mansuras . in q̃b₃ sun̄ . ii . soch.

7 i . borđ p̃tinent ad Stochas . Tra n̄ hñt.

Ilbt caluniat sup ep̃m . R . tra pbri.

7 in Stoches caluniat q̃rta parte uitt.

★ m̃ In Elvestvn . h̃b Goduin . vi . bou tre ad gld̃.

Tra . iḭi . car̃ . Arnegri de Ilbto tenet . 7 ibi h̃t . i . car̃.

7 iii . soch de . ii . bou tre . 7 i . uitt 7 v . borđ hñtes . ii . car̃.

Ibi . xxx . aĉ p̃ti . T.R.E. uat xl . sot . m̃ xxv . sot.

m̃ In Aslachetone . h̃b Leuing . i . bou træ ad gld̃ . Tra dim̃

car̃ . Vluric tenet de Ilbto . 7 ibi h̃t . ii . bou arant . 7 ii.

soch 7 i . borđ . hñtes dim̃ car̃ . 7 viii . aĉs p̃ti . T.R.E. uat

. ii . v . sot 7 iiii . den . m̃ similit.

m̃ In Crophille . h̃br Vluiet . ii . bou tre ad gld̃ . Tra . ii . car̃.

De hac tra fuit saisit Ilbt de Laci . sed q̃do Rog̃ pict

accepit tra . saisiuit istud m̃ sup Ilbt . Wapentac port̃

teſtim̃ Ilbt fuiſſe saisit . m̃ . ē in manu regis . p̃t tcia

parte 7 Tainu q̃ eſt cap̃ manerii quē tenet Ilbtus.

Ibi m̃ in dñio . i . car̃ . 7 iiii . soch hñtes ix . bou in car̃.

7 vi . aĉ p̃ti . T.R.E. uat xvi . sot . m̃ . x . sot.

3 Freemen with ½ b. of land; 16 smallholders who have
   3 ploughs.
The third part of 1 mill, 10d; meadow, 10 acres.
The fourth part of this land belongs to the church of this
   manor. A priest there.
[Value] before 1066 and now 30s.

2 S. In SHELTON, ALVERTON, KILVINGTON and THOROTON, jurisdiction. 3 b.
of land taxable. Land for 1 plough.
   6 villagers and 1 smallholder have 2 ploughs.
   Meadow, 30 acres.

3 M. In (East) STOKE Thorkell had 5 b. of land taxable. Land for 2 ploughs.
Manfred holds from Ilbert; he has ½ plough and
   3 Freemen and 5 smallholders who have 1 plough and 2
     ploughing oxen.
   Meadow, 64 acres.
Value before 1066, 20s; now 15[s].

4   In ELSTON Ilbert has 3 dwellings in which are 2 Freemen and 1
smallholder who belong to (East) Stoke. They have no land.
Ilbert claims the priest's land against Bishop Remigius,
and in (East) Stoke he claims the fourth part of the village.

5 M. In ELSTON Godwin had 6 b. of land taxable. Land for 3 ploughs.
Arngrim holds from Ilbert; he has 1 plough and
   3 Freemen with 2 b. of land; 1 villager and 5 smallholders
     who have 2 ploughs.
   Meadow, 30 acres.
Value before 1066, 40s; now 25s.

[BINGHAM Wapentake]

6 M. In ASLOCKTON Leofing had 1 b. of land taxable, with full jurisdiction.
Land for ½ plough. Wulfric holds from Ilbert. He has 2
ploughing oxen and
   2 Freemen and 1 smallholder who have ½ plough.
   Meadow, 8 acres.
Value before 1066, 5s 4d; now the same.

7 2 M. In CROPWELL (Butler) Wulfgeat and Godric had 4 b. of land
taxable. Land for 2 ploughs. Ilbert of Lacy was in possession of
this land, but when Roger of Poitou received (his) land he took
possession of this manor, against Ilbert. The Wapentake bears
witness that Ilbert was in possession. Now it is in the King's
hands, except for the third part, and a thane; which is the head
of the manor which Ilbert holds.
Now in lordship 1 plough and
   4 Freemen who have 9 oxen in a plough.
   Meadow, 6 acres.
Value before 1066, 16s; now 10s.

In *Echelinge* . iii . car̄ træ 7 dim̄ ad glđ . Turchil 7 Goduin

tenuer̄ p̄ . ii . Ꝏ . Tra . viii . car . In dn̄io s̄t . iii . car̄ . 7 iiii . ſochi

7 xxiii . uilli cū . i . borđ hn̄t . vi . car̄ . Ibi . cc ꞁ ac̄ p̄ti .

Olim . vi . liƀ . Modo ual . iiii . liƀ .

.XXI. TERRA BERENGERIJ DE TODENI.

In *Stoches* h̄b Sbern croc . ii . bou træ 7 dim̄

ad glđ . Tra . i . car̄ . Berenger de Todeni h̄t . Ra

dulf h̄ō ej tenet ꞉ Ibi h̄t ꞉ i . car̄ . 7 ii . uilł 7 iii . borđ .

arantes . ii . boƀ . Ibi xl . ac̄ p̄ti . T.R.E. ual . xii .

ſol . m̄ . x . ſol .

In *Sirestvn* . h̄b Sbern croc . ii . bou træ 7 dim̄

ad glđ . Tra . i . car̄ . Goduin de Bereng tenet . 7 ibi h̄t

. i . car̄ . 7 i . ſoch 7 ii ꞉ uilł cū dim̄ car̄ ꞉ Ibi . x . ac̄ p̄ti .

T.R.E. ual . xxx . ſol . m̄ xx . ſol .

In Brodeholm h̄br Turgot 7 Halden . v . bou t̄re

ad glđ . Tra . ii . car̄ . Waſta . ē ꞉ Modo hn̄t Berenger

de todeni . 7 Wilłs de p̄ci . Tra jacet ad Neuuerce .

ſed op̄ uillanoꝝ p̄tin ad Saxebi in Lincoleſcira .

Ibi . xxx . ac̄ p̄ti . Silua past . i . q̄ꝗ lḡ . 7 altera lat ꞉

.XXII. TERRA HVGONIS FILIJ BALD .

In *Chelvingtvne* 7 Aluriton . h̄b . Colegrim . iii .

bou t̄re ad glđ . Tra . ii . car̄ . Hugo fili Baldrici h̄t .

Anſger tenet . 7 ibi h̄t . ii . car̄ . 7 i . ſoch de dim̄ bou t̄re .

7 iii . uilł 7 ii . borđ hn̄tes . ii . car̄ . 7 xx . ac̄s p̄ti . T.R.E.

ual . xxx . ſol . m̄ . xx . ſol .

In *Crchenai* . h̄b Suen . ii . car̄ træ ad glđ . Tra . iiii . car̄ .

Ricard tenet de Hugone . 7 ibi h̄t . ii . car̄ in dn̄io . 7 iii .

ſoch de . ii . bou t̄re . 7 x . uilł 7 v . borđ . hn̄tes . iii . car̄ .

Ibi p̄br 7 æccła . 7 ii . mol viii . ſolidoꝝ . Silua past

iiii . q̄ꝗ lḡ . 7 iiii . q̄ꝗ lat . T.R.E. 7 m̄ ual . xxx . ſol .

8   In HICKLING 3½ c. of land taxable. Thorkell and Godwin
held it as two manors. Land for 8 ploughs. In lordship 3 ploughs.
4 Freemen and 23 villagers with 1 smallholder have 6 ploughs.
Meadow, 200 acres.
Formerly £6; value now £4.

21   LAND OF BERENGAR OF TOSNY   291 c

[NEWARK Wapentake]

1 M. In (East) STOKE Esbern Crook had 2½ b. of land taxable.
Land for 1 plough. Berengar of Tosny has it. Ralph, his man,
holds it. He has 1 plough and
2 villagers and 3 smallholders who plough with 2 oxen.
Meadow, 40 acres.
Value before 1066, 12s; now 10s.

2 M. In SYERSTON Esbern Crook had 2½ b. of land taxable. Land
for 1 plough. Godwin holds from Berengar. He has 1 plough and
1 Freeman and 2 villagers with ½ plough.
Meadow, 10 acres.
Value before 1066, 30s; now 20s.

3   In BROADHOLME Thorgot and Haldane had 5 b. of land taxable.
Land for 2 ploughs. Waste. Now Berengar of Tosny and William
of Percy have it. The land lies with Newark, but the villagers'
work belongs to Saxilby in Lincolnshire.
Meadow, 30 acres; woodland pasture 1 furlong long and
another wide.

22   LAND OF HUGH SON OF BALDRIC

[NEWARK Wapentake]

1 M. In KILVINGTON and ALVERTON Colgrim had 3 b. of land taxable.
Land for 2 ploughs. Hugh son of Baldric has it.
Anser holds from him. He has 2 ploughs and
1 Freeman with ½ b. of land; 3 villagers and 2
smallholders who have 2 ploughs.
Meadow, 20 acres.
Value before 1066, 30s; now 20s.

[BASSETLAW Wapentake]

2 M. In CUCKNEY Swein had 2 c. of land taxable. Land for 4 ploughs.
Richard holds from Hugh. He has 2 ploughs in lordship and
3 Freemen with 2 b. of land; 10 villagers and 5 smallholders
who have 3 ploughs.
A priest and a church; 2 mills, 8s; woodland pasture 4
furlongs long and 4 furlongs wide.
Value before 1066 and now 30s.

.XXIII. ## TERRA HVGON DE GRENTEMAISN.

In *EDWOLTVN* . ħƀ Gode . vı . bou træ ad glđ . Tra . ıı . car
7 dim . Ibi Hugo de grentemaifnil ħⵏ in đnio . ıı . car
7 vı . foch 7 ı . uilł hntes . ı . car 7 dim . 7 xx . acs pti.
T.R.E. ual . x . . fol . m̃ . xx . fol . Ad Stoctun jacet.

In *TVRMODESTVN* . ı . bou 7 dim ad glđ . Tra . ı . car . Ibi . ıı . fochii 7 ıı . borđ
cũ . ıı . car . 7 ııı . ac pti . In *SANDIRIACA* iacet.

291 d
.XXII. ## TERRA HENRICI DE FEREIRES.

In *LECCHE* . ħƀ Siuuard . ıı . car træ ad glđ . Tra
vı . car . Ibi Henric de ferrariis ħⵏ in đnio . ıııı.
car . 7 xvı . foch . 7 xvı . uilł hntes xvıı . car.
Ibi pƀr 7 æccła . 7 ı . molin . ıı . folid . 7 L . ac pti . 7 filuæ
min . ıı . q̃ɀ lg . 7 ı . lat . T.R.E. ual . vı . liƀ . m̃ . vıı . liƀ.
Ad hoc Man adjacet BEREW Lecche . ubi funt
ıı . car tre ad glđ . Ħ iacet in pluntre hunđ.

In *BONNITON* . ħƀ Siuuard . ı . bou træ 7 dim ad glđ.
Tra . ıııı . bou . Ibi . ııı . uilł hnⵏ . ı . car 7 dim . 7 ııı . acs
pti . T.R.E. ual . vı . fol . m̃ fimilit.

In Wilgebi . ı . bou træ ad glđ . Tra . ııı . bou . SOCA
in Badeleie . Wafta . ẽ . Ibi . vı . acs pti.

.XXV. ## ROBERTI MALET.

In *BRADEMERE* . ħƀ Azor . xıı . bou træ ad glđ.
Tra . ııı . car . Ibi Rotƀr malet in đnio ħⵏ . ııı . car.
7 xvı . uilł 7 vııı . borđ . hntes . v . car . T.R.E. 7 m̃
ual . Lx . folid.

Ṣ In Rodintone . ı . bou tre . 7 ııı . pars . ı . bou ad glđ . Tra
ıı . bou . SOCA in Brademere.

23   # LAND OF HUGH OF GRANDMESNIL

[RUSHCLIFFE Wapentake]

1 In EDWALTON Countess Gytha had 6 b. of land taxable. Land
for 2½ ploughs. Hugh of Grandmesnil has in lordship 2 ploughs and
6 Freemen and 1 villager who have 1½ ploughs.
Meadow, 20 acres.
Value before 1066, 10s; now 20s.
It lies with Stockerston   (in Leicestershire).

2 In THRUMPTON 1½ b. taxable. Land for 1 plough.
2 Freemen and 2 smallholders with 2 ploughs.
Meadow, 3 acres.
It lies in Sandiacre (lands) (in Derbyshire).

24   # LAND OF HENRY OF FERRERS   291 d

[RUSHCLIFFE Wapentake]

1 M. In LEAKE Siward had 2 c. of land taxable. Land for 6 ploughs.
Henry of Ferrers has in lordship 4 ploughs and
16 Freemen and 16 villagers who have 17 ploughs.
A priest and a church; 1 mill, 2s; meadow, 50 acres;
underwood 2 furlongs long and 1 wide.
Value before 1066 £6; now £7.
To this manor is attached the outlier of Leake, where there
are 2 c. of land taxable. It lies in Plumtree Hundred.

2 In (Sutton) BONINGTON Siward had 1½ b. of land taxable.
Land for 4 oxen.
3 villagers have 1½ ploughs.
Meadow, 3 acres.
Value before 1066, 6s; now the same.

3 In WILLOUGHBY (-on-the-Wolds) 1 b. of land taxable. Land
for 3 oxen. Jurisdiction in Bathley. Waste. Meadow, 6 acres.

25   # [LAND] OF ROBERT MALET

[RUSHCLIFFE Wapentake]

1 M. In BRADMORE Azor had 12 b. of land taxable. Land for 3 ploughs.
Robert Malet has in lordship 3 ploughs and
16 villagers and 8 smallholders who have 5 ploughs.
Value before 1066 and now 60s.

2 S. In RUDDINGTON 1 b. of land and the third part of 1 b. taxable.
Land for 2 oxen. Jurisdiction in Bradmore.

.XXVI. DVRANDI MALET.

ⱳ In OVETORP . ħɓ Rolf dim̄ car̄ træ ad glđ . Tra
Tra . iii . car̄ . Ibi Durand malet ħ̄ . i . car̄ . 7 iiii .
focħ 7 iii . uiłł hn̄tes . ii . car̄ . Ibi . xii . ac̄ p̄ti . T.R.E .
ual . xxx . fol . m̄ xx . fol .

292 a

XXVII TERRA OSBERNI FILIJ RICARDI.

ⱳ In GRENEBI ħɓ Algar . iii . car̄ træ ad glđ .
Tra . x . car̄ . Ofɓn fili Ricardi m̄ ħ̄ . Roɓt de olgi
de eo
tenet . 7 ibi ħ̄ . iiii . car̄ . 7 xx . ii . focħ 7 xiiii . uiłł . 7 viii .
borđ . hn̄tes . x . car̄ . Ibi p̄ɓr 7 æccła . 7 ii . molin̄ . x .
folidoȥ . 7 x . ac̄ p̄ti . T.R.E . ual viii . liɓ . m̄ xv . liɓ .
§ In Wiuretone . iii . bou træ 7 dim̄ ad glđ . Tra . i . car̄ .
Ibi . vii . focħ hn̄t . ii . car̄ . Soca in Coletone .
B In Saltreford . vi . bou træ ad glđ .
Wafta . ē . BEREW in Coletone . Silua paft . i . lev lḡ .
7 iiii . q̄ȥ lat̄ .

XXVIII ROBERTI FILII WILLI.

ⱳ In STANFORD ħɓ Ælfag . x . bou træ ad glđ . Tra
iiii . car̄ . Ibi Roɓt filius Wiłłi ħ̄ . i . car̄ . 7 iiii . focħ
7 vii . uiłł 7 ii . borđ . hn̄tes . vii . car̄ . Ibi fed molend̄
7 xv . ac̄ p̄ti . T.R.E . ual . xl . fol . SOCA IBIDĒ .
§ In Stantone . i . bou træ ad glđ . Tra . iiii . bou . Ibi . ii .
LEGHE
focħ hn̄t . i . car̄ . Ad Stanford ptin̄ .
ⱳ In BROCHELESTOV . ħɓ Godric . iii . bou træ ad glđ .
Tra . iii . bou . Ibi Roɓt ħ̄ . i . car̄ . 7 i . uiłł . Silua min̄
i . q̄ȥ lḡ . 7 i . lat̄ . T.R.E . ual xvi . fol . m̄ . viii . fol .

26 [LAND] OF DURAND MALET

[BINGHAM Wapentake]

1 M. In OWTHORPE Rolf had ½ c. of land taxable. Land for 3 ploughs.
Durand.Malet has 1 plough and
4 Freemen and 3 villagers who have 2 ploughs.
Meadow, 12 acres.
Value before 1066, 30s; now 20s.

27 LAND OF OSBERN SON OF RICHARD

292 a

[BINGHAM Wapentake]

1 M. In GRANBY Earl Algar had 3 c. of land taxable. Land for 10 ploughs.
Osbern son of Richard has it now. Robert d'Oilly holds from
him. He has 4 ploughs and
22 Freemen, 14 villagers and 8 smallholders who have 10 ploughs.
A priest and a church; 2 mills, 10s; meadow, 10 acres.
Value before 1066 £8; now £15.
2 S. In WIVERTON 3½ b. of land taxable. Land for 1 plough.
7 Freemen have 2 ploughs.
Jurisdiction in Colston (Bassett).
3 B. In SALTERFORD 6 b. of land taxable. Waste. An outlier
in Colston (Bassett).
Woodland pasture 1 league long and 4 furlongs wide.

28 [LAND] OF ROBERT SON OF WILLIAM

[RUSHCLIFFE Wapentake]

1 M. In STANFORD (-on-Soar) Alfheah had 10 b. of land taxable.
Land for 4 ploughs. Robert son of William has 1 plough and
4 Freemen, 7 villagers and 2 smallholders who have 7 ploughs.
A mill site; meadow, 15 acres.
Value before 1066, 40s.
Also Jurisdiction there.
2 S. In *STANTON*, LEAKE 1 b. of land taxable. Land for 4 oxen.
2 Freemen have 1 plough.
It belongs to Stanford.

[BROXTOW Wapentake]

3 M. In BROXTOW Godric had 3 b. of land taxable. Land for 3 oxen.
Robert has 1 plough and
1 villager.
Underwood 1 furlong long and 1 wide.
Value before 1066, 16s; now 8s.

WILLELMI HOSTIARIJ.

In *BRVNCOTE*. ħƀr Vlchel Godric Aluric 7 Leuric
XII. bou tre ad glđ. Tra. XII. boū. Ibi Wilłs hosti
arius ħ. I. car. 7 IIII. uilł 7 I. borđ. hñtes. III. car
7 dim. T.R.E. uał. LX. soł. m̄. XX.

In *TORWALLE*. ħƀ Vctebrand. I. car træ 7 dim ad
glđ. Tra XII. boū. Ibi Wilłs hostiari ħ. I. car.
7 VI. uilł. cū. IIII. car. Ibi pƀr 7 æccła dimid. 7 VI. ac̄
p̄ti. T.R.E. uał. C. soł. m̄ XX. soł.

XXX. TERRA TAINORVM.

BERNESEDELAWE. *WAPENT*.

In *OSBERNESTVNE.*
ORMESTVNE. ħƀr Eluuine 7 Vluiet
. I. car træ ad glđ. Tra. IIII. car. Modo Suan
7 Vluiet tenex̄ de rege. 7 Ibi hñt. V. soch hñtes
IIII. car. 7 æcctam. 7 XX. ac̄s p̄ti. Silua past. VI. q̄ɀ
lḡ. 7 III. lat. T.R.E. uał. LX. soł. m̄. X. soł.

In *CARLENTVNE* ħƀ Vlchel. III. bou træ ad glđ.
Tra. VI. boū. Alden ħ de rege. Ibi. II. borđ. hñt
III. bou arant. 7 X. ac̄ p̄ti. Silua past. II. q̄ɀ lḡ. 7 dim
lat. T.R.E. uał X. soł. m̄. V. soł 7 IIII. den.

★ **In** *CHENAPETORP*. ten Alden de rege. II. bou
træ ad glđ. Tra. VI. bou. Ibi ħ. I. car. 7 IIII. borđ.
hñtes. I. bouē in car. 7 IIII. ac̄s p̄ti. Silua pastił
II. q̄ɀ lḡ. 7 I. lat. T.R.E. 7 m̄ uał X. soł 7 VIII. den.

In *CRVNWELLE*. tenet Alden de rege. II. car træ
7 VI. bou ad glđ. Tra. IIII. car. Ibi ħ. I. car. 7 V. soch
de. I. car huj træ. 7 VIII. uilł 7 II. borđ. hñtes. IIII. car
7 dim. Ibi æccła 7 I. molin̄. XII. den. 7 I. piscar.
P̄ti. VI. q̄ɀ lḡ. 7 III. lat. T.R.E. uał. LX. soł. m̄. XL.

In *LABELEIA*. ħƀ Vlchet. II. car træ 7 II. bou ad
glđ. Tra. III. car. Alden tenet de rege. 7 ibi ħ. I. car.

29 [LAND] OF WILLIAM THE USHER

[BROXTOW Wapentake]

1 4 M. In BRAMCOTE Ulfkell, Godric, Aelfric and Leofric had 12 b. of land
taxable. Land for 12 oxen. William the Usher has 1 plough and
4 villagers and 1 smallholder who have 3½ ploughs.
Value before 1066, 60s; now 20[s].

2 M. In TROWELL Uhtbrand had 1½ c. of land taxable. Land for 12 oxen.
William the Usher has one plough and
6 villagers with 4 ploughs.
A priest and half a church; meadow, 6 acres.
Value before 1066, 100s; now 20s.

Blank column   292 b

30 LAND OF THE [KING'S] THANES   292 c

BASSETLAW Wapentake

1 2 M. In OSBERTON Alwin and Wulfgeat had 1 c. of land taxable.
Land for 4 ploughs. Now Swein and Wulfgeat hold from the King.
They have
5 Freemen who have 4 ploughs.
A church; meadow, 20 acres; woodland pasture 6 furlongs
long and 3 wide.
Value before 1066, 60s; now 10s.

[LYTHE Wapentake]

2 M. In CARLTON(-on-Trent) Ulfkell had 3 b. of land taxable.
Land for 6 oxen. Haldane has it from the King.
2 smallholders have 3 ploughing oxen.
Meadow, 10 acres; woodland pasture 2 furlongs long and ½ wide.
Value before 1066, 10s; now 5s 4d.

3 M. In KNAPTHORPE Haldane holds from the King 2 b. of land taxable.
Land for 6 oxen. He has 1 plough and
4 smallholders who have 1 ox in a plough.
Meadow, 4 acres; woodland pasture 2 furlongs long and 1 wide.
r   Value before 1066 and now 10s 8d.

4 M. In CROMWELL Haldane holds from the King 2 c. of land and 6 b.
taxable. Land for 4 ploughs. He has 1 plough and
5 Freemen with 1 c. of this land; 8 villagers and 2 smallholders
who have 4½ ploughs.
A church; 1 mill, 12d; 1 fishery; meadow, 6 furlongs long
and 3 wide.
Value before 1066, 60s; now 40[s].

[THURGARTON Wapentake]

5 M. In LAMBLEY Ulfketel had 2 c. of land and 2 b. taxable.
Land for 3 ploughs. Haldane holds from the King and
has 1 plough and

7 xx . uiłł 7 iii . borđ hñtes . iiii . car . 7 iii . ſoch cū . i . car. ⟨de dīm car tre.⟩

Ibi . ii . moł . xx . ſoliđ . 7 xx . ac̄ p̃ti . Silua paſtił

i . lev łḡ . 7 iiii . q̃ʒ łat . T.R.E . 7 m̃ uał . lx . ſoł.

ⓂIn VDEBVRG . h̃ƀ Vlchel . iii . bou træ ad glđ . Tra . i . car.

Ibi h̃t Aldene . iii . uiłł . hñtes dim car . T.R.E . 7 m̃

uał v . ſoł 7 iiii . den.

ⓂIn NORDMVSCHA . h̃ƀ Siuuard . iii . bou træ ad glđ.

Tra . iii . car . Ibi iſđ h̃t Siuuard . ii . borđ . 7 i . moł . x . ſoł.

7 xii . ac̄ p̃ti . T.R.E . uał . xl . ſoł . m̃ . xvi . ſoł.

ⓂIn COLVI . Aluric 7 Buge . v . bou træ ad glđ . Tra . i . car.

Ip̃ſi teneʒ de rege . 7 ibi hñt . ii . car . 7 i . ſoch de . i . bou.

7 vi . uiłł 7 i . borđ . cū . ii . car . Ibi . xxxi . ac̄ p̃ti . 7 viii.

ac̄s ſiluæ min . T.R.E . uał . xxv . ſoł . 7 iiii . den.

ⓂIn VDEBVRG . h̃ƀ Vlchel . iii . bou træ ad glđ . Tra . ii.

car . Idē ten de rege . 7 ibi h̃t . i . car . 7 iii . uiłł 7 i . borđ.

cū . i . car 7 dim . 7 i . moliñ . xx . ſoliđ . 7 i . uirg p̃ti . Silua

paſt . ii . lev łḡ . 7 v . q̃ʒ łat . T.R.E . xx . m̃ xxx . ſoł.

ⓂIn NORMENTVN . h̃ƀ Arnui . v . bou tre ad glđ . Tra

★ ii . car . Waſta . c̃.

ⓂIn ODESTORP . h̃ƀ Vlmer . ii . bou tre 7 dim ad glđ . Tra

. i . car . Ibi in dñio . i . car . 7 dim moł . iiii . ſoliđ . 7 x . ac̄

p̃ti . T.R.E . uał xl . ſoł . m̃ . iiii . ſoł.

In CALVRETONE Aluric . iii . bou træ ad glđ . Tra . i . car . Ibi . ii . ſochi

7 iiii . uiłłi hñt . ii . car . Olī . xvi . ſoł . m̃ uał . x . ſoliđ . Idē tenet.

292 d

RISECLIVE WAPENTAP

ⓂIn NORMANTVN . h̃ƀ Oſgod . iii . bou tre 7 dim

20 villagers and 3 smallholders who have 4 ploughs;
3 Freemen with ½ c. of land and 1 plough.
2 mills, 20s; meadow, 20 acres; woodland pasture 1 league
long and 4 furlongs wide.
Value before 1066 and now 60s.

6 M. In WOODBOROUGH Ulfkell had 3 b. of land taxable.
Land for 1 plough. Haldane has
3 villagers who have ½ plough.
Value before 1066 and now 5s 4d.
[LYTHE Wapentake]

7 M. In NORTH MUSKHAM Siward had 3 b. of land taxable.
Land for 3 ploughs. Siward also has
2 smallholders.
1 mill, 10s; meadow, 12 acres.
Value before 1066, 40s; now 16s.
[THURGARTON Wapentake]

8 M. In COLWICK Aelfric, 3, and Bugg, 2, [had] 5 b. of land taxable.
Land for 1 plough. They hold it themselves from the King.
They have 2 ploughs and
1 Freeman with 1 b; 6 villagers and 1 smallholder with 2 ploughs.
Meadow, 31 acres; underwood, 8 acres.
Value before 1066, 25s 4d.

9 M. In WOODBOROUGH Ulfkell had 3 b. of land taxable. Land for 2 ploughs.
He also holds from the King. He has 1 plough and
3 villagers and 1 smallholder with 1½ ploughs.
1 mill, 20s; meadow, 1 virgate; woodland pasture 2 leagues
long and 5 furlongs wide.
[Value] before 1066, 20[s]; now 30s.

10 In WOODBOROUGH Aelfric has 5 b. taxable. Land for 2 ploughs,
which are there, with
3 villagers and 1 smallholder.
1 mill, 20s.
He also held it as a manor before 1066.

11 M. In NORMANTON (by Southwell) Ernwy the priest had 5 b. of
land taxable. Land for 2 ploughs. Waste.

12 M. In 'ODSTHORPE' Wulfmer had 2½ b. of land taxable.
Land for 1 plough. In lordship 1 plough.
½ mill, 4s; meadow, 10 acres.
Value before 1066, 40s; now 4s.

13 In CALVERTON Aelfric [had] 3 b. of land taxable. Land for 1 plough.
2 Freemen and 4 villagers have 2 ploughs.
Formerly 16s; value now 10s.
He also holds it (now).
RUSHCLIFFE Wapentake   292 d

14 M. In NORMANTON (-on-Soar) Osgot had 3½b. of land taxable.

ad glđ . Tra . I . car . Ibi . II . uiłł 7 II . ač p̄ti . T.R.E. xx . s.

B̃ In Būnitone . I . bou tre 7 dim ad glđ.　　　　Ḟ m̃ vı . soł.

Tra dim car . Ad Norm̃tun ptiñ . Ibi . v . uiłł cū . I .

car . 7 III . ač p̄ti . T.R.E. 7 m̃ . vı . soł.

M̃ In ead Norm̃tun . Rauen . II . bou træ ad glđ.

M̃ In SVTONE . h̃b Leuuord . III . bou træ ad glđ.

Siuuard teñ de rege.

M̃ IBIDĒ Coleman . I . bou træ 7 dim ad glđ.

M̃ In CHINESTAN . h̃b Ælgar . III . bou træ ad glđ.

Tra . II . car . Sauuin teñ de rege . 7 ibi h̃t . II . uiłł .

cū . I . car . 7 sed molini . 7 x . ač p̄ti . T.R.E. xx . soł.

M̃ In RADECLIVE . h̃b Osgod . x . bou tre　　Ḟ m̃ x . soł

7 IIII . part . I . bou ad glđ . Tra . vı . car . Sauuin

de rege teñ . 7 ibi h̃t . II . car . 7 lx . uiłł . 7 III . borđ .

h̃ntes . II . car . Ibi p̄br 7 æccła . 7 I . moliñ x . soł .

7 vı . ač p̄ti . T.R.E. uał . c . soł . m̃ lx . soł

S̃ In Chineſtan . I . car træ ad glđ . Tra . II . car . Ibi . vIII .

soch 7 III . uiłł h̃nt . III . car .

M̃ IBIDĒ h̃b Vlchet . I . bou træ 7 dim ad glđ . Tra . I .

car . Ibi Godric m̃ ten . f̷ hões patriæ nesciuɴ p̷ quē .

quom̃ . Ibi . I . uiłł . 7 vı . ač p̄ti . T.R.E. uał xx . soł.

M̃ In BARTONE . h̃b Ælgar . I . bou tre 7 dim　Ḟ m̃ . III . soł.

7 IIII . partē . I . bou ad glđ . Tra . I . car . Ibi Sauuin h̃t

I . uiłłs . 7 II . borđ cū . III . bob arant . 7 III . ač p̄ti . T.R.E.

uał . x . soł . m̃ . III . soł.

M̃ In GATHĀ . h̃b Godric . III . bou tre 7 dim . 7 I . ač

ad glđ . Tra . I . car . Waſta . ē . Sauuin h̃t . Ibi . xII . ač

p̄ti . T.R.E. uał . x . soł . m̃ . II . soł.

In CLIFTVN . h̃t Vlchel de rege . I . bou træ ad glđ .

Ibi h̃t . I . uiłł cū . II . bob arant . 7 I . ač p̄ti.

Land for 1 plough.
   2 villagers.
   Meadow, 2 acres.
  [Value] before 1066, 20s; now 6s.

5   B.   In (Sutton) BONINGTON 1½ b. of land taxable. Land for ½ plough. It belongs to Normanton.
   5 villagers with 1 plough.
   Meadow, 3 acres.
  [Value] before 1066 and now 6s.

6   M.   Also in NORMANTON (-on-Soar) Raven, 2 b. of land taxable.

7   M.   In SUTTON (Bonington) Leofward had 3 b. of land taxable. Siward holds from the King.

8   M.   There also Colman, 1½ b. of land taxable.

9   M.   In KINGSTON (-on-Soar) Algar had 3 b. of land taxable. Land for 2 ploughs. Saewin holds from the King. He has
   2 villagers with 1 plough.
   A mill-site; meadow, 10 acres.
  [Value] before 1066, 20s; now 10s.

0   M.   In RATCLIFFE (-on-Soar) Osgot had 10 b. of land and the fourth part (?) of 1 b. taxable. Land for 6 ploughs. Saewin holds from the King. He has 2 ploughs and
   9 villagers and 3 smallholders who have 2 ploughs.
   A priest and a church; 1 mill, 10s; meadow, 6 acres.
  Value before 1066, 100s; now 60s.

1   S.   In KINGSTON (-on-Soar) 1 c. of land taxable. Land for 2 ploughs.
   8 Freemen and 3 villagers have 3 ploughs.

2   M.   There also Ulfketel had 1½ b. of land taxable. Land for 1 plough. Godric now holds, but the local men do not know through whom or how.
   1 villager.
   Meadow, 6 acres.
  Value before 1066, 20s; now 3s.

3   M.   In BARTON (-in-Fabis) Algar had 1½ b. of land and the fourth part of 1 b. taxable. Land for 1 plough. Saewin has
   1 villager and 2 smallholders with 3 ploughing oxen.
   Meadow, 3 acres.
  Value before 1066, 10s; now 3s.

4   M.   In GOTHAM Godric had 3½ b. of land and 1 acre taxable. Land for 1 plough. Waste. Saewin has it.
   Meadow, 12 acres.
  Value before 1066, 10s; now 2s.

25   In CLIFTON Ulfkell has from the King 1 b. of land taxable. He has
   1 villager with 2 ploughing oxen.
   Meadow, 1 acre.

§ In Willebi Algar . II . bou træ 7 dim ad glđ . Soca ^{in Torp.}

Ibi . II . foch cū . III . car . 7 III . ač p̃ti.

Ꝝ In *CHIRCHEBI* . h̃b Aluric . II . bou træ ad glđ . Tra

II . bou . Idē tẽ de rege . 7 ibi h̃t . I . car̃ . T.R.E . v . fot.

Ꝝ In Bafeford . h̃b Aluric . I . bou ad glđ . Wafta . ē ^{7 Efcul . I . bou . wafta ē} ⌐m̃ . II . fot.

In *PAPLEVVIC* . h̃br Aluric 7 Alfa 7 Ælric . II . car̃

træ 7 III . bou ad glđ . Wafta funt H̃ . Ibi Silua paſt

I . lev lg̃ . 7 dim lat . T.R.E . uat . xx . fot.

Ꝝ In *TORWALLE* h̃b Vlchel dim car træ ad glđ

Tra . IIII . bou . Wafta . ē . Alden h̃t . Ibi . II . ač p̃ti.

T.R.E . x . fot uat m̃ . v . folid 7 IIII . den.

Ꝝ In *STADELIE* ^{SRAELIE} . h̃b Vlchel . III . bou træ ad glđ.

293 a

Tra . III . bou . Nc̄ Vlfi 7 Goduin tẽ de rege . 7 hñt

ibi . IIII . uilt 7 I . borđ .   T.R.E . uat . II . fot . m̃ . III . S.

Ꝝ In *NVTEHALE* . h̃b Afchil . III . bou træ 7 dim ad

glđ . Tra . III . bou 7 dim . Aluric tẽ de rege . 7 ibi h̃t

VI . uilt cū . II . car̃ . T.R.E . uat . x . fot . m̃ vi . fot 7 viii ^{to} . den.

Ꝝ In *ELDESVORDE* h̃b Vlchete dim car træ ad glđ.

Aldene tenet.

Ꝝ In *BASEFORD* h̃b Aluric IIII . bou tre ad glđ . Tra.

dim car . Idē tẽ de rege . 7 ibi h̃t . I . uillañ cū . I . car̃.

7 I . ač p̃ti . 7 II . molin . xvi . folid . 7 Siluæ min . I . ač.

T.R.E . 7 m̃ uat . xx . folid.

Ꝝ In *WILGEBI* . h̃b Sbern ^{7 Vlmer} . III . bou træ ad glđ . Tra . III . bou.

Eluuin de rege tẽ . Wafta . ē . Ibi . v . ač p̃ti . T.R.E . uat ^{7 Ernuin 9} ^{7 v . borđ.}

x . fot . 7 IIII . den . m̃ . II . fot . *BINGAMESHOV WAP.*

Ꝝ In *LABECOTES* . h̃b Vlchel . v . bou træ 7 III . parte ^{ciam}

uni bou ad glđ . Aldene de rege tẽ . 7 h̃t ibi . I . car̃

in dñio . 7 vi . ač s p̃ti . T.R.E . uat x . fot . m̃ . v . fot.

Ꝝ In *ASLACHESTONE* . h̃b Leuric . I . bou tre ad glđ.

Tra . IIII . bou . Vluric tẽ de rege . 7 ibi h̃t . II . bou in car̃.

26 S. In WILLOUGHBY (-on-the-Wolds) Algar, 2½ b. of land taxable.
Jurisdiction in Thorpe (-in-the-Glebe).
    2 Freemen with 3 ploughs.
    Meadow, 3 acres.
[BROXTOW Wapentake]

27 M. In KIRKBY (-in-Ashfield) Aelfric had 2 b. of land taxable.
Land for 2 oxen. He also holds from the King. He has 1 plough.
[Value] before 1066, 5s; now 2s.

28 2 In BASFORD Aelfric had 1 b. taxable. Waste. Aswulf 1 b. Waste.
29 M. In PAPPLEWICK Aelfric, Alfsi and Alric had 2 c. of land and 3 b.
taxable. Waste.
    Woodland pasture 1 league long and ½ wide.
    Value before 1066, 20s.

30 M. In TROWELL Ulfkell had ½ c. of land taxable. Land for 4 oxen.
Waste. Haldane has it.
    Meadow, 2 acres.
    Value before 1066, 10s; now 6s 8d.

31 M. In STRELLEY Ulfkell had 3 b. of land taxable. Land for 3 oxen.
Now Wulfsi and Godwin hold from the King. They have   293 a
    4 villagers and 1 smallholder.
    Value before 1066, 4s; now 3s.

32 M. In NUTHALL Askell had 3½ b. of land taxable. Land for 3½ oxen.
Aelfric holds from the King. He has
    6 villagers with 2 ploughs.
    Value before 1066, 10s; now 6s 8d.

33 M. In AWSWORTH Ulfketel had ½ c. of land taxable. Haldane holds it.
34 M. In BASFORD Aelfric had 4 b. of land taxable. Land for ½ plough.
He also holds from the King. He has
    1 villager with 1 plough.
    Meadow, 1 acre; 2 mills, 16s; underwood, 1 acre.
    Value before 1066 and now 20s.

35 2 In WILLOUGHBY (-on-the-Wolds) Esbern and Wulfmer had 3 b. of
  M. land taxable. Land for 3 oxen. Alwin and Ernwin hold from
the King. Waste.
    5 smallholders.
    Meadow, 5 acres.
    Value before 1066, 10s 4d; now 4s.
BINGHAM Wapentake

36 M. In LAMCOTE Ulfkell had 5 b. of land and the third part of 1 b.
taxable. Haldane holds from the King. He has 1 plough in lordship.
    Meadow, 6 acres.
    Value before 1066, 10s; now 5s.

37 M. In ASLOCKTON Leofric had 1 b. of land taxable. Land for 4 oxen.
Wulfric holds from the King. He has 2 oxen in a plough and

7 ii.focħ 7 i.borđ cū dim̃ caŕ.Ibi.viii.ac̃ p̃ti.T.R.E
7 m̃.ual.v.fol 7 iiii.den.

Ⓜ In *CHINELTONE*.ħɓ Azor.i.bou træ ad glđ.Tra.iii.boū.
Nc̃ fili⁹ azor ten de.rege.7 ibi ħ̃.iii.uilł.iii.bob⁹ arant.
7 iii.ac̃s p̃ti.T.R.E.ual.x.fol.m̃.ii.fol 7.viii.den.

In *CLAVREBVRG* ħɓ Vlmer.i.bou tre 7 dim ad glđ
cū faca 7 foca fine aula.Tra.iii.bou.Idē de rege
tenet.7 ibi ħ̃.ii.uilł 7 iii.borđ.cū dim caŕ.7 iii.ac̃s
p̃ti.Silua paſt.vi.q̃ʒ lḡ.7 iii.lat.T.R.E.ual.iii.fol
m̃.ii.fol.   *NEWERCE WAP.*

Ⓜ In *SIRESTVNE*.ħɓ Turuert.ii.bou træ ad glđ.Tra
v.boū.Ibi.ii.uilł 7 i.borđ hn̄t.i.caŕ.7 v.ac̃s p̃ti.
T.R.E.ual x.fol.m̃.v.fol.

Ⓜ In *ELCHESLEIE*.ħɓ Afchil.iiii.bou træ ad glđ.Tra.ii.caŕ.
Ernuin ten de rege.Ibi.iiii.uilł hn̄t.i.caŕ 7 dim.T.R.E
ual.viii.fol.m̃.x.fol.In *NORTMORTVN*.iii.boū ad glđ.vaſt eſt.

Ⓜ In *MISNA*.ħɓ Cnut.i.bou tre 7 dim ad glđ.Tra.iii.boū.
Ernuin⁹ ħ̃ ibi.iiii.uilł cū dim caŕ.7 ii.focħ cū.i.caŕ.
7 piſcaŕ.iii.folid.Silua paſt.i.q̃ʒ lḡ.7 i.lat.Valet.viii
Ṣ Ibidē.iii.bou træ ad glđ.Soca de Chi|cheton.   Ƒfol.
Ibi.vi.uilłi hn̄t.iii.caŕ.   Ƙ Tra.vi.boū.

Ⓜ In *CALVN*.ħɓ Vlchel.i.bou træ 7 ii.part.i.bou ad glđ.
Ibi ħ̃ Aldene ii.uilł 7 ii.borđ cū.i.caŕ.7 vi.ac̃s p̃ti.
Silua min viii.q̃ʒ lḡ.7 viii.uirg lat.T.R.E.xx.fol.m̃.x.
Ⓜ In *MVSCHA* ħɓ Sortebrand vi.bou træ ad glđ.
293 b
Tra.i.caŕ 7 dim.Seric⁹ tenet de rege.7 ibi ħ̃.i.focħ
7 ii.borđ.cū.ii.bob⁹ in caŕ.7 xii.ac̃ p̃ri.Silua paſt
i.q̃ʒ lḡ.7 i.lat.T.R.E.ual.xvi.fol.m̃.v.fol.

2 Freemen and 1 smallholder with ½ plough.
Meadow, 8 acres.
Value before 1066 and now 5s 4d.

M. In KINOULTON Azor had 1 b. of land taxable. Land for 3 oxen.
Now Azor's son holds from the King. He has
3 villagers with 3 ploughing oxen.
Meadow, 3 acres.
Value before 1066, 10s; now 2s 8d.

[OSWALDBECK Wapentake]
In CLARBOROUGH Wulfmer had 1½ b. of land taxable, with full
jurisdiction, without a hall. Land for 3 oxen. He also holds
from the King. He has
2 villagers and 3 smallholders with ½ plough.
Meadow, 3 acres; woodland pasture 6 furlongs long and 3 wide.
Value before 1066, 3s; now 2s.

NEWARK Wapentake

M. In SYERSTON (which) is the King's, Thorferth had 2 b. of land
taxable. Land for 5 oxen.
2 villagers and 1 smallholder have 1 plough.
Meadow, 5 acres.
Value before 1066, 10s; now 5s.

[BASSETLAW Wapentake]
M. In ELKESLEY Askell had 4 b. of land taxable. Land for 2 ploughs.
Ernwin the priest holds from the King.
4 villagers have 1½ ploughs.
Value before 1066, 8s; now 10s.

In NORTH MORTON Askell held and Ernwin holds 3 b. taxable. Waste.

M. In MISSON Canute had 1½ b. of land taxable. Land for 3 oxen.
Ernwin has
4 villagers with ½ plough and 2 Freemen with 1 plough.
A fishery, 3s; woodland pasture 1 furlong long and 1 wide.
Value 8s.

S. There also 3 b. of land taxable. Jurisdiction of Kirton (-in-Lindsey).
6 villagers have 3 ploughs.

[LYTHE Wapentake]
M. In KELHAM Ulfkell had 1 b. of land and two parts of 1 b. taxable.
Land for 6 oxen. Haldane has
2 villagers and 2 smallholders with 1 plough.
Meadow, 6 acres; underwood 8 furlongs long and 8 virgates wide.
[Value] before 1066, 20s; now 10[s].

M. In (South) MUSKHAM Swartbrand had 6 b. of land taxable.
Land for 1½ ploughs. Seric holds from the King. He has   293 b
1 Freeman and 2 smallholders with 2 oxen in a plough.
Meadow, 12 acres; woodland pasture 1 furlong long and 1 wide.
Value before 1066, 16s; now 5s.

Ⓜ) In *WIMARSPOLD* .ħƀ Wills.xi.bou̷ træ̷ ad glđ̷ . Tra̷

ii.car̷.Aldene ħ̄ ibi.xiiii.focħ.7 ii.uiłł 7 ii.feruos.

cū.vi.car̷.7 xx.ac̷s p̷ti.T.R.E.uał.xl.foł.ṁ.xxx.fol

Iƀidē ħƀr.iiii.taiɲi.vi.bou̷ træ̷ ad glđ̷.Tra̷.i.car̷.

Alden ħ̄ ibi.i.focħ cū.iii̷ᵇ.boƀ in car̷.7 vi.ac̷s p̷ti.

T.R.E.uał xxi.foł.ṁ.vi.foł.

Ⓢ In Gunnulfeftone ħƀ Erᵖᵗᵉ̄rnuin cū.iiii.focħ.v.bou̷

træ̷ ad glđ̷.Tra̷ xii ؛ bou̷.Soca in Ernehale.Ibi.iiii.

focħ hn̄t.i.car̷.7 v.ac̷s p̷ti.7 xvi.ac̷s filue miɲ̷.

Ⓜ In *ꝄOVVALLE* ħƀ Aluric dim̷ car̷ tre̷ ad glđ̷.Tra̷.ii.boƀ.

Idꝫ de rege tenet.7 ħ̄ ibi.iii.uiłł cū.ii.car̷.7 ii.ac̷s p̷ti.

T.R.E.7 ṁ uał.ix.foł.

Ⓜ Iƀidē ħƀ Vluric dim̷ car̷ træ̷ ad glđ̷.Tra̷ dim̷ car̷.

Ernuin ħ̄.i.borđ 7 i.uiłł cū.i.car̷.7 ii.ac̷s p̷ti.T.R.E.

uał x.foł.ṁ.v.foł 7 iiii.deɲ̷.Ibi jacet.i.bou træ̷.Soᴄᴀ.ᵂᵃⁿᵗᵃ·ᵉ̄

Ⓜ In *ESꝄECILLEWELLE*.ħƀ Dunninc.v.bou træ̷ ad glđ̷.Tra̷

v.bou̷.Ernuin ħ̄ ibi.i.uiłł cū dim̷ car̷.7 xii.ac̷s p̷ti.

T.R.E.v.foł 7.iiii.deɲ̷.ṁ.iii.foł 7 iiii.deɲ.

In *WARESHOPE*.ten̷ ꝗđā cecus.i.bou in elemofina de rege.

In *CLAVREBVRG*.ii.bou̷ træ̷ ad glđ̷.Tra̷.ii.car̷.Archil tenuit

Ernuin teɲ.Ibi.ii.uiłł 7 vi؛ac̷ p̷ti.Valuit.iiii.foł.ṁ.ii.foł.

·In *SVTONE* Aluric 7 Brun.xii.bou̷ træ̷ ad glđ̷.ꝑ.ii.Ⓜ tenuer̷.

7 Vlfi.i.car̷ 7 dim̷ ad glđ̷.foca jacet in Ollaueftone.Tra̷.ē.iii.car̷.

In *OꝝDESHALE*.i.bou̷ ad glđ̷.Tra̷.iiii.boƀ.Ernui teɲ̷. ꝼ Vafta.ē.

47 M. In WIDMERPOOL William had 11 b. of land taxable. Land for 2 ploughs.
Haldane has
    14 Freemen, 2 villagers and 2 slaves with 6 ploughs.
    Meadow, 20 acres.
Value before 1066, 40s; now 30s.

48 There also 4 thanes had 6 b. of land taxable. Land for 1 plough.
Haldane has
    1 Freeman with 3 oxen in a plough.
    Meadow, 6 acres.
Value before 1066, 21s; now 6s.

49 S. In GONALSTON Ernwin the priest, with 4 Freemen, had 5 b. of
land taxable. Land for 12 oxen. Jurisdiction in Arnold.
    4 Freemen have 1 plough.
    Meadow, 5 acres; underwood, 16 acres.

[BROXTOW Wapentake]

50 M. In TROWELL Aelfric had ½ c. of land taxable. Land for 4 oxen.
He also holds from the King. He has
    3 villagers with 2 ploughs.
    Meadow, 2 acres.
Value before 1066 and now 9s.

51 M. There also Wulfric had ½ c. of land taxable. Land for ½ plough.
Ernwin has
    1 smallholder and 1 villager with 1 plough.
    Meadow, 2 acres.
Value before 1066, 10s; now 5s 4d.
    1 b. of land lies there. Jurisdiction. Waste.

52 M. In EAST CHILWELL Dunning had 5 b. of land taxable. Land
for 5 oxen. Ernwin has
    1 villager with ½ plough.
    Meadow, 12 acres.
[Value] before 1066, 5s 4d; now 3s 4d.

[BASSETLAW Wapentake]

53 In WARSOP a blind man holds 1 b. in alms from the King.

[OSWALDBECK Wapentake]

54 In CLARBOROUGH 2 b. of land taxable. Land for 2 ploughs.
Arkell held it. Ernwin holds it.
    2 villagers.
    Meadow, 6 acres.
The value was 4s; now 2s.

[BROXTOW Wapentake]

55 In SUTTON (Passeys) Aelfric and Brown held 12 b. of land
taxable as 2 manors and Wulfsi 1½ c. taxable. The jurisdiction
lies in Wollaton. Land for 3 ploughs. Waste.

[BASSETLAW Wapentake]

56 In ORDSALL 1 b. taxable. Land for 4 oxen. Ernwy holds it.

NOTES

ABBREVIATIONS used in the notes. DB... Domesday Book. DG... H.C. Darby and G.R.Versey *Domesday Gazeteer* Cambridge 1975. EPNS... English Place-Name Society Survey, 17, 1940 (Notts.). MS...Manuscript. OEB... G.Tengvik *Old English Bynames* Uppsala 1938. PNDB... O.von Feilitzen *Pre-Conquest Personal Names of Domesday Book* Uppsala 1937. VCH...Victoria County History (Notts., vol.1).

The editor is grateful to Mr. J.D. Foy for collating the place identifications with the Lay Subsidy Rolls.

The manuscript is written on leaves, or folios, of parchment (sheepskin), measuring about 15in. by 11in.(38 by 28 cm), on both sides. On each side, or page, are two columns, making four to each folio. The folios were numbered in the 17th century, and the four columns of each are here lettered a,b,c,d. The manuscript emphasises words and usually distinguishes chapters and sections by the use of red ink. Underlining here indicates deletion.

NOTTINGHAMSHIRE. In red, across the top of the page, spread above both columns, *SNOTINGH(AM)SCIRE* (*SNOTINGHA(M)SCIRE*, 289 ab); omitted, blank page 282 ab.

B 1   75s 7d. Old English currency lasted for a thousand years until 1971. The pound contained 20 shillings, each of 12 pence, abbreviated as £(*ibrae*), s(*olidi*), d(*enarii*).

B 3   THE SHERIFF of Nottingham was also Sheriff of Derby until the later 16th century, and was already so before 1086, since his returns were attested by the 'witness of the two Shires' (Derby B 15, the Latin, here given, in column 280 b). In 1086 Alstoe and Martinsley Wapentakes of Rutland were also 'attached to the Sheriffdom of Nottingham for the King's tax', Alstoe equally divided between Thurgarton and Broxtow, with which it had no geographical connection; these Wapentakes are therefore entered immediately after Notts. (283 c - 294 a). The other Sheriffs between 1066 and 1100 were Harding, Hugh of Port, Ernwy and William Peverel.

B 9   HORSEMEN'S HOUSES. Probably of *milites,* in garrison immediately after 1066; William Peverel was or had been keeper of Nottingham Castle.

B 16   FRAIL. OEB 313.

B 20   DYKE. Possibly the Fosse Way; more probably either a defence work linking the old Borough with the new Borough built in 924 south of the Trent, or the great ditch that joined the Norman Castle to the old Borough.

S   THE SHIRE CUSTOMS transcribe an English record, since they speak of the Earl, though there was no Earl in 1086.

S 1   18 HUNDREDS. The clause, repeated in the customs of Lincolnshire and Yorkshire, is discussed by Round *Feudal England* p.73 (1964 reprint p.68). This 'Hundred' was a unit of 12 carucates. £8 is the equivalent of 12 silver marks (note S 3 below) and also of a 'long hundred' (120) of *ora*, at 16d to the *ora.* These small Hundreds, of 12 carucates, explained in the Lindsey Survey of c.1115, or multiples thereof, are confined to Nottingham and adjacent Shires. See also notes 5,9; 9,90; 11,17; 18,6; 24,1. See also 18,1.

S 3   DEATH-DUTY. The *relevatio, relevum,* the 'relief' or 'heriot', was paid by the heir on taking up his inheritance. The scale of rates was laid down in the law codes, especially 2 Canute 71 and 'Laws of King William' 20. The *villanus* paid an ox, cow or horse, the *censarius* (10,3 note) a year's tribute.
SILVER MARK. 13s 4d, making 3 marks to £2.

S 5   MARKET RIGHTS. *Thaim,* jurisdiction over disputed 'warranty'; in connection with 'toll', probably concerned with the seller's title to cattle and other goods taken to market.
MARKEATON and the other places named are in Derbyshire, except for Collingham, Granby and Worksop.
COUNTESS GYTHA. See 10,5 note.

L   EARLS and Counts are listed before Bishops and Abbots, contrary to custom.
RUTLAND. The Wapentakes attached to Nottingham, see B 3 note.

1,1   WAPENTAKE. Equivalent of the Hundred in Danish areas. The Notts. Wapentakes are normally entered in the same order in each chapter, see Index to Places. DB enters headings for manors only. Dependencies are often in different Wapentakes.
CARUCATE. Equivalent in the Danish areas of the hide; comprising 8 bovates. The abbreviations c. and b. are here used. 96 or 48 c. to the Wapentake seems to be the Notts norm

1,6   HEADON. Corrected from Grove; underlining, or scoring through with double lines, indicates deletion.

1,9   FURLONGS WIDE. MS *l(on)g,* in error.

1,11	MORTON. DB distinguishes Morton, North Morton, and 'the other Morton'. There are now six adjacent Mortons, covering about 5 square miles, none of them now called 'North'. The most northerly are Morton (here mapped) and Morton Hall.
1,21	BESTHORPE. Also 1,24 and 12,9. Some of the references may be to Besthorpe (82 64), opposite Carlton-on-Trent.
1,24	TOTAL. The sum of the details does not correspond.
1,30	RANBY. Deleted, a duplicate of 1,14; deletion of Bothamsall accidentally omitted.
1,44	BYCARR'S DYKE. In Misterton, EPNS 1.
1,64	MEERING In Newark in the Lay Subsidy Rolls; added with, 1,65-66, with thin initials, not reddened.
2,10	LEVERTON and Tresswell (2,9), see 9,129 note.
3,3	SUTTON BONINGTON. Two places, amalgamated in the 14th century, EPNS 256.
3,4	2 M. Two manors before 1066, one in 1086; so frequently in Notts. DB.
4,1	HALDANE. Perhaps of Cromwell, 30,4 note.
5,1	FERRY. Less valuable than the Trent ferry at Fiskerton (11,20); probably over the Great.
5,2	MUSKHAM. See Lincs. C W 15 (376 c) 'The Shire witnesses that at King Edward's death and later Askell had these three manors, Scotton, Scotter, and Raventhorpe, in his own free possession *(in propria libertate)*, from King Edward; he had Muskham in Nottinghamshire similarly'. He gave Muskham to Peterborough, where his brother Brand was Abbot.
5,4	LANEHAM. See Lincs. 2,26 (340 a) 'In Newton (-on-Trent) the Archbishop (of York) has 100 acres of meadow which belong to Laneham'.
5,5-6	WRITTEN in three lines across both·columns, the beginning of each line here exdented.
5,7	LOUND substituted for Mattersey.
5,8	SCAFTWORTH 1c. *Car(ucata)* is normally abbreviated with a zig-zag upright in Notts., *car(uca)* with a horizontal line; as here, the convention is not consistent.
5,9	BLIDWORTH. In Broxtow Wapentake, EPNS 115; in Thurgarton in the Lay Subsidy Rolls of 1334; the places apparently attached to Blidworth are in Thurgarton in DB, see 18,6 note.
5,12	RANSKILL. The entry is inserted into the MS in small lettering.
5,14	OSMANTHORPE. MS *Osuuitorp* for *Osmutorp*.
6,1	AND 56 BURGESSES. The duplicate '7' in Farley seems to be an insertion mark in the MS.
6,3	BARNBY. The interlinear marks below *ii bo* and above *ar* are not, as Farley, *tre*; they are probably the remnant of an incomplete erasure.
6,15	WITH A THIRD. Either read *cum* for *et*, or add abbreviation marks for (m).
	THE WRITING goes round a hole in the parchment, beautifully mended in antiquity.
[7]	CHAPTERS 7-11 are misnumbered 6-10 in the MS.
7,6	NEPHEW. Or possibly grandson.
9,1	R in the margin, for *r(equire)*, 'look into this'.
9,18	COTTAM. Not Cotham, in Newark Wapentake, as VCH 260, followed by EPNS 212 and DG, since all the other 50 places in this chapter are placed in their right Wapentakes. Cottam in Bassetlaw was *Cotum* in 1280, EPNS 29.
9,19	4 M. The *iiii* is written against the top of the *I* of *In*, not against the previous line, as in Farley; so throughout Notts.
9,20	SIXTH PART. MS *vi* for *vi tam*, as often in Notts.
	THE WRITING avoids the hole in the parchment, see 6,15 note.
9,24	IN GROVE. Accidentally repeated in the MS.
9,28	WEST MARKHAM, or Little Markham, now Markham Clinton, EPNS 56, and OS.
9,35	COLD COATES. Not, as VCH 261 and DG, Oldcoates, whose spellings derive from 'owl', not 'cold', EPNS 99; probably a lost place.
9,49	BLYTH. In 1088 Roger of Bully and his wife Muriel founded Blyth Priory. Its cartulary (Thoroton Society 27, 1968, ed. R.T.Timson) includes its foundation charter (folio 100 b), which gives a detailed list of *consuetudines*, exactly contemporary with DB. Roger granted *ecclesiam de Blida et totam villam integre cum omnibus appendiciis suis et consuetudinibus, sicuti homines eiusdem ville michi faciebant, scilicet arare, karare, falcare, bladum meum secare, fenum meum facere, marchetum dare, stangnum* (sic) *molendini facere* (the church of Blyth and the whole village entire, with all its dependencies and the customary dues, as the men of the village used to perform for me, namely ploughing, carting, mowing, reaping my corn, making my hay, paying marriage-dues, making the mill pond). The grant included tolls, ferry and market and *omnes dignitates quas habebam in eadem villa, scilicet soc et sac, tol et them, et infangethief, ferrum et fossam, et furcas, cum aliis libertatibus, uti tunc temporis tenebam de rege* (all the privileges I had in this village, namely full jurisdiction, market rights, thief-taking, iron and ditch, and gallows, with the other freedoms that I then had from the King). 'Hanging Field' in the adjoining parish of Styrrup (EPNS 304) might have been the gallows site. Roger also granted Elton (9,110), Barnby (probably 9,54), and Beighton (Derby 16,13 ... 278 b), as well as tithes from numerous other places. The

'privileges' of sentencing men to ordeal by iron and ditch (i.e. water) and to be hanged were not accorded to all landholders.

9,53 PLOUGHS... AZOR. *bi* of *Ibi* missing from the MS.

9,64 DENA. PNDB 223.
FULK. MS *Fulo* for *Fulco*.

9,66 ULFKETEL. Possibly identical with Ulfkell, see 10,47 note.

9,70 6½b. (? 6b.). Probably 7 *dim* should also have been underlined for deletion.

9,74 TOLLS... SHIP. Gunthorpe is on the Trent, opposite East Bridgford, already so-called in DB, where the bridge may have marked the limit of navigation for sea-going vessels.
EXACTIONS. Paid to the lord. *Tailla* in DB, unlike later *tallagium*, is normally confined to larger manors with *sochemanni*, especially in north-east Mercia. The word is regularly explained as *exactio*; see texts cited in Du Cange *Glossarium* Tallia 8

9,82 HAD. *hb* for normal plural *hbr*.
WITH. Either a word is missing, or *de* is superfluous.

9,84 WULFHEAH. *Unfac*, understood as Old Swedish *Ofegh* in PNDB 334. A misspelling of *Ulfac* (9,82), comparable with *Unlof* for *Ulnot* (10,24) is more probable.

9,90 BROXTOW WAPENTAKE. The manors in the five places named, with the exception of part of Willoughby (16,5 note), are entered under Broxtow in four separate chapters, although separated from it geographically by Rushcliffe. Since the total assessment of these Broxtow lands is ¼ bovate short of 12 carucates, they may have originally formed a small Hundred (S 1 note, above).

9,102 THIRD PART, rather than 'three parts of'. Normally, the upright zigzag abbreviates *partes*, a horizontal line *partem*; but the usage is not consistent, see 5,8 note above.

9,105 WARBOROUGH. The name is preserved by Warby Gate in Plumtree, EPNS 240.

9,109 ERNWIN. See 16,5 note.

9,113 SPARROWHAWK. PNDB 369, citing instances of the name, still used as a surname.

9,129 TRESWELL and Leverton, adjoining places, both equally divided with Count Alan (2,9).

10,3 TRIBUTARIES. *Cens(it)ores, censarii,* chiefly in north-east Mercia, Yorkshire, Essex and Dorset, paid tribute in money, not work; see S 3 note.

10,5 COUNTESS GYTHA. In most of his Northants. holdings, William Peverel succeeded (Countess) Gytha (*Gitde*); at Adstock in Bucks. (16,8 ... 148 b) his predecessor was 'Gytha (*Gethe*) wife of Earl Ralph (of Hereford, nephew of King Edward)'; and at Woolley in Berks. (24,1 ... 61 a) he succeeded Earl Ralph. His Notts. predecessor Gountess 'Goda' is therefore a misspelling of 'Gytha'. She is evidently also the Goda who held Edwalton (23,1), since Edwalton belonged to Stockerston (Leics. 13,15 .. 232 a), also formerly held by Earl Ralph. She named her son Harold, and is easily confused with her namesake, Countess Gytha, wife of Earl Godwin and mother of King Harold.

10,15 THANELAND. Land reserved by a lord, commonly a church, for the maintenance of a thane, armed and mounted; usually inalienable, and not automatically heritable.

10,17 MORTON. By Nottingham, VCH 270.

10,18 NEWBOUND. *Neubold*, in the middle of 50 consecutive Broxtow entries, is unlikely to be Newbold in Bingham (1,58), as DG and EPNS (237). It is probably Newbound, by Teversal, in Broxtow, called Newbold until the 18th century, EPNS 136.

10,24 WULFNOTH. *Unlof*, explained as 'Olaf', PNDB 335; but in the next line called *isdem Ulnod* (Wulfnoth). Wulfnoth is also spelt *Ulnof* in Dorset (Exon. 60a), and in Kent the same person is given as *Unlot* and *Ulnot* (5,158;167...10 c,d), see 9,84 note.

10,31 VILLAGER WHO HAS. *i vill habentes* is either an error for *habens*; or else a figure, or an entry of *bordarii*, has been omitted.

10,47 GRIMKETEL. Possibly identical with Grimkell. Spellings with a 't' are here rendered by -ketel, those without a 't' by -kell.

10,55 BINGHAM WAPENTAKE. Radcliffe is listed in Bingham (11,33), Holme Pierrepont (9,80) in Rushcliffe; Adbolton (10,12; 56) therefore seems equally divided between the Wapentakes, as was Willoughby, 16,5 note.

10,64 MANTON and 10,65-66 are added in thinner lettering, with larger plain initials.

11,11 OXTON. Spelling emended to *Ostune*, as in 5,11 and 9,76.

11,13 TITHBY. Added at the foot of the column, interrupting 11,12; the initial I is abnormally tall and thin, matched in Notts. only in 23,2, a similar addition.

11,17 SOUTHWELL HUNDRED and Blidworth and Plumtree Hundreds (18,6; 24,1) may be survivals of small Hundreds (S 1 note above).

11,33 RADCLIFFE. In the MS there is a wide gap, equivalent to 5 or 6 letters, between RA and DE..; Farley indicates the gap in the lines above and below; see 14,3.

12,1 2c. OF LAND. Farley *iii c.* MS *ii,* followed by a small hole in the parchment, with what might be the bottom of a third stroke below it; the hole was perhaps caused in the course of a deliberate alteration from *iii* to *ii.*

13,1 TWO CHILWELLS. Not distinguished from each other, later or now, EPNS 142.

13,6 2c. OF LAND. Farley, in error, *iii c.*

14,3 THE GAP corresponds to the gap at 11,33, on the other side of the page.

THESE...MANORS. *Hos*, here treating *manerium* as masculine, perhaps on the analogy of *locus*, place, which may normally be masculine or neuter in the plural, occasionally in the singular.

14,5 QUARTER. *Ferding*, a fourth part; often a 'furlong'.

14,6 4c. OF LAND deleted, with correction above the line.

15,8 OGGA. PNDB 335.

16 ROGER OF POITOU had forfeited his lands into the King's hands in most counties; either he retained his Notts. lands, or the Survey was drafted before his forfeiture was known.

16,5 WILLOUGHBY. Here in Rushcliffe Wapentake; so perhaps also 10,10, attached to Clifton in Rushcliffe, see 9,90 note. Adbolton also seems to have been divided by a Wapentake boundary, 10,55 note.

ERNWY. Possibly Ernwy the priest, who held from Roger of Poitou in Lincs. and the future Lancashire; and from the King in Notts. 30,11. He may also be identical with Ernwin the priest, and some or all of the other persons entered as Ernwy or Erwin in Notts.

17,1 BASSETLAW WAPENTAKE. MS Newark, in error.

ULF. Probably Ulf Fenman (*Fenisc*), Gilbert's predecessor in Derbyshire (13,1-2), Hunts (B 2) and elsewhere. In Notts. a blank space is left after his name wherever it occurs, except 17,14-15, perhaps intended for the insertion of his byname.

17,12 WELLOW. *Creilege* or *Cratela* (EPNS 65) appears to be the old name of Wellow, VCH 280, citing Thoroton, 3,200.

17,13 VILLAGERS HAVE. *h....,* probably for *habent*, perhaps for *habentes.*

17,17 HAWKSWORTH. Spelling error corrected in the MS.

18,1 [£] 6. The MS is blotted.

18,5 IT DID NOT BELONG. *q(ua)e*, with singular verb, evidently referring to *terra*, perhaps intending only the land of the 'senior' thane.

18,6 ALWOLDESTORP. Identified with Caythorpe (SK 68 45; first mentioned c. 1170, EPNS 159) by Thoroton, cited VCH 281, followed by DG, not noted in EPNS. Possibly the deserted medieval village immediately north of Caythorpe (SP 69 46).

BLIDWORTH HUNDRED. Probably referring to *Alwoldestorp*, which adjoined Blidworth lands, if rightly identified, rather than Staythorpe, remote from Blidworth and separated from it by Southwell Hundred. Blidworth (5,9) held the mill at Lowdham, which bordered on Caythorpe, and with the villages between, Salterford, Oxton, which 'lay in Blidworth' (5,11), Calverton, Woodborough and Epperstone, the area was assessed at exactly 12 carucates, the extent of a small Hundred, see S 1 note, above. The lands of Lowdham were attached to Gunthorpe (9,75).

20,4 BISHOP REMIGIUS. Of Lincoln.

20,5 6b. OF LAND. In the MS a space of about two or three letters is left between *bou* and *tre.*

20,7 THANE. The grammar is confused. The emendations suggested by VCH, of *tainum* to *tainagium* (233) or to *tainlanda* (282) are not parallelled, and neither word could be masculine. Perhaps a MS error for *tainum qui habet.*

23,1 COUNTESS GYTHA. See 10,5 note.

24,1 SIWARD. Probably Siward Bairn.

OUTLIER . . . LEAKE. DB does not otherwise distinguish between East and West Leake. PLUMTREE HUNDRED. See 11,17 note.

24,3 BATHLEY. Not entered in DB.

27,2 COLSTON BASSETT. Not entered in DB; so also 27,3.

28,2 STANTON. Underlining for deletion, present in the MS, is missing in the facsimile, followed by VCH 284.

30,1 OSBERTON. Spelling error corrected in the MS.

30,3 MARGINAL R. Omitted by Farley; see 9,1 note.

30,4 HALDANE. Ancestor of the medieval Cromwells, from whom Thomas and Oliver may or may not derive. Possibly identical with the Haldane(s) who held before 1066 (10,25;40. 21,3).

30,11 ERNWY. A small space in the MS between *Arnui* and *v bou.*

30,31 STRELLEY. Spelling error corrected in the MS.

30,40 THE KING'S. Inserted to distinguish this land from other Syerston holdings.

30,55 ERNWY. Probably identical with Ernwin, named half a dozen times in this chapter; who may however be Ernwy the priest, see 16,5 note.

INDEX OF PERSONS

Familiar modern spellings are given when they exist. Unfamiliar names are usually given in an approximate late 11th century form, avoiding variants that were already obsolescent or pedantic. Spellings that mislead the modern eye are avoided where possible. Two, however, cannot be avoided; they are combined in the name 'Leofgeat', pronounced 'Leffyet' or 'Levyet'. The definite article is omitted before bynames, except where there is reason to suppose that they described the individual. The chapter numbers of listed landholders are printed in italics. The Rutland landholders are indexed in the Rutland volume.

Churches and Clergy. Archbishop (of York)...Thomas. **Bishop**...of Bayeux 7. Chester S 5. Lincoln 6, see also Remigius. **Abbeys**...Burton S 5. Peterborough 8. S 5. **Churches**...St. Mary's, Southwell 5,3;13. **Priest**...Aitard, Azor, Ernwin, Ernwy, Godwin, Norman.

Secular Titles. Count *(comes)*...Alan, of Mortain, Robert. **Countess** *(comitissa)*...Aelfeva, Godiva, Gytha. **Earl** *(comes)*...Algar, Hugh, Tosti. **Sheriff** *(vicecomes)*...Baldric. **Usher** *(hostiarius)*...William. **Young** *(cilt)*...Swein, Wulfric, Wulfsi.

The name of each place is followed by (i) the initial of its Hundred and its location on the Map in this volume; (ii) its National Grid reference; (iii) chapter and section references in DB. Bracketed figures denote mention in sections dealing with a different place. Unless otherwise stated, the identifications of EPNS and the spellings of the Ordnance Survey are followed for places in England; of OEB for places abroad. Inverted commas mark lost places with known modern spelling; unidentifiable places are given in DB spelling, in italics. The National Grid reference system is explained on all Ordnance Survey maps, and in the Automobile Association Handbooks; the figures reading from left to right are given before those reading from bottom to top of the map. All places in Nottinghamshire are in the 100 kilometere grid square lettered SK. The Nottinghamshire Wapentakes are Bassetlaw (Ba); Bingham (Bn); Broxtow (Br); Lythe (L); Newark (N); Oswaldbeck (O); Rushcliffe (R); Thurgarton (T).

	Map	Grid	Text
Clifton	N 3	81 71	6,8;10-12. 9,3;5
Clipston	Bn 24	63 34	9,104
Clipstone	Ba 74	60 64	9,39
Clown	Ba 45	57 73	1,24
Clumber	Ba 33	62 74	1,24. 9,41;(42)
Coddington	N 15	83 54	6,3; 6-7. 7,3-4.
'Cold Coates'	Ba -	-	9,35
Collingham	N 10	82 61	S 5. (7,5). 8,1. 14,8
Car Colston	Bn 4	72 43	1,56. 9,107. 11,24
Colston Bassett	Bn 31	70 33	(27,2-3)
Colwick	T 30	61 40	10,1. 12,17. 30,8
Cossall	Br 24	48 42	10,36. 13,12
Costock	Br 42	57 26	9,94. 10,11; 53. 15,5
Cotgrave	Bn 25	64 35	15,8-10. 16,7
Cotham	N 24	79 47	6,4. 7,1. 11,4
Cottam	Ba 43	81 80	9,18
Cromwell	L 11	79 61	18,2. 30,4
Cropwell Bishop	Bn 26	68 35	5,3
Cropwell Butler	Bn 19	68 37	11,32. 16,6. 20,7
Cuckney	Ba 57	56 71	9,36. 22,2
'Dallington'	N 27	(77 43)	11,3
Danethorpe	N 12	84 57	14,4
Darlton	Ba 53	77 73	1,1
Doveridge (Derbyshire)			S 5
East Drayton	Ba 40	77 75	1,2
West Drayton	Ba 37	70 74	9,(30); 31. 16,11
Dunham	Ba 56	81 74	1,1; (8).
Eakring	Ba 80	67 62	1,24. 12,5. 17,7-8
Eastwood	Br 14	46 46	10,32
Eaton	Ba 31	71 78	5.8. (9,9); 9,20 (21; 25; 30)
Ednaston (Derbyshire)			S 5
Edwalton	R 8	59 35	16,4. 23,1
Edwinstowe	Ba 68	62 66	1,24; 28
Egmanton	Ba 73	73 68	9,14-15
Elkesley	Ba 35	68 75	1,10. 9,32. 30,41
Elston	N 23	76 48	6,3; 5. 9,1. 20,4-5
Elton	Bn 16	77 39	9,110
Epperstone	T 16	65 48	9,73. 14,5
Everton	O 4	69 91	5,8. 9,117; 124
Farndon	N 17	76 51	6,1
Farnsfield	T 2	64 56	1,22. 11,17
Fenton	O 20	79 83	1,33. 9,112-113
Finningley	Ba 1	67 99	18,3
Fiskerton	T 10	73 51	11,15; 20-21
Flawborough	N 30	78 42	9,2. 11,1; 3; 5
Fledborough	Ba 66	81 72	6,13
Flintham	Bn 2	74 46	1,61. 9,108-109. 11,26
Gamston	Ba 36	71 76	9,9. 16,1-2
Gamston	R 6	60 37	10,14
Gedling	T 27	61 42	9,72. 12,16-1?
Gibsmere	T 20	72 48	13,13
Girton	N 7	82 66	6,4
Gleadthorpe	Ba 58	59 70	9,38
Gonalston	T 17	68 47	10.3. 14,6. 30,49
Gotham	R 14	53 30	4,3. 30,24
Granby	Bn 22	75 36	S 5. 11,26. 27,1
Grassthorpe	L 6	79 67	9,62
Greasley	Br 16	49 47	10,29-30
Grimston	Ba 76	69 65	1,17-18; 24; 27
Gringley-on-the-Hill	O 5	73 90	9,122
Little Gringley	O 18	73 80	1,4; 43. 5,8
Grove	Ba 32	73 79	9,22; (24; 30)
Gunthorpe	T 25	68 44	9,74; (75)
Harby	N 5	87 70	6,4; 9
Harwell	O 3	68 91	9,117;124
Harworth	Ba 4	61 91	9,55
Haughton	Ba 48	68 72	16,9
Hawksworth	Bn 6	75 43	11,23. 17,17
Hawton	N 18	78 51	6,3. 11,7 14,1-3
Headon	Ba 38	74 77	1,6. 9,7;26
Hempshill	Br 21	52 44	10,50
Hickling	Bn 34	69 29	5,3. 11,30. 20,8
Hockerton	L 21	71 56	5,17. 9,60. 11,8
Hodsock	Ba 9	58 86)	
Hodsock	Ba 14	61 85)	9,46-48
Holme Pierrepont	R 2	62 39	9,80-(81)
Horsepool	T 9	(69 50)	11,12
Hoveringham	T 24	69 46	11,14
Hucknall Torkard	Br 13	53 49	10,49. 15,4
Inkersall	Ba 81	63 60	17,6
Kelham	L 23	77 55	9,59. 11,19. 15,3. 18,4. 30,45
Kersall	L 12	71 62	17,9
Keyworth	R 17	61 30	4,7. 9,87-88. 10,10. 13,7
Kilvington	N 28	80 42	6,3. 20,2. 22,1
Kimberley	Br 19	49 44	10,47-48;(63)
Kingston-on-Soar	R 21	50 27	3,4. 30,19; 21-22
Kinoulton	Bn 33	67 30	11,31. 30,38
Kirkby-in-Ashfield	Br 6	49 56	13,9. 30,27
Kirklington	T 4	67 57	17,13
Kirton	Ba 64	69 69	1,19; 24. 9,13. 12,2. 17,2
Kirton-in-Lindsey (Lincs)			(1,65. 30,44)
Knapthorpe	L 18	74 58	11,9. 12,7. 22. 30,3
Kneesall	Ba 78	70 64	17,9
Kneeton	Bn 1	71 46	1,62. 2,7-8. 9,102;(109)

	Map	Grid	Text
Lambley	T 21	63 45	30,5
Lamcote	Bn 18	64 38	9,96. 15,7. 30,36
Laneham	Ba 42	80 76	5,4; (8)
Langar	Bn 27	72 34	10,59. 11,28
Langford	N 11	82 58	19,1
Laughton (Lincs)	01	54 97	(1,66)
Laxton	Ba 72	72 67	12,1; (3)
Leake	R 22	55 26	4,4. 9,89. 24,1. 28,2
Lenton	Br 33	55 39	1,48. 10,19; 24
Leverton	O 19	78 82	1,32. 2,10. 5,4. 9,130
Linby	Br 10	53 50	10,20
Littleborough	O 21	82 82	1,34
Lound	Ba 17	69 86	1,16. 5,7. 9,51
Lowdham	T 23	66 46	(5,9). 9,75
Mansfield	Br 4	53 61	1,(17); 23; (26;30). (9,47)
Manton	Ba 27	60 78	10,64
Maplebeck	L 13	71 60	1,24; 29. 17,11
Markeaton (Derbyshire)			S 5
East Markham	Ba 52	74 72	1,3. 9,6;(7-9);10-11
West Markham	Ba 50	72 72	9,28-30
High Marnham	L 2	80 70	9,64
Low Marnham	L 4	80 69	9,65
Martin	Ba 3	63 94	9,56
Mattersey	Ba 13	69 89	1,15. 9,132
Meering	N 8	81 65	1,64
Milton	Ba 49	71 73	10,3
Misson	Ba 2	69 95	1,65-66. 9, 21. 30,43-44
Misterton	O 1	76 94	1,38. 9,121; 123
Morton	Br 34	56 38	10,17
Morton	Ba 23	67 80	1,11
North(?) Morton (Hall)	Ba 23	?65 80	9,34. 30,42
Little Morton	Ba 23	67 78	1,11 note
Morton (-in-Fiskerton)	T 11	72 51	11,16. 13,13
North Muskham	L 19	79 58	5,2. 8,2. 12, 11-13. 30,7
South Muskham	L 20	79 57	5,5. 30,46
Newark	N 14	80 53	6,1. (21,3)
'Newbold'	Bn 32	68 31	1,58
Newbound	Br 1	49 63	10,18-(19)
Newthorpe	Br 15	48 46	4,8. 10,33; 62-63
Newton	Bn 8	68 41	9,97. 12,20
Normanton-by-Clumber	Ba 34	65 74	1,8
Normanton-on-Soar	R 24	51 23	3,2. 4,1. 9,78. 30, 14; 16
Normanton-by-Southwell	T 8	70 54	17,14. 30,11
Normanton-on-Trent	L 3	79 68	6,14. 9, 68-69
Normanton-on-the-Wolds	R 12	62 32	9,84-85 10,10
Nottingham	Br 35	57 39	B 1-20. (1,22)
Norwell	L 9	77 61	5,13. (12,22)
Nuthall	Br 20	51 44	10,40. 30,32
'Odsthorpe'	T -	-	1,12. 9,42; 71. 30,12
Ollerton	Ba 69	65 67	9,17. 17,3
Ompton	Ba 77	68 65	1,24. 12,6. 15,2. 17,10
Ordsall	Ba 30	70 79	1,5;12. 9,19; 23. 30,56
South Ordsall	Ba 30	70 79	1,13
Orston	Bn 17	77 41	1,51
Osberton	Ba 29	62 79	30,1
Osmanthorpe	T 3	67 56	5,14
Ossington	Ba 79	75 64	15,1
Owthorpe	Bn 30	67 33	9,111. 12, 21. 26,1
Oxton	T 6	63 51	5,11. 9,76. 11,11
Papplewick	Br 11	54 51	10,21. 30,29
Perlethorpe	Ba 61	64 70	1,24; 26; 30. 9,37
Pilsley (Derbyshire)			S 5
Plumtree	R 11	61 33	9,82; (85-87)
Plumtree Hundred			24,1
Radcliffe on-Trent	Bn 11	64 39	10,55. 11,33
Radford	Br 29	55 40	10,15
Ragnall	Ba 55	80 73	1,1
Rampton	O 23	79 78	9,131
Ranby	Ba 22	65 81	1,13-14; 30. 9,24-25
Ranskill	Ba 11	65 87	5,12
Ratcliffe	R 20	49 28	30,20
Rayton	Ba 28	61 79	1,24; 30
Rempstone	Br 44	58 24	9,94. 10,54. 15,6
Retford	Ba 25	70 81	5,8. 9,42; 71
Rolleston	T 12	74 52	5,6. 7,5. 11,18
'Roolton'	Ba 20	?63 81	9,44
Ruddington	R 10	57 33	2,6. 9,83. 17,15. 25,2
Rufford	Ba 75	64 64	17,4
Rutland			B 3 note
Salterford	T 5	60 52	27,3
Sandiacre (Derbyshire)	03	47 63	(23,2)
Saundby	O 10	78 88	1,44. 5,4. (9,118)
Saxilby (Lincs)	02	88 75	(21,3)
Saxondale	Bn 12	68 39	9,103
Scaftworth	Ba 5	66 91	5,8
South Scarle	N 9	84 64	6,4
Scarrington	Bn 9	73 41	1,52
Scofton	Ba 21	62 80	1,24; 30
Screveton	Bn 5	73 43	1,55. 7,6. 9,106

Places not in Nottinghamshire Indexed Above

Places outside Britain (see Index of Persons)

Aincourt...Walter.   Bayeux...Bishop.   Bully...Roger.   Buron...Ralph.   Ferrers...Henry.
Ghent...Gilbert.   Grandmesnil...Hugh.   La Guerche...Geoffrey.   Lacy...Ilbert.
Limesy...Ralph.   Mortain...Count of, Robert.   Moutiers...Robert.   Oilly...Robert.
Percy...William.   Poitou...Roger.   Tison...Gilbert.   Tosny...Berengar.

SYSTEMS OF REFERENCE TO DOMESDAY BOOK

The manuscript is divided into numbered chapters, and the chapters into sections, usually marked by large initials and red ink. Farley however did not number the sections. References have therefore been inexact, by folio numbers, which cannot be closer than an entire page of column. Moreover, half a dozen different ways of referring to the same column have been devised. In 1816 Ellis used three separate systems in his indices; (i) on pages i-cvii; 435-518; 537-570; (ii) on pages 1-144; (iii) on pages 145-433 and 519-535. Other systems have since come into use, notably that used by Vinogradoff, here followed. This edition numbers the sections, the normal practicable form of close reference; but since all discussion of Domesday for three hundred years has been obliged to refer to page or column, a comparative table will help to locate references given. The five columns below give Vinogradoff's notation, Ellis' three systems, and that employed by Welldon Finn and others. Maitland, Stenton, Darby and others have usually followed Ellis (i).

Vinogradoff	*Ellis (i)*	*Ellis (ii)*	*Ellis (iii)*	*Finn*
152 a	152	152a	152	152ai
152b	152	152a	152.2	152a2
152c	152b	152b	152b	152bi
152d	152b	152b	152b2	152b2

In Nottinghamshire, the relation between the Vinogradoff column notation, here followed, and the chapters and sections is

280a	B1 - B 20	285a	9,29 - 9,40	290a	15,1 - 15,10		
b	Derby	b	9,40 - 9,53	b	16,1 - 16,12		
c	S1 - S 6	c	9,54 - 9,65	c	17,1 - 17,12		
d	Landholders	d	9,66 - 9,76	d	17,13 - 17,18		
281a	1,1 - 1,12	286a	9,76 - 9,93	291a	18,1 - 19,1		
b	1,13 - 1,31	b	9,94 - 9,106	b	20,1 - 20,8		
c	1,32 - 1,50	c	9,107 - 9,118	c	21,1 - 23,2		
d	1,51 - 1,66	d	9,118 - 9,127	d	24,1 - 26,1		
282a	blank column	287a	9,128 - 9,132	292a	27,1 - 29,2		
b	blank column	b	10,1 - 10,15	b	blank column		
c	2,1 - 3,4	c	10,15 - 10,28	c	30,1 - 30,13		
d	4,1 - 4,8	d	10,29 - 10,46	d	30,14 - 30,31		
283a	5,1 - 5,6	288a	10,46 - 10,60	293a	30,31 - 30,46		
b	5,7 - 5,19	b	10,61 - 10,66	b	30,46 - 30,56		
c	blank column	c	11,1 - 11,12				
d	6,1 - 6,11	d	11,12 - 11,26				
284a	6,11 - 6,15	289a	11,26 - 11,33				
b	7,1 - 8,2	b	12,1 - 12,19				
c	9,1 - 9,21	c	12,19 - 13,11				
d	9,15 - 9,28	d	13,11 - 14,8				

NOTTINGHAMSHIRE NORTHERN
WAPENTAKES

Bassetlaw (Ba)
1 Finningley
2 Misson
3 Martin
4 Harworth
5 Scaftworth
6 Styrrup
7 Serlby
8 Scrooby
9 Hodsock Grange
10 Blyth
11 Ranskill
12 Torworth
13 Mattersey
14 Hodsock
15 Barnby Moor
16 Sutton
17 Lound
18 Carlton-in-Lindrick
19 Bilby
20 'Roolton'
21 Scofton
22 Ranby
23 Morton
24 Babworth
25 Retford
26 Worksop
27 Manton
28 Rayton
29 Osberton
30 Ordsall
31 Eaton
32 Grove
33 Clumber
34 Normanton
35 Elkesley
36 Gamston
37 West Drayton
38 Headon
39 Upton
40 East Drayton
41 Stokeham
42 Laneham
43 Cottam
44 'Swanston'
45 Clown
46 Carburton
47 Bothamsall
48 Haughton
49 Milton
50 West Markham
51 Askham
52 East Markham

53 Darlton
54 Wimpton
55 Ragnall
56 Dunham
57 Cuckney
58 Gleadthorpe
59 Budby
60 Thoresby
61 Perlethorpe
62 Walesby
64 Willoughby
64 Kirton
65 Tuxford
66 Fledborough
67 Warsop
68 Edwinstowe
69 Ollerton
70 Wellow
71 Boughton
72 Laxton
73 Egmanton
74 Clipstone
75 Rufford
76 Grimston
77 Ompton
78 Kneesall
79 Ossington
80 Eakring
81 Inkersall
82 Bilsthorpe

Lythe (L)
1 Skegby
2 High Marnham
3 Normanton-on-Trent
4 Low Marnham
5 Weston
6 Grassthorpe
7 Sutton-on-Trent
8 Carlton-on-Trent
9 Norwell
10 Willoughby
11 Cromwell
12 Kersall
13 Maplebeck
14 Besthorpe
15 Caunton
16 Bathley
17 Winkburn
18 Knapthorpe
19 North Muskham
20 South Muskham

21 Hockerton
22 Averham
23 Kelham

Newark (N) (North)
1 Thorney
2 Broadholme
3 Clifton
4 Wigsley
5 Harby
6 Spalford
7 Girton
8 Meering
9 South Scarle
10 Collingham
11 Langford
12 Danethorpe
13 Winthorpe
14 Newark
15 Coddington

Oswaldbeck (O)
1 Misterton
2 Bycarr's Dike
3 Harwell
4 Everton
5 Gringley-on-the-Hill
6 Walkeringham
7 Beckingham
8 Wiseton
9 Clayworth
10 Saundby
11 Bole
12 Wheatley
13 Sturton-le-Steeple
14 West Burton
15 Tiln
16 Welham
17 Clarborough
18 Little Gringley
19 Leverton
20 Fenton
21 Littleborough
22 Treswell
23 Rampton

Lincolnshire
01 Laughton
02 Saxilby
Not Mapped.
'Cold Coates' (Ba)
Simenton(e) (O)

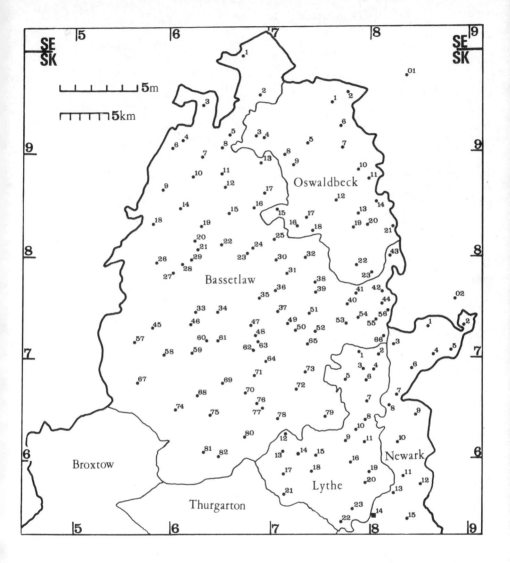

NOTTINGHAMSHIRE NORTHERN WAPENTAKES

The County Boundary is marked by thick lines; Wapentake boundaries (1086) by thin lines.

National Grid 10-kilometre squares are shown on the map border.

Each four-figure grid square covers one square kilometre, or 247 acres, approximately 2 hides, at 120 acres to the hide.

NOTTINGHAMSHIRE SOUTHERN WAPENTAKES

Bingham (Bn)
1 Kneeton
2 Flintham
3 East Bridgford
4 Car Colston
5 Screveton
6 Hawksworth
7 Shelford
8 Newton
9 Scarrington
10 Thoroton
11 Radcliffe-on-Trent
12 Saxondale
13 Bingham
14 Aslockton
15 Whatton
16 Elton
17 Orston
18 Lamcote
19 Cropwell Butler
20 Tithby
21 Wiverton
22 Granby
23 Tollerton
24 Clipston
25 Cotgrave
26 Cropwell Bishop
27 Langar
28 Barnstone
29 'Warborough'
30 Owthorpe
31 Colston Bassett
32 'Newbold'
33 Kinoulton
34 Hickling
35 Upper Broughton

Broxtow (Br)
1 Newbound
2 Teversal
3 Skegby
4 Mansfield
5 Sutton-in-Ashfield
6 Kirkby-in-Ashfield
7 Selston
8 Wansley
9 Annesley
10 Linby
11 Papplewick
12 Brinsley
13 Hucknall Torkard
14 Eastwood
15 Newthorpe
16 Greasley
17 Watnall

18 Awsworth
19 Kimberley
20 Nuthall
21 Hempshill
22 Bulwell
23 Arnold
24 Cossall
25 Strelley
26 Bilborough
27 Broxtow
28 Basford
29 Radford
30 Trowell
31 Sutton Passeys
32 Wollaton
33 Lenton
34 Morton
35 Nottingham
36 Sneinton
37 Stapleford
38 Bramcote
39 Beeston
40 Chilwell & East Chilwell
41 Toton
42 Costock
43 Wysall
44 Rempstone
45 Thorpe-in-the-Glebe
46 Willoughby-on-the-Wolds

Newark (N) (South)
16 Barnby-in-the-Willows
17 Farndon
18 Hawton
19 Balderton
20 East Stoke
21 Thorpe
22 Syerston
23 Elston
24 Cotham
25 Sibthorpe
26 Shelton
27 'Dallington'
28 Kilvington
29 Staunton
30 Flawborough
31 Alverton

Rushcliffe (R)
1 Adbolton
2 Holme Pierrepont
3 Bassingfield
4 Wilford
5 West Bridgford
6 Gamston

7 Clifton
8 Edwalton
9 Barton-in-Fabis
10 Ruddington
11 Plumtree
12 Normanton-on-the-Wolds
13 Thrumpton
14 Gotham
15 Bradmore
16 Bunny
17 Keyworth
18 Stanton-on-the-Wolds
19 Widmerpool
20 Ratcliffe-on-Soar
21 Kingston-on-Soar
22 Leake
23 Sutton Bonington
24 Normanton-on-Soar
25 Stanford-on-Soar

Thurgarton (T)
1 Blidworth
2 Farnsfield
3 Osmanthorpe
4 Kirklington
5 Salterford
6 Oxton
7 Southwell
8 Normanton
9 Horsepool
10 Fiskerton
11 Morton
12 Rolleston
13 Staythorpe
14 Calverton
15 Woodborough
16 Epperstone
17 Gonalstone
18 Thurgarton
19 *Alwoldestorp*
20 Gibsmere
21 Lambley
22 Bulcote
23 Lowdham
24 Hoveringham
25 Gunthorpe
26 Burton Joyce
27 Gedling
28 Carlton
29 Stoke Bardolph
30 Colwick

Derbyshire
03 Sandiacre
Not mapped. 'Odsthorpe' (T)

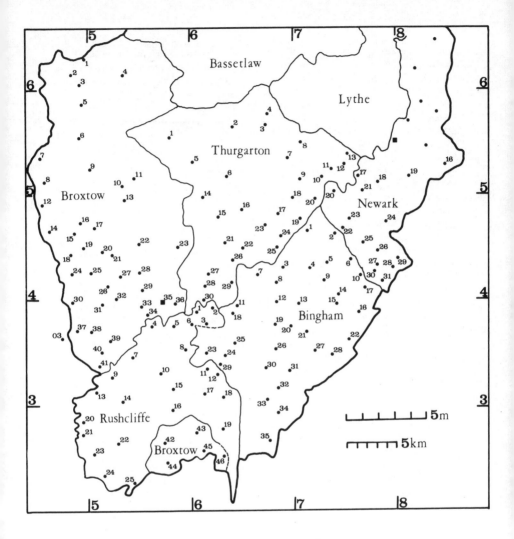

NOTTINGHAMSHIRE SOUTHERN WAPENTAKES

The County Boundary is marked by thick lines; Wapentake boundaries (1086) by thin lines.

National Grid 10-kilometre squares are shown on the map border.

Each four-figure grid square covers one square kilometre, or 247 acres, approximately 2 hides, at 120 acres to the hide.

TECHNICAL TERMS

Many words meaning measurements have to be transliterated. But translation may not dodge other problems by the use of obsolete or made-up words which do not exist in modern English. The translations here used are given in italics. They cannot be exact; they aim at the nearest modern equivalent.

B. Marginal abbreviation for berewic; an outlying place, attached to a manor. *o u t l i e r*
BORDARIUS. Cultivator of inferior status, usually with a little land. *s m a l l h o l d e r*
BOVATA. One eighth of a carucate. *b.*
CARUCA. A plough, with the oxen who pulled it, usually reckoned as 8. *p l o u g h*
CARUCATA. The unit of land measurement in Danish areas. *c.*
CENSORES. See 10,3 note. *t r i b u t a r i e s*
DOMINIUM. The mastery or dominion of a lord *(dominus)*; including ploughs, land, men, villages, etc., reserved for the lord's use; often concentrated in a *home farm* or *demesne*, a 'Manor Farm' or 'Lordship Farm'. *l o r d s h i p*
FRANCUS HOMO. Equivalent of *liber homo* (free man). *f r e e m a n*
GELDUM. The principal royal tax, originally levied during the Danish wars, normally at an equal number of pence on each *hide* of land. *t a x*
HIDA. The English unit of land measurement or assessment, often reckoned at 120 acres; see Sussex, Appendix. *h i d e*
HUNDRED. In English Shires a district within a shire, whose assembly of notables and village representatives usually met about once a month. In and about Nottinghamshire, see S 1 note. *H u n d r e d*
LEUGA. A measure of length, usually about a mile and a half. *l e a g u e*
M. Marginal abbreviation for *manerium*, manor. *M.*
SACA. German *Sache*, English *sake*, Latin *causa*, affair, lawsuit; the fullest authority normally exercised by a lord. *f u l l   j u r i s d i c t i o n*
SOCA. 'Soke', from *socn*, to seek, comparable with Latin *quaestio*. Jurisdiction with the right to receive fines and a multiplicity of other dues. District in which such *soca* is exercised; a place in a *soca*. *j u r i s d i c t i o n*
SOCHEMANNUS. 'Soke man', exercising or subject to jurisdiction; free from many villagers' burdens; before 1066 often with more land and higher status than villagers (see e.g. Bedfordshire, Middlesex Apppendices); bracketed in the Commissioners' brief with the *liber homo* (free man). *F r e e m a n*
TAINUS, TEGNUS. Person holding land from the King by special grant; formerly used of the King's ministers and military companions. *t h a n e*
T.R.E. *tempore regis Edwardi,* in King Edward's time. *b e f o r e   1 0 6 6*
VILLA. Translating Old English *tun*, town. The later distinction between a small *village* and a large *town* was not yet in use in 1086. *v i l l a g e* or *t o w n*
VILLANUS. Member of a *villa*, usually with more land than a *bordarius*. *v i l l a g e r*
VIRGATA. A quarter of a hide, reckoned at 30 acres. *v i r g a t e*
WAPENTAC. Equivalent of the English Hundred in Danish areas. *w a p e n t a k e*